ZEN AND THE UNSPEAKABLE GOD

COMPARATIVE
INTERPRETATIONS
OF MYSTICAL
EXPERIENCE

ZEN and the
UNSPEAKABLE
GOD

JASON N. BLUM

THE PENNSYLVANIA STATE UNIVERSITY PRESS
UNIVERSITY PARK, PENNSYLVANIA

Library of Congress Cataloging-in-Publication Data

Blum, Jason N., 1977– , author.
Zen and the unspeakable god : comparative
interpretations of mystical experience / Jason N. Blum.
pages   cm
Summary: "An interpretive approach to the study of
mystical experience. Compares the experiences of
Meister Eckhart, Ibn Arabi, and Hui-neng to reveal
commonalities that have provocative implications
for our understanding of consciousness"—
Provided by publisher.
Includes bibliographical references and index.
ISBN 978-0-271-07079-7 (cloth : alk. paper)
ISBN 978-0-271-07080-3 (pbk : alk. paper)
1. Mysticism.
2. Ibn al-'Arabi, 1165–1240.
3. Eckhart, Meister, –1327.
4. Huineng, 638–713.
I. Title.

BL625.B58   2015
204'.22—dc23
2015016516

FOR VANA,

the condition of possibility for this,

and so much else.

CONTENTS

ACKNOWLEDGMENTS

This book would not exist without the help—intellectual, material, and emotional—of more than a few people, and I can only hope to name them all here. Steve Dunning, Ann Matter, Talya Fishman, and David Hufford provided invaluable advice and guidance in the early stages. I want to thank them for asking the hard questions, for pushing when pushing was necessary, and of course for their feedback on early versions of the manuscript. Steve, especially, deserves credit for always demanding close and careful textual engagement, and for equally close and careful feedback on (multiple) rough drafts.

I am grateful for generous financial support from The American University in Cairo and the University of Pennsylvania. My friends and colleagues at The American University in Cairo—Ian Morrison, Jason Beckett, Mate Tokić, Mike Ryan, Surti Singh, Anne Justus, Ananya Chakravarti, Justin Kolb, Julia Seibert, Chris Spatz, Ryder Kouba, Sean McMahon, Kim Fox, and many others—provided the intellectual environment necessary for good thinking and writing, and the occasional distractions and camaraderie that are also necessary for good thinking and writing. Omar Amin, my research and teaching assistant at AUC during the final stages of preparing the manuscript, was invaluable, particularly in editing the Arabic terms in the book.

Kathryn Yahner, Charlee Redman, and everyone else at Penn State University Press made this book better through both their patience and their skill. I owe them thanks for seeing the book in the manuscript, and for their talent and professionalism in nurturing that metamorphosis. Suzanne Wolk also did an excellent job copyediting the manuscript. The two outside readers provided exceptionally detailed and carefully considered feedback and encouragement, and are great examples of how to engage with and critique others' work.

My students' efforts, insight, energy, and curiosity have buoyed me along the way, and have often reminded me why I got into this business in the first place.

My friends Jeff Palmer, Scott Sifton, and Scott Rosen have helped me stay on track through our monthly get-togethers. I have a few more books to write, so you'd better be available. Jay Arnold has commiserated with me over the joys and agonies of writing and life, and is always there when either proves more vexing than usual. I thank Chantal Auger for always taking my e-mails in exactly the way I intended them. Grant Potts has been a persistently grounding influence, and I thank him for that.

My parents, Claude and Laurel, and my sister, Jessica, and brother-in-law, Jim, have been my pillars of support. My father always says that he doesn't understand my work, but I hope he does understand how vital his and the rest of our family's emotional support has been, from the very beginning of this process to the very end. I would not have begun on this path without you. Andrea, Cathy, Jim, and many other members of my family also gladly listened and supported my work. I wish I could have shared this with Grandpa Sam, Grandpa Jaime, and Aunt Debbie. I know that Aunt Debbie and Grandpa Jaime, especially, would have been proud to see this project come to fruition. Debbie's consistent and sincere interest in my work and career, and the intellectual legacy of Grandpa Jaime, have both provided inspiration when it was needed.

We often visited my wife's family in Albania—my parents-in-law, Lavdije and Asqeri, and my sisters-in-law and their husbands, Enkelejda, Nertila, Altin, and Heris—during short breaks from writing and teaching. Although my poor command of Albanian prevented us from discussing the finer points of neo-Kantian epistemology, their love and support provided just the energy I needed to continue working.

My wife, Silvana, is the unsung hero of this book. Without her incisive critiques and constant emotional support (often, fortunately, offered simultaneously), this book would not have been written. Vana, thank you for that, and for so much else that made this journey—among so many others—not only possible but worthwhile. And that, of course, is only the beginning of what I need to thank you for. I love you, and we have time for the rest.

Finally, some credit must also go to Lila, our dearly departed cat, for the companionship she provided by inserting herself between me and my laptop at every conceivable angle while much of this book was written. Her younger stepbrother Chewie deserves credit for inspiring at least one good laugh per day.

Cairo, Egypt, October 2014

Theory versus Interpretation

Robert Forman and Jensine Andresen once described the theoretical debate that has suffused the study of mysticism for more than thirty years as a "methodological war."[1] In many ways, the description is apropos. Since the late 1970s, the study of mysticism has been dominated by unrelenting debate over the nature—both actual and possible—of human experience generally, and of mystical experience in particular. Although many studies of mysticism are replete with references to mystical texts and thinkers from numerous traditions, they are usually controlled by scholars' own epistemological theories or models of experience; having first articulated a theory as to what mystical experience is and how it functions, that theory is then used as a template for analyzing mystics' accounts of their experiences. In this sense, methodology has overshadowed subject matter, and the empirical study of texts describing mystical experience has been made subservient to prior philosophical commitments.

On one side of the debate is the contextualist position, which has been dominant in theoretical discussions of the study of mystical experience since it was endorsed in 1978 by Steven Katz. According to this position, which is based on an extrapolation of Kantian epistemology, experience is always influenced and constrained by prior experience, learning, and language. The mystic, in engaging on his course of study and pursuing his mystical path, immerses himself in the teachings, doctrines, and concepts of his religion; in this manner he builds up an array of expectations (often unintentionally and subconsciously) concerning what his mystical experience will be like, and when he finally does achieve his goal, it turns out to be precisely what one would expect. Because this perspective assumes that experience is essentially conceptual and linguistic in nature, it is inevitably shaped by ideas, concepts, and beliefs ingested from learning, culture, and historical setting. Context (broadly construed) thereby sets the boundaries and limits of experience. Mystical experiences, according to this perspective, are identical in structure to all other kinds of consciousness.

This position was initially articulated as a response to essentialism—the claim that all mystical experiences are fundamentally the same. The essentialist thesis was later revised, largely as a response to the critique offered by Katz and others, into a more nuanced form that became the primary counterposition to contextualism. This position, defended most prominently by Robert Forman, holds that while the contexualist thesis may describe the vast majority of experience, there is a certain subset of experiences—rare, but significant nonetheless—that partake of a different structure altogether. These experiences, which Forman refers to as "pure consciousness events," are *not* fundamentally linguistic and conceptual in nature, nor are they influenced by context or prior expectation. They are essentially empty or "pure," meaning that they are unsullied by any of the cognitive functions and background assumptions that contextualists claim shape all experience.

Since 1978, these two positions have represented the poles of debate in the study of mystical experience. Theoretical reflection on the study of mystical experience has therefore been framed in epistemological terms: two models for the structure of consciousness and nature of experience are offered, each is defended on the basis of certain philosophical traditions and schools of thought, and each is then deployed as a template for analyzing mystical experience. Theoretical scholarship on mystical experience has generally followed this epistemological trajectory for the past three decades, formulating the methodological question of how to study mystical experience as a matter of articulating and defending an independent model of consciousness, which is brought to experiential accounts as a kind of guide or template.

I argue that this epistemological framing of the problem has become the primary hindrance to progress in the study of mystical experience. Regardless of the particular theory employed, reliance on prior assumptions about the nature of consciousness and mystical experience runs the risk of obscuring those aspects of an experiential account that do not accord with it. As counterexamples, consider the following passages:

> One way to describe the manner in which meaning is created in theosophical-theurgical Kabbalah is to assume that the authors and their readers understood specific terminology as symbolic. However, the term "symbol" itself requires more precise definition. . . . *The way in which modern scholarship under the impact of [Gershom] Scholem,*

Johann Reuchlin and Franz Molitor understands symbols is informed by the German Romantic approach rather than by Kabbalah. . . . I have taken issue with this simplistic application of the German Romantic view of symbolism to the variegated literature of Kabbalists.[2]

One of the first problems we face in investigating [Ibn al-ʿArabi's] voluminous writings is how to deal with his interpretive biases. It would be tempting to try to leave aside his theorizing and go straight to his experience. But then we would be forced to interpret his interpretation in terms of our own theoretical categories, and there is no reason to suppose that such an approach would bring us any closer to an understanding of what is at issue.[3]

In the first passage, Moshe Idel notes that much influential scholarship on Jewish mysticism has been designed with interpretive principles drawn from German romanticism, and that these principles therefore have no necessary relation or application to Kabbalah (Jewish mysticism). While symbols do play an undeniably important role in kabbalistic literature, Idel reminds us that there is no reason to expect that they function in a manner comparable to the role of symbols in German romanticism. Therefore, use of the latter to interpret the former, Idel argues, is unwarranted and potentially misleading. Rather, he suggests, kabbalistic symbolism must be interpreted according to the code represented by the ten *sefiroth*— an interpretive frame derived from Kabbalah itself.[4]

Similarly, William Chittick suggests that in order to correctly understand the writings of the Sufi mystic and theologian Ibn al-ʿArabi, the scholar cannot ignore the native interpretive framework that suffuses Ibn al-ʿArabi's writing, within which he explicates his understanding of mystical experience. Like Idel, Chittick recognizes that while it is possible to interpret Ibn al-ʿArabi according to any number of frameworks or "theoretical categories," there is no reason to suppose that any such interpretation or framework would be appropriate for understanding Ibn al-ʿArabi's texts. Rather, Chittick implies, the interpreter must examine *both* the reported mystical experience *and* the interpretive framework in which the experiential description is already immersed in order to understand either.

Both scholars recognize that mystic experiential accounts are already embedded in and permeated by their own philosophical assumptions. Mystic experiential accounts do not stand in a vacuum. Rather, they usually appear as part of a tradition of writing and thought that, significantly, includes its own assumptions about the nature of consciousness and the structure of mystical experience—its own inherent epistemology. And given the significant differences in historical context between most of history's mystics and their contemporary interpreters, those assumptions are often vastly different from those with which today's scholars operate. This indicates that the imposition of prior theoretical assumptions about the functionality of experience—whether those assumptions be contextualist, essentialist, or of any other sort—may do more harm than good in understanding mystics' accounts of their experiences. Because mystic experiential accounts are typically already embedded in their own set of emic assumptions about the nature of experience, interpreting them through another set of (often divergent if not contradictory) assumptions runs the risk of obfuscating or misconstruing the original text.

Context does matter, and in order to understand the nature of mystical experience as described by its often eloquent and sometimes perplexing heralds, we must take context into account. In this sense, Katz's contextualist thesis is correct. However, incorporating context into analysis by means of an epistemological theory that assumes that context sets parameters that necessarily constrain the content and character of experience is deeply problematic. At the very least, such an approach still fails to unearth the understanding of experience with which a given mystic operates, instead relying on its own epistemological theory in order to derive the nature of mystical experience. In doing so, the understanding of experience that is already embedded in an experiential account is obscured behind the interpreter's own assumptions about the nature of consciousness, resulting in an analysis of mystical experience that reflects the interpreting scholar's epistemological theory rather than the mystic's own experience and understanding of it.

I propose a different approach. Improving the study of mystical experience is not a matter of articulating and applying the right epistemological theory or experiential model, but of developing an effective *interpretive* method that reveals the understanding of experience that is already embedded within specific experiential accounts. Rather than filter accounts of mystical experience through the philosophical assumptions of one or another etic theory or model of consciousness, I develop a hermeneutic approach—derived from phenomenology of religion and semantic holism—that unearths fundamental assumptions about experience that are already embedded in mystical thought and literature and harnesses these assumptions as interpretive guides.

I apply this approach to the experiential accounts of three mystics: Meister Eckhart, Ibn al-'Arabi, and Hui-neng. This comparison reveals a number of intriguing similarities. I do not argue that all mystical experience is the same, or even necessarily similar. However, the commonalities that I reveal do represent similarities in mystical experience that transcend boundaries of culture, tradition, and historical context. These similarities demonstrate the dual errors of assuming that context necessarily delimits the boundaries of experience and that mystic experiential accounts arising in different traditions and contexts will not share important similarities. These similarities are suggestive for further study, and they have provocative implications for both the study of mystical experience and our own understanding of the nature of consciousness and experience in general.

Throughout the book, I employ a heuristic vocabulary that is intended to be sufficiently inclusive so as to facilitate cross-cultural comparison while presupposing as little as possible about mystical experience. To a degree, my adopted terms are therefore intentionally underdefined. I define a mystic experiential account as *a report of an encounter between a mystic and ultimacy that is more intimate than that afforded by religious practice as performed by the larger, general religious community.* Such accounts appear in a number of genres, including poetry, discursive first-person reports, and didactic texts. I use the term "ultimacy" as a placeholder for that which a mystic holds to be of greatest value.[5] This typically takes the form of a deity (e.g., the Abrahamic god) or a state of being (nirvana) that is of paramount importance to a mystic's tradition, practice, and theology. "Mysticism," then, consists broadly of practices, texts, and beliefs related to, and experiential reports of, an encounter between a mystic and ultimacy. The term "encounter" signals any sort of interaction between a mystic and ultimacy; this often indicates an experience of union entailing some degree of identity between mystic and ultimacy, but it need not do so necessarily.

While this definition is designed to cast a broad net, I do not address a significant subset of mystical experiences: those described in terms of visual or auditory sensory impressions, such as visions of deities or saints or audible locutions attributed to the same. Such experiences clearly play an important role in mystical and religious traditions and have received ample scholarly treatment. They have not, however, been centrally relevant to the contemporary debate that is the impetus for this book. In the past thirty-plus years, debate over the interpretation of mystical experience has been focused on the controversial possibility of similarity or identity of experiences across traditional, cultural, and historical boundaries. Visions and locutions of deities and other religious entities have not played a significant role in this debate. To my knowledge, there are no extant reports of these types of sensory experiences that involve a mystic of one tradition encountering a deity or saint of another tradition of which the mystic did not have demonstrable previous knowledge. Such an instance would, of course, raise very interesting questions. However, because of the absence of any such examples, sensory mystical experiences have not been implicated in the methodological issues concerning epistemology and experience that have galvanized contemporary debate, with which this study is primarily concerned. Therefore, while their importance to mystical and religious traditions is undisputed, they remain outside the purview of this project.

Chapter 1 lays out the problem I seek to solve. I describe the contested role that context plays in contemporary debate about mystical experience, and focus on the work of Steven Katz, whose work largely initiated the epistemological trajectory of contemporary theoretical work on mystical experience, and whose position has been dominant for more than thirty years. Katz relies on a neo-Kantian epistemology that suggests that mystical experience is "overdetermined" by context; this, he claims, indicates that there will be "necessary" differences between mystical experiences in different traditions.[6] This epistemology undergirds a causal explanatory relationship that Katz establishes between context and experience wherein the former delimits and powerfully influences the latter. Since his initial publication on mysticism in 1978, this epistemology has motivated Katz to argue systematically for various related theses concerning mystical experience.[7]

Responses to Katz's contextualist thesis have been varied, including both vehement criticism and enthusiastic endorsement. His historically sensitive method resonates with the general tenor of contemporary scholarship and postmodern philosophy, which emphasize the historically rooted nature of subjectivity, the fundamentally linguistic nature of conception, and the cultural conditioning that limits theory. Numerous scholars—many of whom have contributed to Katz's edited volumes on the topic—have endorsed this approach.[8] However, partially because of the unequivocal tone in which it is articulated, Katz's work has also been the subject of sometimes strident criticism. The contextualist approach, while helpfully highlighting the importance of context for understanding mystical experience, results in a number of misleading claims concerning the nature of mystical experience and the possibility of similarities across historical and traditional boundaries. This analytical method assumes that mystic experiential accounts will be compatible with the basic doctrines of the religious traditions out of which they arise, and that therefore similarities between experiential accounts of different traditions should not occur. *Pace* Katz, my analysis of mystic experiential accounts suggests that both conclusions are mistaken, and that they seriously impair any approach to the study of mystical experience that accepts them as guiding assumptions.

Chapter 1 briefly considers some additional problems regarding the relationship Katz constructs between context and experience. Although context does play an important role in both the representation and interpretation of mystical experience, assuming a close explanatory relationship between context and experience is not a methodologically sound way to incorporate context into analysis. The use of context in studying mystical experience requires more careful theorization in order to be effective without importing prior conclusions that mislead analysis.

In chapter 2, I develop a new approach to the study of mystical experience that responds to these needs. This method fundamentally revises the study of mystical experience by shifting analysis from an epistemological paradigm to a hermeneutical one. Rather than base analysis on a model of experience or a theory about the nature of consciousness, my approach starts with close reading of mystical literature itself that is designed to unearth the mystic's own assumptions and beliefs about the nature of mystical experience. I begin by suggesting a theoretical bifurcation between interpretation and explanation. Whereas an explanation of a mystical experience typically proposes causal factors—examples could include God, psychosis, or a combination of contextual cues and self-suggestion—an interpretation of a mystical experience seeks instead to produce an account of an experience that unearths and accurately reflects the perspective and embedded assumptions of the mystical subject.

Having separated interpretive and explanatory endeavors, I then develop an interpretive approach to the study of mystical experience. First, I draw on the notion of semantic holism, which situates an experiential account within a "notional context" of related sources and texts. Semantic holism regards meaning as something that arises not from individual sentences or terms but from the interrelations of a subject's statements, beliefs, and other, nondiscursive attitudes and emotions with one another. Second, I recommend the principle of charity, a basic hermeneutical principle that makes interpretation possible by assuming that a subject's discourse has a minimal degree of internal consistency such that it has interpretable meaning. Taken together, holism and the principle of charity allow context to be harnessed as an interpretive guide to a mystical text or experiential account without importing assumptions about the structure of the experience itself.

Drawing on the work of Hans-Georg Gadamer, I also suggest a procedure for "checking" the interpreter's preconceptions about the meaning of an experiential account against the emergent meaning of the text itself. This procedure goes hand in hand with phenomenological *epoché*, the hermeneutical principle that an interpreter must temporarily bracket or suspend his own philosophical commitments for purposes of interpretation. Phenomenological *epoché* foregrounds emic mystical assumptions about the nature of experience, which then serve as guides to the interpretation of specific experiential accounts.

Having articulated my approach, chapters 3, 4, and 5 put this method into practice. In each chapter, I focus on the work of one prominent mystic—Ibn al-'Arabi, Meister Eckhart, and Hui-neng—in which he describes the nature of mystical experience. All of these figures both exerted significant influence on the mystical traditions of which they are a part and were influenced by those traditions. The understandings of mystical experience that they articulate, therefore, represent important trends within their respective traditions. And while Eckhart and Ibn al-'Arabi shared certain historical influences important to all three Abrahamic religions, Hui-neng did not; this ensures that any similarities between all three mystical authors cannot be attributed to common historical sources or influences.

Beginning with a key passage from each mystic, I employ my hermeneutic method to interpret it. Each chapter organizes my interpretation into the two categories of epistemology and ontology. For purposes of this project, I employ the terms "ontology" (and its close analogue, "metaphysics") and "epistemology" without reference to any specific philosophical theory or school of thought. Rather, in order to facilitate comparison across traditions, I define these terms in their most basic senses. Ontology refers to a theory concerning the fundamental nature and/or structure of reality, including the character or basic nature of the being of both an aspiring mystic and ultimacy. In the context of this project, ontology most often refers to the metaphysical status or nature of the mystic's soul (or its cognate, depending on the religion under consideration), the deity or form of ultimacy with which the mystic is concerned, and the encounter between the two. Epistemology, on the other hand, refers to the modality by which a mystic comes to know or experience ultimacy.

Organizing interpretation into these two categories allows me to unearth fundamental aspects of mystical experience in all three cases: what is the nature of the encounter between mystic and ultimacy (i.e., is this an experience of identity or union, or not)? And what is the mode or type of knowing involved (i.e., is this mode of knowing linguistic, conceptual, and/or mediated)? Applying these two categories to my analyses of all three mystics facilitates comparison between them.

Chapter 3 focuses on the mystical experience of Ibn al-ʿArabi, arguably the most influential Sufi thinker and writer in the history of Islam. The chapter begins with a key passage from *The Meccan Revelations* in which he describes the apex of his own mystical journey, an experience the sheikh refers to as the "Muhammadan station." Although brief, the passage is densely packed with idiosyncratic references to Ibn al-ʿArabi's own thought and theology. In order to interpret the passage, I first draw on other sections of *The Meccan Revelations*. Then I consider other works of the Sufi master's, especially *The Bezels of Wisdom*, another masterpiece that many consider the culmination of Ibn al-ʿArabi's thought on religion and mystical practice. Finally, I consider Ibn al-ʿArabi's reported experience in light of the broader context of Sufism, including common Sufi themes such as *fanāʾ* and *baqāʾ*, and the works of other Islamic mystics such as Mansur ibn Muhammad al-Hallaj and Abu Yazid al-Bistami.

Chapter 4 considers the mystical experience of Meister Eckhart, the medieval Dominican preacher and mystic who famously and controversially claimed that "God's ground is my ground, and my ground is God's ground."[9] First, I examine the remainder of the sermon in which Eckhart makes this striking claim. I then consider other examples from Eckhart's substantial body of work, including sermons, biblical commentaries, and longer essays, all of which provide essential guidance in interpreting the key passage. I draw on both his vernacular works, many of which were intended as sermons to be preached to the public, and his scholarly Latin works, which were addressed to more educated audiences. Finally, I reflect on other influential Christian mystics, including Pseudo-Dionysius and the anonymous author of the *Cloud of Unknowing*, who offer further interpretive guidance to Eckhart's major themes.

Chapter 5 shifts focus to the Buddhist tradition, and specifically the enlightenment of Hui-neng, the ancient Chinese monk and esteemed patriarch of Zen Buddhism. He advocates a particular approach to Zen thought and practice that is the heart of the "sudden enlightenment" school of Chan (Zen) Buddhism. Hui-neng's account of his own enlightenment serves as my key passage in this chapter. This account—along with other teachings of the Zen master—is found in *The Sutra of Hui-neng* (also called *The Platform Sutra*), the first resource I use in unraveling the patriarch's understanding of mystical experience. I then consider *The Diamond Sutra*, a separate text that, according to Hui-neng, sparked his own enlightenment, and Hui-neng's commentary on it. Finally, I turn to other sources of Zen teaching, such as the *Blue Cliff Record* and Nagarjuna's *The Fundamental Wisdom of the Middle Way*. Although the philosophical context and basic assumptions with which Hui-neng operates are significantly different from those of Meister Eckhart and Ibn al-'Arabi, the categories of epistemology and ontology still prove useful for organizing my interpretation of his work.

The conclusion summarizes and discusses the comparative findings of chapters 3 through 5. Although neither epistemology nor ontology is a category explicitly used by these mystical authors themselves, the two categories capture areas of thought that are deeply relevant to their understandings of mystical experience. They also serve my purpose of disclosing fundamental assumptions about experience that define their experiential accounts, and of comparing these with their counterparts in other mystical traditions. Through these categories, I identify a number of intriguing common themes between the three mystics. Ontologically, a significant structural similarity obtains in all three traditions. Each mystic experiential account depicts what I call an "ontological resonance" between mystic and ultimacy: however the metaphysical character of ultimacy is described, that character is represented as also constituting the most basic nature of the mystic's self. The ontological nature of ultimacy is thus deeply connected with, if not identical to, the ontological nature of the mystic.

In addition, all three mystics describe their experiences as nonconceptual, nonlinguistic, and unmediated by context, training, or even their own religious traditions. This is not to say that these mystical writers simply dismiss the importance of religious education, doctrine, and scripture in pursuing their respective paths. However, they all concur that these discursive dimensions of experience and thought are ultimately surpassed at the pinnacle of the mystical journey. This indicates that mystical experience is typically characterized in ways that run directly counter to dominant trends in modern Western philosophy, and further underscores the risks involved in relying on an etic (Western) model of experience as an interpretive guide to studying mystical experience. These cross-cultural similarities do not warrant the claim that all mystics have identical experiences, or that they are experiencing the same divine reality, but they do represent intriguing commonalities that transcend differences of tradition, history, and context. These commonalities suggest provocative directions for further research in religious studies and philosophy.

Twenty-five years ago, Sallie B. King warned of a strange sort of procrustean bed developing out of academic insistence on its own interpretive theories. At that time, the works of Hans Penner and Steven Katz on mysticism were representative of her concern:

> The danger of Katz's and Penner's approach is that it reduces mystical experience to mystical language for reason of methodological convenience. There is a parallel situation in psychology with respect to methodological and theoretical behaviorism. Starting from the observation that the so-called "inner world" is inaccessible to scientific observation, behaviorists limited themselves to what their scientific methodology could adequately study: human behavior. What began as a concern with methodological propriety, however, resulted in theoretical reductionism such that many behaviorists explained away mental and emotional phenomena altogether, "mind" became a four-letter word, and human beings were reduced to a set of material functions and processes. . . . We run a similar risk with the question of mystical experience. . . . I would very much regret seeing the kind of reductionism which has plagued psychology become normative in religious studies. It would be better, if necessary, to frankly acknowledge that the phenomena of mystical experience are beyond our reach and live with the consequences of that admission than to reduce mysticism to less than it is for the sake of method.[10]

Although King was concerned specifically with analyses of language in mysticism, her warning is germane to the field in general. Steven Katz, Robert Forman, and many other scholars have sought to bring a greater degree of methodological rigor and theoretical sophistication to the study of mysticism, and they have drawn on various philosophical resources in doing so. This was necessary, given the lack of theoretical reflection demonstrated by much early work on mysticism thoughout the early and mid-twentieth century. There is the danger, however, of overemphasizing the power of theory. Overreliance on theories of consciousness (which, after all, are derived from their own contextually and culturally delimited perspectives) and the epistemological importance of context has created a situation in which interpretation of mystic experiential accounts is largely replaced by theoretical deductions based on interpreters' own philosophical positions. In this sense, theory has become overly influential in interpretation and has limited the semantic horizons of mystical experience to possibilities predetermined by analysts' own understandings of context and the nature of consciousness.

We can marshal a better response than the humble admission that mystical experience must remain beyond our theoretical grasp. Rather than impose theoretical constraints on the boundaries of experience or the meanings of texts, hermeneutics should open up source material for interpretation, and lay bare that which is implicit or assumed within it. Theory must not trump interpretation. Through both the proper application and the restraint of theory, an interpretive method can be devised that discloses the inner dynamics of mystical experience as described by its subjects. When thus applied, interpretation reveals complex and surprising similarities in mystical experience that contradict some of our most well worn theories and assumptions. Rather than straining to explain mystical experiences within the comfortable boundaries inscribed by our theories, it may be that these accounts demonstrate the necessity of revising the theories themselves.

1

THE PROBLEM OF CONTEXT

The role of context in both the formation and the analysis of mysticism is a contentious topic, and it has played a predominant role in theoretical debates about the interpretation and explanation of mystical experience. Steven Katz, the foremost representative of the contextualist approach, argues for a strong causative relationship between context and experience wherein the former delimits the possible forms of the latter and is largely responsible for its character and content.[1] Here, "context" refers to a broad collection of factors thought to influence mystical experience: language, education, historical setting, and internalization of doctrine and tradition (to name a few). As a result of this proposed relationship, Katz suggests that a proper analysis of mystical experience requires thorough study of the context of any experiential account.

While I concur that context plays a necessary role in understanding mystical literature—including experiential accounts—the role that context plays in analysis must be defined with precision. In arguing for the "necessary" differences between mystical experiences in different traditions, Katz orients his work around what he calls a "preinterpretive" question: why are mystical experiences the experiences they are?[2] In formulating his inquiry in this fashion (with a "why" question), Katz shapes his project with an explanatory trajectory that precedes and directs his interpretation of mystical literature. He answers his "why" question with the "single epistemological assumption" that all experience is unavoidably mediated: mystical experiences are the way they are because they are mediated by context. As such, and given the apparent differences between the contexts of different mystical texts and experiential accounts, Katz argues that mystical experiences arising from different contexts and traditions will predictably be different.

This investigative structure requires revision. As a result of this analytical orientation, Katz's representations of mystical experience are informed primarily by his own predetermined explanatory hypothesis rather than by interpretation of mystical texts themselves. By using the assumption of a strong explanatory relationship between context and experience as a guide to interpreting mystic experiential accounts, this method fosters misleading characterizations of mystical experience and prejudges the possibility of similarity between experiential accounts of different traditions.

As an example of the former, Katz states that Jewish mysticism will only characterize mystical experience in conformity with the basic Jewish teaching that God and humanity are ontologically distinct; Jewish mysticism, therefore, will not include the notion of unity or ontological commingling between human and divine. However, as demonstrated below, that assumption is not borne out by examination of Jewish mystical literature. Some mystical Jewish texts clearly include claims of union between the mystic and supernatural entities; others describe various ontological relationships between humanity and the divine that, while falling short of union, still suggest a profound metaphysical connection between the two. All of these texts describe relationships between humanity and the divine in which the ontological distinction between man and God is at least blurred, if not overcome. As an additional example, this chapter also briefly shows that Islam—which places equal if not greater emphasis on God's uniqueness—has also produced metaphysical theories and mystic experiential accounts that clearly suggest a commingling of human and divine essences. These examples indicate that the assumption of conformity between mystical experience and mainstream religious doctrine is incorrect.

The contextualist hypothesis also suggests that mystic experiential accounts from different traditions should not demonstrate significant similarities. If the content and character of mystical experience can be explained largely through context and, as Katz emphasizes, the contexts of distinct mystical experiences differ, then similarities between mystical experiences arising from different cultures and traditions should not occur. As I demonstrate in chapters 3, 4, and 5, however, significant themes are shared among distinct mystical traditions. These similarities do not efface significant differences between traditions and individual experiential accounts. However, they do suggest that the assumption that the close relationship between experience and context ensures differences between experiential accounts in different traditions is also incorrect.

Finally, I point out, following Katz, that mystical understandings of religious teachings and doctrine are often novel and polyvalent. As such, the "meaning" of scripture—which, according to Katz, defines and delimits mystical experience—is unstable. The meaning of the doctrine or teaching with which mystical experience supposedly conforms is often subject to what Katz describes as "radical hermeneutics"—interpretive strategies that stretch the meanings of scripture in unexpected directions.[3] The assertion that mystical experience will be compatible with basic tenets of religious tradition therefore may offer little in terms of interpretive guidance. While mystics may claim that their experiences are in conformity with scripture, that claim may be simultaneous with divergent or unorthodox interpretations of it.

The "preinterpretive" adoption of context as a filter for predicting the nature of mystical experience leads to misrepresentations of mystical experience and erroneous conclusions about comparability across traditions. In underscoring the importance of context for understanding mystical experience, Katz points scholarship on mysticism in the right direction. But additional methodological refinement is required in order to incorporate context into our understanding of mystical experience without interpolating ulterior, misleading assumptions into interpretation.

The original impetus for Katz's work was his criticism of previous research on mystical experience. In this regard, he mentions William James, Evelyn Underhill, Aldous Huxley, and Rudolf Otto, among others.[4] Many of these earlier scholars supposed that, beneath the external trappings of religious doctrine and merely incidental aspects of different religious practices, mysticism represented some sort of universal commonality that was ultimately shared among all the world's faiths. This is the original essentialist thesis that Katz seeks to dismantle. This essentialist program, Katz argues, arose from an "ecumenical desire" to find commonalities between the world's religious traditions, and the hope of restoring vitality to them.[5] While he recognizes the debt of contemporary scholars to those who initiated the modern study of mysticism, Katz states that neither of these motivations was sound for the study of mystical experience. Following this initial group, Katz credits more recent students of mysticism with raising "the debate as to the nature, content, and philosophical relevance of mysticism to a new level of sophistication."[6] Even these later scholars, however—namely, Ninian Smart, R. C. Zaehner, and W. T. Stace—had not yet articulated a method for the study of mystical experience that was acceptable. Katz states that the positions of these scholars were still "unsatisfactory because they try to provide various cross-cultural phenomenological accounts of mystical experience which are phenomenologically as well as philosophically suspect."[7]

Ultimately, Katz suggests that existing methods for the study of mystical experience were too often controlled by a priori commitments on the part of interpreting scholars that facilitated the production of reductive interpretations of mystical experience. These methods resulted in the "discovery" of similarities in mystical experiences of different religions and historical contexts through dubious interpretive procedures that artificially separated mystical experiences from the contexts in which they occurred and were recorded. These criticisms have motivated Katz's project with regard to mystical experience; the primary assumption against which Katz argues is that mystical experiences from different contexts and traditions are ultimately the same, or at least similar enough to be captured by a limited typology of two or three different types. Katz states this intention explicitly in his seminal 1978 article: "Our primary aim has been to mark out a new way of approaching the data, concentrating especially on disabusing scholars of the preconceived notion that all mystical experience is the same or similar."[8] In 2000—the year in which *Mysticism and Sacred Scripture*, his latest edited collection of essays on mysticism, was published—Katz again defined the "contextualist paradigm" as arguing against the older essentialist model, which consists, in his estimation, of two primary assumptions: "(a) mystical experience was essentially independent of the sociocultural, historical, and religious context in which it occurred and (b) all mystical experience, at its highest and purest level, was essentially the same."[9] Katz's entire project, then, spanning more than twenty years of scholarship, can be described by the motivation he ascribes to himself in his first essay on the topic: a "plea for the recognition of differences."[10]

The essentialist assertion that all mysticism was fundamentally the same depended largely on the claim that the language, symbols, and other contextually informed ways in which mystics described their experiences were ultimately unimportant to the experience itself: beneath and behind

these historical differences lurked a single, universal experience (or a limited set of experiential types) that appeared in the clothing of different
languages and cultures. While the essentialist position eventually fell by
the wayside, a weaker, more defensible version of its central claim later
emerged as the "pure consciousness event." Rather than reject contextualism wholsesale, Robert Forman and others argued that while contextualism might describe the majority of human experience, distinct exceptions
to this contextually defined modality of experience could be found, and
found in a variety of religious and mystical contexts. Rather than claim
that *all* mystical experience was at root identical, the argument became
that *some* mystical experiences partook of a different epistemological
structure and were not subject to the contexualizing influences that Katz
and others insisted upon—thereby carving out logical space for cross-
cultural similarities in at least some mystical experiences.[11] The heart of
this argument—like the earlier essentialism—rejects the strong contextualist thesis that all experience is necessarily filtered by context.

In arguing against the essentialist thesis (in both its earlier and later
forms), Katz contends that the historical, cultural, and doctrinal differences between mystical traditions must be recognized. This argument
takes the form of a "single epistemological assumption" that both prompts
his project and validates its overarching procedure. The relevance of this
methodological statement for the contextualist project requires that he be
quoted at length:

> Let me state the single epistemological assumption that has exercised
> my thinking and which has forced me to undertake the present
> investigation: *There are NO pure (i.e. unmediated) experiences.* Nei-
> ther mystical experience nor more ordinary forms of experience give
> any indication, or any grounds for believing, that they are unmedi-
> ated. That is to say, *all* experience is processed through, organized by,
> and makes itself available to us in extremely complex epistemologi-
> cal ways. The notion of unmediated experience seems, if not self-
> contradictory, at best empty. This epistemological fact seems to me to
> be true, because of the sorts of beings we are, even with regard to the
> experiences of those ultimate objects of concern with which mystics
> have intercourse, e.g. God, Being, nirvāna, etc. This "mediated"
> aspect of all our experience seems an inescapable feature of any epis-
> temological inquiry, including the inquiry into mysticism, which has

to be properly acknowledged if our investigation of experience, including mystical experience, is to get very far. . . . A proper evaluation of this fact leads to the recognition that in order to understand mysticism it is *not* just a question of studying the reports of the mystic after the experiential event but of acknowledging that the experience itself as well as the forms in which it is reported is shaped by concepts which the mystic brings to, and which shape, his experience.[12]

Katz was not the first to put forth the claim that mystical experiences are contextually influenced. Ten years earlier, Michel de Certeau, citing Herskovits, wrote, "experience is always defined culturally, even if such experience is mystical. It receives its form from a milieu that structures it before all explicit consciousness. It obeys the law of language."[13] But it was Katz's development of this thesis, in numerous essays and edited volumes, that shaped the study of mysticism and mystical experience for the next thirty-plus years. His original methodological statement is repeated verbatim in his 1983 article in *Mysticism and Religious Traditions*, and again in 2004.[14]

The mediation thesis represented by his "single epistemological assumption" functions to link mystical experience indissolubly to context, including (for example) the collection of concepts, expectations, and assumptions that a mystic will have internalized through enculturation in his sociohistorical context, immersion in the teachings of his religious tradition, and guidance by a teacher or guru. As a result of these formative factors, Katz asserts that "the forms of consciousness which the mystic brings to experience set structured and limiting parameters on what the experience will be, i.e. on what will be experienced, and rule out in advance what is 'inexperienceable' in the particular given, concrete, context."[15] Katz is explicit about the fact that this prior conditioning plays a powerful causative, and therefore explanatory, role in the experience of any mystic: "What I wish to show is only that there is a *clear causal connection* between the religious and social structure one brings to experience and the nature of one's actual religious experience."[16]

Various objections to the contextualist thesis have been voiced. More sympathetic critics either point out that Katz's theoretical approach extends a Kantian epistemology in ways that Kant himself never intended, or suggest that Katz's theory is incomplete in that it does not specify exactly which concepts filter which experiences, or precisely what the mechanism of filtering is.[17] Others raise more fundamental objections by identifying types of mystical experience that, they argue, Katz's theory cannot explain. Forman, for example, draws attention to the example of "untrained mystics"—individuals who have "undeniably mystical experiences" without previously having been immersed in any religious or mystical training.[18] In a similar vein, both Forman and Michael Stoeber cite examples of mystics who have experiences that in some significant fashion contradict either their own expectations or the teachings of their traditions. These examples of mystical heresy, Forman and Stoeber argue, represent counterexamples to Katz's theory that experience is always contextually delimited.[19] This criticism has also been raised by Francis Clooney, James Robertson Price, and others.[20]

The single most prevalent objection to Katz's work is the charge that his epistemological theory is dogmatic and empirically unsupported. Donald Evans states the point directly: "I have criticized Katz for dogmatically ruling out the possibility of pure consciousness. . . . My basic criticism of Katz is that he insists on a view of human nature such that no human being *could* ever have pure consciousness. As a good Kantian, it is obvious to Katz that no human ever could be so changed as to become free of 'conditioned existence' and thereby bring *no* conceptual or linguistic framework to an experience, thereby becoming pure consciousness. . . . [However,] Katz, as an academic, is not in a position to dictate what mystics can or cannot do."[21] Others echo this objection, pointing out that the question of the modes of consciousness available to mystics is an empirical one that cannot be settled by a priori theorization.[22]

Partly as a result of the conviction with which he sets forth his claims, Katz has sometimes been read as a complete reductionist—i.e., as dissolving mystical experience into nothing but religious doctrine.[23] Such a reading of Katz is incomplete. While Katz is unequivocal about the delimiting influence of context on experience—an influence he takes to be both powerful and unavoidable—he is careful to assert that this influence is only partially constitutive of the experience itself. As Katz states early in his 1978 article, "it is *not* being argued either that mystical experiences do not happen, or that what they claim may not be true. . . . One would be both dogmatic and imprudent to decide *a priori* that mystical claims are mumbo-jumbo, especially given the wide variety of such claims by men of genius and/or intense religious sensitivity over the centuries as well as across all cultural divisions. Nor does it seem reasonable to reduce these multiple and variegated claims to mere projected 'psychological states' which are solely the product of interior states of consciousness."[24]

A radically reductionist reading of Katz is injudicious. However, while Katz does not argue that context alone *causes* a mystical experience, he is quite clear about both the depth and the inevitability of the *shaping and delimiting influence* of the mystic's contextual and conceptual background on the character and content of experience: "mystical experience is 'overdetermined' by its socio-religious milieu: as a result of his process of intellectual acculturation in its broadest sense, the mystic brings to his experience a world of concepts, images, symbols and values which shape as well as colour the experience he eventually and actually has" (46). Although Katz is careful to allow that context is not the sole causative ingredient of experience, he clearly holds that context plays a dominant role in shaping it. Indeed, it is not going too far to claim that, for Katz, contextual input is a *necessary* dimension of any mystical experience: "This much is certain: the mystical experience *must* be mediated by the kinds of beings we are. And the kinds of beings we are *require* that experience be not only instantaneous and discontinuous, but that it also involve memory, apprehension, expectation, language, accumulation of prior experience, concepts, and expectations, with each experience being built on the back of all these elements and being shaped anew by each fresh experience" (emphasis added) (59).

This mediation thesis implicitly satisfies Katz's "plea for the recognition of differences" (25). Because the doctrines, teachings, and historical milieus of religious and mystical traditions are different (as even cursory analysis shows), the mediation thesis predicts that mystical experiences will also be different, and necessarily so. Katz emphasizes that the fundamental tenets of religious traditions play a central role in this regard: "mystical experience(s) are rooted in established religious communities, and grow out of, *and are compatible with*, the basic elements of those positive traditions" (emphasis added).²⁵ As such, Katz's thesis suggests that it is possible to predict or deduce, in broad outline, the limits within which mystical experience within any given tradition will be expressed; enculturation and social conditioning determine, prior to experience, "what is 'inexperienceable' in the particular given, concrete, context" (26).

Katz assumes the predictive power of this method with regard to numerous mystical traditions. Here, I focus on his application of this deductive method to Judaism. After canvassing Katz's assessment of the basic elements of Jewish tradition, which, he states, "define in advance" Jewish mystical experience, I offer a number of examples—quoted from Jewish mystical texts and interpreted by scholars of that tradition—that contradict the predictions of the mediation thesis.

Katz states that in "the cultural-social sphere the Jewish mystic will have learnt and been conditioned in all kinds of ways up from childhood." He then lists ten fundamental tenets that characterize the background of Jewish mystics. These include such uncontroversial beliefs as "(1) there is more to reality than this physical world," and "(8) that God entered into special covenants with Abraham and his heirs, Israel." Katz also includes, however, the following two theses: "(6) that even in covenants he [God] remains distinct [from men]; (7) that God's being and man's being are ontologically distinct" (33). Katz then describes the role these tenets play in Jewish mysticism and mystical experience:

> Moreover, the Jewish mystic will have learnt to fit all these items into a special "mystical theology" known by the broad term of Kabbalah. . . . All these cultural-social beliefs and their attendant practices . . . clearly affect the way in which the Jewish mystic views the world, the God who created it, the way to approach this God, and what to expect when one does finally come to approach this God. . . . These images, beliefs, symbols, and rituals, define, *in advance*, what the experience *he wants to have*, and which he then does have, will be like. . . . That this complex pre-experiential pattern affects the actual experience of the Jewish mystic is an unavoidable conclusion. (33–34)

According to the mediation thesis, and this synopsis of the basic tenets of Jewish thought, Jewish mystics should have mystical experiences and/or describe relationships with God *only* in such a fashion that the mystic and God remain ontologically distinct. The mystic's prior, enculturated belief in the absolute ontological distinction between humanity and God will cause his experience to manifest in a fashion that corroborates that distinction. Katz reasserts this principle numerous times, claiming that "all Jewish mystical testimonies conform to [the] pattern" of a strict ontological duality between human and God (36, 35).[26] Wayne Proudfoot appears to endorse this argument. Citing this example in *Religious Experience*, Proudfoot also highlights the explanatory relationship assumed to link experience and doctrine: "The fact that Jewish mystics do not experience union with God is best explained by references to parameters set by the tradition that has formed their beliefs about persons and God and their expectations for such experiences."[27]

This characterization of Jewish mysticism follows the assessment put forth by Gershom Scholem, who also holds that Jewish mysticism does not demonstrate the kinds of union or commingling of divine and human selves known to other forms of mysticism.[28] This broad characterization of Jewish mystical experience has, however, been challenged by a number of contemporary scholars. Moshe Idel argues for "an alternative view on expressions of *unio mystica* in Kabbalah": "far from being absent, unitive descriptions recur in Kabbalistic literature no less frequently than in non-Jewish mystical writings, and the images used by the Kabbalists do not fall short of the most extreme forms of other types of mysticism."[29] Seth Brody and Eitan Fishbane support Idel's argument that human-divine union is a distinct form of Jewish mystical experience.[30] *Pace* Katz, Proudfoot, and Scholem, Jewish mystical texts and experiential accounts include numerous descriptions of encounters and varied metaphysical theories in which divine and human ontologies are intimately related—often metaphysically linked or commingled—in apparent contradiction of mainstream Jewish thought and the predictions of the contextualist thesis.

The ways in which Jewish mystical theology links divine and mundane ontologies are numerous and complex. For present purposes, a number of salient examples suffice to show that contextualism's predictive characterization of Jewish mysticism is misleading. In an early text, *Sefer Yetsirah*, dated to between the third and sixth centuries C.E., the ten *sefiroth* are described as the fundamental building blocks of reality. Building on the account of creation offered in Genesis, *Sefer Yetsirah* describes the *sefiroth* as the fundamental metaphysical elements out of which reality—in its physical, temporal, and moral dimensions—was initially created. Jewish mystical thought is equivocal about the nature of the *sefiroth*; they are sometimes represented as innate aspects of the divine, and sometimes as related to—but not actually *of*—the divine itself.[31] But their immanence in creation, as described in *Sefer Yetsirah*, and their intimate relation to divinity suggest at least the possibility of an ontological connection between the mundane and supernal realms. This possibility is also suggested by R. Barzilai, an early kabbalist thinker: "The world and all the creatures were created by means of the ten *ma'amarot*, and they are [immanent] in everything like the juice in a bunch of grapes, and they are the ten Sefirot, linked to each other."[32] As human beings are among the creatures created by means of the *sefiroth*—and given the fact that the *sefiroth* themselves represent some aspect or manifestation of the divine—the possibility of an ontological connection between man and God is present. Seth Brody locates a similar theme of divine immanence in the thought of the Hasidic master R. Dov Ber, Maggid of Mezherich, who taught that there is "no existence save God's," suggesting that all of existence, including humanity, is ultimately rooted in the divine.[33] While these examples do not indicate that humanity is or becomes unified with God, they do suggest that characterizing humanity and the divine as always or entirely ontologically distinct overlooks certain dimensions of Jewish mysticism.

The foundational meaning of the *sefiroth* was later expanded in the *Zohar*, a seminal work for Jewish mysticism. Here, the ten entities become, in essence, a structural blueprint for the various aspects or levels of reality. In Scholem's own words,

> The spiritual outlook of the *Zohar* might well be defined as a mixture of theosophic theology, mythical cosmogony and mystical psychology and anthropology. God, the universe and the soul do not lead separate lives, each on its own plane. The original act of creation in fact knows nothing of such clear-cut division. . . . The close interrelation of all three which we find in the *Zohar* is also characteristic of all later Kabbalism. Reference to one often shades off imperceptibly into talk of the other. Later Kabbalists have sometimes tried to deal separately with them, but as far as the *Zohar* is concerned its fascinating appeal to the mind is to a large extent bound up with its unique combination of the three elements into a colorful though not unproblematic whole.[34]

"Theosophic theology," "mythical cosmogony," and "mystical psychology and anthropology" refer to three interrelated planes of existence. In terms of "theology," the *sefiroth* are taken to describe elements of the divine being itself, most often as dimensions or faculties of his psyche or power: *Gevurah* (sometimes also called *Din*) is God's judgment; *Hesed* is God's grace; *Tiferet* is God's splendor, and so forth.[35] In terms of "cosmogony," the *sefiroth* are still, as in *Sefer Yetsirah*, understood as the foundational elements of the created universe. And in terms of "psychology and anthropology," the *sefiroth*, most tellingly, are construed as elements of the human person, or the human spiritual self. Therefore, as Scholem writes, "God, the universe and the soul do not lead separate lives, each on its own plane. . . . [Rather, there is a] unique combination of the three elements into a colorful though not unproblematic whole."

The *sefiroth*, in this formulation, represent a shared ontological structure or reflection that connects God, the universe, and the human person at a basic level. As Scholem indicates, the profound connection between the three signals not only a similarity in structure but the fact that action on one plane has the ability to effect changes on another. As Katz notes, the *sefiroth*, according to some sources, are sometimes related in a correspondence with human deeds; rigorous ethical behavior has the ability to affect the divine itself, and to facilitate relation with it (34).[36] The shared *sefirothic* structure between man and divine may be seen as the reason that human ethical behavior has this power to affect God, and to achieve relation with him.

This recapitulated *sefirothic* arrangement provides only one of numerous ways in which a profound ontological connection with divinity is established by certain trends of Jewish mystical thought. Another strategy is genealogical in nature, wherein the human soul or intellect is seen as descended or generated from the *sefiroth*. This genealogical notion takes at least two forms in mystical Jewish thought. In the first, the soul is construed as the offspring of *Binah*, the *sefirah* of understanding or discernment. This genealogical relationship may establish the basis for the ability of Enoch—a figure important to Jewish mysticism—to merge with *Binah*: "And when he [Enoch] adhered to it, his soul longed to attract the abundance of the upper [spheres] from the [*sefirah* of] wisdom, until his soul ascended to and was bound by the [*sefirah* of] discernment, and the two of them became as one thing."[37] Note that, according to the text, Enoch becomes "as one" with *Binah*. The text clearly describes a kind of experience in which the mystic, Enoch, achieves unity with one of the *sefiroth*.

In the second formulation of this mystical-genealogical origin, the soul is described not as descended from *Binah* alone in a kind of supernal parthenogenesis, but as the offspring of a divine union between two of the *sefiroth*, *Tiferet* and *Malkuth*, also called *Shekinah*. In the *Zohar*, *Tiferet* is characterized as male while *Shekinah*, the "daughter" of *Binah*, is described as female, and the human soul arises from a kind of *hieros gamos* between the two.[38] The existence of these two distinct *sefirothic* lineages of the human soul indicates a lack of consensus about the details, but it also underscores the importance of this notion for kabbalistic thinkers. Both suggest the importance or the attractiveness of the notion of a genealogical relationship of the soul to the divine for kabbalistic thought.

This notion of the divine origin of the soul is repeated, in different form, in Lurianic Kabbalah. Echoing gnostic influences, the human soul is viewed as a piece of the divine, a "spark" whose ultimate home is with God: "all his [the kabbalist's] intention must be to link his soul and bind her to the supernal source by means of Torah . . . as when studying Torah man must intend to link his soul and to unite her and make her cleave to her source above."[39] Note that the supernal realm is referred to twice as the "source," indicating that the divine spark of the human soul ultimately originates from that realm. The goal of kabbalistic practice therefore is to "bind" or "unite" that spark with the original source. Again, the ultimate descent of the soul from the divine may be seen as justification for the mystic's ability to achieve union with it.

Neoplatonic thought, influential in the mystical traditions of all three Abrahamic religions, provides a final model of the close ontological relation between man and God.[40] Rabbi Isaac of Acre's *Me'irat 'Einayyim* details the descent of the human soul from the "Divine Intellect." Through numerous emanations, the divine intellect descends until it reaches its final manifestation in the human person: "We therefore find that the Divine Intellect, which is within the human soul, is called the soul." Harnessing a common Neoplatonic theme, the mystic is enabled to encounter God by reversing this process of emanation, returning up through the hierarchy by progressively "cleaving" or "attaching" to higher emanations and eventually becoming a "Divine man." The text describes this final stage of the mystic's ascent as being "returned to [his] source and root, which is called, literally, the Divine Intellect."[41] Again, the theme of divine origination appears to substantiate the ability of the mystic to encounter— and to merge with—the divine.

These are just a few examples of mystical Jewish theories that suggest a profound ontological link between human and divine and that seem to provide theological justification for the possibility of encountering and, in some cases, merging with God or other supernal entities. Yet Katz characterizes Jewish mysticism as lacking any notion of ontological admixture between human and divine, based on the Jewish tradition's "strong monotheistic emphasis on God's uniqueness . . . understood to entail not only his numerical unity and perfection but also his qualitative, ontological, distinction from his creations" (35). The suggestion is that a doctrinal emphasis on monotheism and God's metaphysical distinctness translates into a mystical tradition wherein experiences of unification or mingling of human and divine ontologies will not obtain.

As shown, this suggestion is misleading in the case of Judaism. If this principle held, it would be reasonable to expect it to obtain in the case of Islam, a tradition that places great emphasis on the singular uniqueness of God. However, this also turns out not to be the case; Islamic mysticism, like its Jewish counterpart, boasts numerous experiential claims and metaphysical theories that link the ontological nature of the aspiring mystic to that of the ultimacy he seeks. Not least among the relevant concepts is Ibn al-'Arabi's doctrine of *wahdat al-wujud*, or the "unity of being." According to the Sufi master, "We ourselves are the attributes by which we describe God; our existence is merely an objectification of His existence. God is necessary to us in order that we may exist, while we are necessary to Him in order that He may be manifested to Himself."[42] Ibn al-'Arabi's sometimes recondite style can complicate interpretation, and numerous readers have described him, because of passages like this, as a pantheist. While that appellation is simplistic, at the very least, it does not seem that Ibn al-'Arabi felt constrained to understand God's ontological otherness in a fashion that excluded the possibility of humanity's sharing an important and intimate ontological relationship with him.

Ibn al-'Arabi was not alone in conceiving of God as more intimately related to humanity than orthodox Muslim theology suggests. Other Sufis, for example, the tenth-century master Junayd, adhered to the "mystery of Divine Unity . . . which meant . . . the existential experience of man's being carried back into the Divine Unity before its bifurcation into Creator and created."[43] Significantly, Junayd also suggests the notion of humanity's original existence as part of the divine as a justifying precondition for the "existential experience" of reactualizing that unity.

Perhaps the most common Sufi doctrine indicating some sort of ontological commingling between human and divine is that of *fanā'* and *baqā'*, the annihilation of the self and subsequent manifestation of divine attributes through the person of the individual mystic.[44] This notion of the replacement of the human self with some aspect of the divine nature grounds some of the most famous mystical pronouncements in the history of Sufism, such as *'Anā al-Haqq* and *subhānī*—meaning, respectively, "I am the Real" (*al-Haqq* being one of the traditional Muslim names for God) and "glory to me." Through the dual notions of *fanā'* and *baqā'*, these ecstatic declarations become not blasphemous assertions of the mystic's own divinity but orthodox affirmations of God's own being, spoken through the mouth of a human mystic in the midst of a moment in which his own being is effaced so that God's being may announce itself through him.

Mystical ontological theories and experiential accounts of unity or merging with ultimacy, in either the Jewish or the Muslim examples described above, should not be interpreted as simple reversals or denials of orthodox teaching in either tradition. Mystical writers are often subtle thinkers whose nuanced theologies allow the retention of apparently opposed or mutually exclusive understandings of the divine. Also, as Katz demonstrates effectively, mystics usually display the sincere desire to remain within the doctrinal and communal boundaries of their religious traditions—even while pushing those boundaries to new limits.[45] However, these brief examples from the Sufi tradition corroborate those from Jewish mysticism: doctrine, context, or background cannot be assumed to set absolute limits to forms of mystical experience. In both traditions, there are numerous examples of mystics who conceive of the encounter with divinity as occurring in an intimate fashion that overcomes, if only temporarily, the metaphysical distinction between humanity and God that is upheld by orthodox doctrine.

In addition to the misrepresentation of individual mystical experiences, the construal of context as overdeterminative of experience implies a second problematic conclusion. In combination with the apparent differences in teaching, doctrine, and context between religious traditions, the contextualist thesis suggests that mystic experiential accounts in different traditions will also be dissimilar. In "The 'Conservative' Character of Mysticism," Katz writes, "the experience of mystics comes into being as the kind of experience it is as a necessary consequence of the linguistic-theological and social-historic circumstances which govern the mystical ascent. And these circumstances are grounded in specific ontological schemata which shape the configuration of the quest and its goal."[46] This passage mentions at least five separate factors that, Katz insists, are determinative of mystical experience: language, theology (including basic doctrinal teachings), social context, historical setting, and ontological "schemata," or the metaphysical assumptions that pervade the religious tradition of which the mystic is a part. Given the "necessary" relationship Katz establishes between context (construed broadly to include these factors) and experience, differences in even one of these categories would seem sufficient to establish incomparability between mystical experiences of distinct traditions.

In fact, Katz seems to suggest that difference in theology alone is sufficient to ensure the distinct character of mystical experiences in different traditions. In addition to the ten basic tenets above attributed to Judaism, in his 1978 article Katz also offers a summary of the basic doctrinal elements of Buddhism—the Four Noble Truths and the Noble Eightfold Path (36). Following this, Katz offers seven features as a brief synopsis of nirvana, echoing the method he employs in summarizing basic Jewish doctrine. Shortly thereafter, Katz states, "Just setting this Buddhist understanding of the nature of things over against the Jewish should, in itself, already be strong evidence for the thesis that what the Buddhist experiences as *nirvana* is different from what the Jew experiences as *devekuth* ("cleaving" to God)" (38). Katz thereby suggests that differences in the doctrinal elements of different religious traditions are largely sufficient to ensure that mystical experiences associated with the relevant traditions will not be comparable. Context determines beforehand what is inexperienceable for a mystic (26).

Careful exegesis and comparison of mystical texts and experiential accounts in different religions fails to bear this claim out in the strong sense that Katz intends it. Although mystical texts tend to use terms and concepts derived from their respective religious traditions, common themes between distinct traditions and experiential accounts do arise. Substantiation of this claim relies on thorough exegetical comparison of mystical texts and experiential accounts; such extensive work requires separate discussion, and is offered in chapters 3, 4, and 5. The presence of these commonalities militates against the assumption that difference in context rules out the possibility of cross-cultural experiential similarities.

The problematic nature of the interpretive assumption that mystical experience will conform with doctrine is further compounded by the imaginative and innovative ways in which mystics interpret scripture. Katz argues convincingly that mystical literature effectively reinforces the authority of canonical scripture. This occurs partially because mystical texts frequently present themselves as commentaries on or extensions of scripture. This claim not only allows mystics to, in a sense, borrow the authority of the canon for their own works but also reconfirms the canonical status of scripture itself. After all, the desire to link their own writings and experiential accounts to their respective canons would not be felt unless mystics regarded these texts as true or authoritative. Ibn al-'Arabi's *Bezels of Wisdom*, for example, employs this conceit. Katz identifies this as a pervasive "conservative" tendency in mysticism, and locates examples in multiple mystical traditions and texts.

Katz is correct that mystics generally do seek to link their works to canonical scripture. Although he states that this "conservative" tendency does not characterize the entirety of mystical literature, his work emphasizes this aspect of it. This emphasis is concurrent with his "plea for the recognition of differences" between mystical experiences and traditions. By underscoring the linkage between mystical and canonical literature, Katz suggests that differences in mystical experience will parallel differences in authoritative religious tradition and doctrine.

This "conservative" aspect of mysticism, however, is complicated by the manner in which mystics interpret the scripture to which they relate their own texts and experiences. Mysticism, while seeking to relate itself to canonical scripture, is also characterized by the motivation to go beyond the modes of encounter with ultimacy afforded by mainstream religious practice. As Katz notes, "This tendency to 'go further' is common to all mystical traditions."[47] It is often manifested through mystics' use of "radical hermeneutics" that construe scripture in creative ways that lend validity to their own, often innovative and even heterodox theories and experiences. Neither Katz nor I mean to suggest that this is a cynical process wherein mystics intentionally contort scripture to their own ends. Rather, the novel ways in which mystics interpret scripture are undergirded by belief in its multivalence:

> Even, or perhaps especially, when they [mystics] offer apparently radical doctrinal views, they most usually do so in terms that relate their doctrines, no matter how novel, to the canonical source of their tradition. They do this for purposes of legitimation—that is, in order to justify their seemingly idiosyncratic claims—and because they sincerely believe that the master text that is appealed to has inexhaustible levels of meaning, the innermost layers of which they alone, rather than the "ordinary" believer or rational exegete, are able to plumb. Precisely because the text is God's Word (Logos, *aql*, *śruti*, or Torah), it carries the inherent possibility, even the necessity, of multiple meanings.[48]

Precisely because the mystic regards scripture as in some way divine, it is understood to embody multiple, if not infinite, potential meanings. Katz states that this understanding of scripture, and the attendant "radical hermeneutics," is present in "nearly all the great mystical traditions."[49]

Katz argues that it is this belief in the polysemy of scripture that substantiates mysticism's "conservative character": "The elaborate exegetical tradition of the Kabbalists is based on precisely this conservative principle, i.e. God's word as revealed in the Torah is inexhaustible in its meaning and meaningfulness. . . . The very novelty of the Kabbalistic interpretation of Scripture is grounded in the first instance in the highly traditional, conservative belief in the authority of the Torah as God's own will."[50] Kabbalists, Katz admits, derive surprising and sometimes counterintuitive meanings from scripture. It is largely for this reason that the mystical Jewish passages and teachings canvassed above should not be regarded as simple contradictions of traditional Jewish teaching. Rather, their authors regard them as commensurate with particular readings of scripture or doctrine, although those interpretations may not have been apparent to those unschooled in mystical thought.

In similar fashion, Katz argues that Sufis regard the meaning of the Qur'an as "endless, bottomless, infinite, containing all wisdom," and he identifies similar examples of belief in the divine polysemy of scripture in Christian and Hindu mystical texts.[51] In all cases, belief in the polyvalent or potentially infinite meanings of scripture allows mystics to put forth innovative doctrines or novel experiential descriptions that can be portrayed as commensurate with accepted teachings and within the bounds of orthodoxy. Katz is correct that this represents a sort of "conservative" tendency in that it serves to ensconce scripture even more powerfully as an authoritative symbol for religious and mystical traditions. However, the method by which this "conservative" dynamic is enacted simultaneously suggests the error of assuming that mystical literature and experiential reports will be compatible with authoritative interpretations of scripture or mainstream doctrine. Although mystics usually do regard scripture as authoritative, the belief that scripture can provide multiple if not infinite meanings renders the attribution of any particular meaning to scripture unstable. The "conservative" relationship of mysticism to canonical scripture is brought about precisely by regarding scripture as subject to multiple if not infinite meanings. This assumption creates a large if not endless semantic field within which the claim that "mystical experience will be compatible with orthodox doctrine" becomes largely meaningless as an interpretive guide or as a predictor of the content or character of experiential accounts. "Doctrine," under these circumstances, could refer to any of a number of different and potentially contradictory beliefs or interpretations.

Therefore, the "conservative" comportment of mysticism vis-à-vis orthodoxy is largely structural rather than substantive. Although scripture is regarded as authoritative and truthful, the content or substance of scripture is rendered unstable by mystics' particular hermeneutical strategies and beliefs. The appearance of orthodoxy is bought at the price of equivocality. This renders problematic Katz's claim that descriptions of mystical experience will be compatible with orthodox doctrine. While this is probably the view of most mystics, the observation offers little guidance as an interpretive principle.

Although context plays an essential role in interpreting mystic experiential accounts, the preinterpretive, explanatory assumption of conformity between the two is problematic in a number of ways. First, as demonstrated by the examples above, Jewish mysticism includes various metaphysical theories by which the ontological distinction between humanity and God—a notion that, as Katz rightly claims, is fundamental to orthodox Jewish thought—is blurred or traversed. Similarly, Islamic mysticism also suggests an ontological relationship between human and divine that would seem to contravene the emphasis on God's uniqueness and radical distinction from human beings. In both traditions, such theories are not uncommon in mystical literature. Some of these accounts entail claims of union with the divine or with other supernal entities, while others suggest deep metaphysical linkages between the mystic and God (still others include both). While this does not indicate that mystical experience should be interpreted in isolation from religious doctrine, it does suggest that the prior assumption of conformity between the two can be misleading.

The assumption that mystical experiences will differ merely as a result of differences in context or religious tradition is also problematic. The propensity of mystic experiential accounts to cross or escape the delimiting boundaries of context is explained in part by the epistemological theories whereby mystics understand and represent their own experiences, as detailed in chapters 3, 4, and 5. Additionally, the difficulty of assuming a close explanatory relationship between context and experience is compounded by the hermeneutical strategies of mystics, which presume multiple meanings of scripture. The divine polysemy of scripture suggests that mystics' understandings of the meaning of the canon may not conform either to mainstream doctrine or to the interpreting scholar's understanding of scripture, rendering the assumption of conformity ineffectual as an interpretive guide.

The problems that arise from Katz's method of analysis are emblematic of any interpretive theory that is based on the prior assumption of an explanatory relationship between context and experience. In assuming that context is sufficient to explain differences between mystical experiences, such an approach makes two problematic presuppositions. First, Katz's "preinterpretive" assumption of difference militates against recognition of similarities between experiential accounts or mystical traditions. Katz closes his influential 1978 article with the following words: "Our primary aim has been to mark out a new way of approaching the data, concentrating especially on disabusing scholars of the preconceived notion that all mystical experience is the same or similar. If mystical experience is always the same or similar in essence, as is so often claimed, then this has to be demonstrated by recourse to, and accurate handling of, the evidence, convincing logical argument, and coherent epistemological principles" (65). In retrospect, "accurate handling of the evidence" would seem to require that scholars, in comparing mystic experiential accounts, seek to interpret their material without assuming *either* sameness *or* difference. Katz describes his interest in refuting the essentialist thesis as "preinterpretive," indicating that his assumption of difference between mystical traditions and experiences precedes his engagement with mystical texts (23). As an interpretive method specifically intended to identify differences in mystic experiential accounts, contextualism, while sufficient to that purpose, leads to misleading conclusions about mystical experience and prejudges the results of comparative inquiry.

Second, Katz embeds an explanatory hypothesis in his attempt to interpret mysticism and mystical experience. In Katz's work, this explanatory hypothesis largely substitutes for the tasks of interpreting and comparing mystic experiential accounts and texts. Rather than characterize mystical experience through hermeneutically sound interpretation of experiential accounts, Katz does so through a deductive explanatory hypothesis—the "single epistemological assumption" that all experience is contextually mediated. This, in combination with synopses of mainstream religious doctrine, largely serves as the basis for Katz's characterizations of mystical experience. As I have shown above, this leads to various problematic presuppositions about mystical experience, both within and between individual traditions.

The difficulties implicated in this approach to the analysis of mysticism can be corrected by distinguishing the task of explaining mystical experience from interpreting it. Without the assumption that the nature of—let alone the differences between—mystical experiences can be explained by context, interpretation can disclose both similarities and differences between mystical traditions and texts. Additionally, interpretation can incorporate context as a hermeneutical aid without interposing prior deductive conclusions about the nature of mystical experience or contested epistemological theories about the structure of consciousness. I suggest a method for such interpretation in the following chapter.

2

AN INTERPRETIVE APPROACH

Wayne Proudfoot's *Religious Experience* has been widely influential in methodological discussions of the study of mystical experience. Proudfoot argues that a certain tradition of "hermeneutic" interpretation in religious studies, whose origins he traces to the work of Friedrich Schleiermacher, has helped foster illegitimate "protective strategies" within religious studies, especially with regard to discussions of religious experience and mysticism. According to Proudfoot, these strategies serve covert apologetic purposes; while they purport to offer theoretically neutral analyses of religious phenomena and experience, they actually function to shield such accounts from scholarly inquiry and particularly from naturalistic explanation. While he argues that a certain essential insight for interpretation has been garnered from this tradition, Proudfoot criticizes the role that such strategies have played in the study of religion and religious experience.

As a corrective, Proudfoot argues that the analysis of religious experience must distinguish between two tasks: descriptive and explanatory reduction. Under this bifurcation an experience "must be identified under the description employed by the subject and with reference to his concepts and beliefs."[1] To identify a mystical experience in terms that ignore or contradict the subject's own concepts and beliefs constitutes "descriptive reduction," which Proudfoot regards as inappropriate. After fulfilling this descriptive requirement, however, the analyst may legitimately engage in "explanatory reduction" of religious experience; she may offer an explanation or causal theory for the experience that *does not* necessarily agree with the subject's perspective.

In addition to this methodological bifurcation, Proudfoot argues in *Religious Experience* for an understanding of experience that is fundamentally conceptual and linguistic in nature, and concurrently denies the possibility of immediate experience. In this regard, his work is in step with that of Steven Katz and other contextualist thinkers. However, in light of the bifurcation Proudfoot draws between description and explanation, this epistemological position is relevant only to his attempt to explain, rather than interpret, mystical experience. I adopt a version of Proudfoot's bifurcation for the analysis of mystical experience; however, that adoption does not indicate my endorsement of either his epistemology or his naturalism.[2]

As Proudfoot notes, the descriptive or interpretive phase of analysis must precede the explanatory one (44, 218). Explanation, Proudfoot emphasizes, may and usually does employ philosophical commitments and theories ulterior to the subject's own experiential account. Therefore, if performed prior to interpretation, the explanatory procedure can lead to alteration of the account under consideration and result in a misleading characterization of experience (i.e., descriptive reduction). The conflation of these two processes is another way of describing the problematic nature of Katz's approach to the study mystical experience.

Although Proudfoot employs the language of "description" and "explanation," I argue that this distinction more broadly describes the difference between *interpretation* and explanation. Proudfoot emphasizes that the subject's identification of his experience as religious or mystical entails an unspoken commitment to the belief that his experience cannot be exhaustively explained in terms of natural causes; the mystic implicitly assumes that his experience is fully explicable only with reference to some supernatural reality (137). For Proudfoot, nonreductive "description" of a mystical experience entails acknowledgment of only this (often implicit) belief. I employ the term "interpretation" to signal that understanding a mystic experiential account is most effective when it considers various additional, often complex beliefs, commitments, and assumptions implicit in an experiential account. For the purposes of this project, I categorize those beliefs and assumptions under the rubrics of ontology and epistemology.

By employing Proudfoot's distinction between description (or interpretation) and explanation, the interpreter is able to foreground philosophical and religious commitments on the part of the subject or text that are intimately related to an experiential account and that should serve as interpretive guides. Expanding on Proudfoot's comments regarding description, I argue that this is achieved through a combination of phenomenological *epoché*, holism, and the principle of charity, which together function to bracket the interpreter's own philosophical commitments (including explanatory theory) and to foreground those of the subject or text for purposes of interpretation. By employing this phenomenological method as a strictly interpretive, rather than explanatory, technique, I contend that this approach does not entail the protective explanatory restrictions that Proudfoot criticizes, and that it provides an effective technique for the interpretation of mystic experiential accounts.

In defending religion against the "cultured despisers" with whom he associated, Friedrich Schleiermacher offers a conception of religion that associates it, first and foremost, with religious experience, and especially the "religious affections" (7). In doing so, Schleiermacher attempts to free religion from association with either doctrine or practice, and thereby to insulate it from objections based on critiques of the "metaphysical beliefs" associated with it. Ultimately, Schleiermacher argues that religion is to be identified not with ecclesiastical institutions or theological doctrines but with an "autonomous moment" of experience that cannot be reduced to either thought or morality (xiii). Proudfoot contends that this conception of religion as sui generis—or as nonreducible to other forms of human life such as belief or practice—has been carried on in a tradition that includes thinkers such as William James and Rudolf Otto, and that it is still employed by some contemporary scholars (7).

Throughout *Religious Experience*, Proudfoot maintains that this "hermeneutic tradition" has contributed an important insight to the study of religion and particularly the study of religious experience. Specifically, this tradition undergirds the descriptive requirement for which Proudfoot argues: that religious experience must be "identified under a description" that accords with the subject's own understanding. However, when combined with warnings against "reductionism," Proudfoot contends, this tradition often serves the apologetic purpose of insulating religious experience from academic inquiry and protecting it from explanation in anything but religious terms. The stance of scholars who employ this covertly apologetic program is, in Proudfoot's words, "that religious experience cannot properly be studied by a method that reduces it to a cluster of phenomena that can be explained in historical, psychological, or sociological terms" (190). Under such conditions, Proudfoot argues, scholarly works that purport to be descriptive or analytical ultimately function apologetically and theologically because they preserve and protect the religious or mystical character of the experience under consideration.

In deconstructing these covert apologetics, Proudfoot points out that "experience" is an ambiguous term that can function in two ways: "When I inquire about what a person has experienced at a certain moment, my question is ambiguous between two meanings: (1) how it seemed to that person at that time; and (2) the best explanation that can be given of the experience" (217). This is a categorical rather than a temporal distinction. In (1), "experience" refers to the subject's perspective on or appraisal of his own experience; it is the subject's own understanding of the experience that is indicated. In (2), "experience" refers more objectively to the most likely or plausible explanation of the experience under consideration. Proudfoot offers a lucid example of the difference between these two senses of "experience." A man is hiking down a path in the woods. He perceives a bear up ahead and accordingly feels fear. Upon later inspection, it turns out that the "bear" he feared was actually a log partially hidden in shadows. In the second sense of experience, what the man "actually" perceived was a log; given further information (in this case, closer examination of the object in question), that is the most accurate description of the event. However, in order to understand the man's initial feeling of fear, it is necessary to describe his experience as that of perceiving a bear rather than a log (192–93). This requires reference to "experience" in the first sense given above.

Proudfoot contends that the hermeneutic tradition to which he objects conflates these two senses of experience by insisting that experience always and only be considered in the first sense, investing the subject's perspective on his experience with comprehensive authority. Under these conditions, Proudfoot argues, the attempt to explain a given experience in terms that would not be amenable to the subject's understanding is considered illegitimate. This constitutes the apologetic or protective program to which Proudfoot objects. In response, Proudfoot suggests a fundamental distinction between descriptive reduction and explanatory reduction. The former, Proudfoot argues, is always illegitimate: "*Descriptive reduction* is the failure to identify an emotion, practice, or experience under the description by which the subject identifies it. This is indeed unacceptable. To describe an experience in nonreligious terms when the subject himself describes it in religious terms is to misidentify the experience, or to attend to another experience altogether" (196). In order to analyze a mystical experience accurately, it is necessary to begin with an account of the experience that retains the character of it as the subject originally describes it. Here, Proudfoot refers in general terms to the religious nature of the experience. Specifically, this descriptive requirement demands that religious or mystical experience "must be specified from the subject's point of view" and include only concepts and beliefs that can be plausibly attributed to the subject (229).

Proudfoot allows that in constructing a description of a mystical experience, the analyst may paraphrase or elaborate on the original account. In doing so, however, she must ensure that the resultant description is one that can be plausibly ascribed to the subject (180). This requires that the experiential description "employ only concepts in the subject's repertoire, and any background beliefs or desires presupposed by the attribution of the experience to the subject must be plausibly ascribed to the subject" (181). In order to ensure that a given experiential description is accurate, the analyst must take care that any concepts or assumptions implied by attributing the experience to its subject can, in fact, be plausibly ascribed to him. Proudfoot repeats this standard numerous times, underscoring its centrality to the descriptive task (73, 193, 209, 234). This is the "chief insight" that Proudfoot derives from the "hermeneutic tradition" (68). As he notes, a similar standard is suggested by William James in *The Varieties of Religious Experience*: "Religious experience must be characterized from the perspective of the one who has the experience. . . . This is rather close to James's circumscription of the topic of his [Gifford] lectures: 'Religion, therefore, I now ask you arbitrarily to take it, shall mean for us the feelings, acts, and experiences of individual men in their solitude, so far as they apprehend themselves to stand in relation to whatever they may consider to be the divine'" (181). Proudfoot later argues that James ultimately expands this method too far, indulging in the protective agenda that Proudfoot critiques. In this instance, however, Proudfoot suggests that James is correct to privilege the perspective of the subject in terms of describing the experience. This "first-person privilege," Proudfoot reminds us, does not imply that the subject has "immediate intuitive access to [his own] mental states versus mediated inferential reasoning" (195).[3]

Beyond these comments, Proudfoot does not describe at great length what is involved in this focus on the subject's perspective for describing experience. Further methodological elaboration is required in order to satisfactorily delineate the interpretive approach that is required. In suggesting that the subject's own perspective should be authoritative in the first phase of analysis, Proudfoot's descriptive requirement may be seen as recommending a phenomenological approach to the interpretation of religion.[4] In describing the descriptive phase of analysis, Proudfoot quotes Mircea Eliade, who suggests that religious data be interpreted "on their own plane of reference" (191). By this, Eliade suggests that the meaning of a religious or mystical statement should be assessed through reference to the notional context from which it arises—the religious or mystical worldview of the subject. To this extent, Proudfoot is in agreement with Eliade. However, for Eliade, phenomenology of religion is also characterized by the search for the "essence" or universal structures of religious phenomena. In this fashion, Eliade perceives a fundamental, if creative, tension between phenomenological and historical approaches to the study of religion.[5] Whereas the phenomenologist, in Eliade's estimation, seeks to discover the common essence within religion, the historian focuses on the particular, individual historical "moments" of religion. The manner in which Eliade seeks to resolve, if only partially, this tension between phenomenological and historical approaches to the study of religion is telling: "if the 'phenomenologists' are interested in the meanings of religious data, the 'historians,' on their side, attempt to show how these meanings have been experienced and lived in the various cultures and historical moments, how they have been transformed, enriched, or impoverished in the course of history. But if we are to avoid sinking back into an obsolete 'reductionism,' this history of religious meanings must always be regarded as forming part of the history of the human spirit."[6] Eliade seeks to subsume the historian's approach to the study of religion within the assumptions of his phenomenological method. The historian's task, as he defines it, is to unearth the specific forms and shapes in which the essential meanings and structures of religion, identified by phenomenological analysis, have been manifested. The presumption of an ahistorical "essence" pervading and linking various religions and religious phenomena has come in for serious criticism since Eliade's time. In this sense, the analytical method that Eliade endorses is an example of the essentialism to which Katz objects.[7] Just as the essentialist scholar of mystical experience seeks the common core of it underneath its culturally inflected forms, Eliade seeks the essential structures of religion underneath the specific forms identified by the historian. In this manner, Eliade seeks to validate the historical dimension of research into religious phenomena while simultaneously making that research subservient to his own search for essences.[8]

Proudfoot is correct that Eliade's formulation of phenomenology of religion, in combination with his criticism of reductionism, results in a problematic approach to the study of religion and mystical experience. This is because Eliade conflates interpretive and explanatory procedures in his formulation of phenomenology of religion. In applauding the work of Gerardus van der Leeuw, Eliade writes, "he remained a phenomenologist insofar as in his descriptions he respected the religious data and their peculiar intentionality. He pointed out the irreducibility of religious representations to social, psychological, or rational functions, and he rejected those naturalistic prejudices which seek to explain religion by something other than itself."[9] It is the categorical rejection of "naturalistic prejudices" that is problematic. Eliade regards resistance to any explanation that would "reduce" religious phenomena to naturalistic causes as essential to the phenomenological method. In rejecting both the interpretation *and the explanation* of religious phenomena through naturalistic notions, Eliade restricts or eliminates the process of explanatory reduction that Proudfoot defends, and protectively privileges a specifically religious understanding of religious phenomena.

Pace Eliade, I argue that this explanatory delimitation is not necessary to phenomenology of religion. Within the structure of the analytical bifurcation that Proudfoot draws between description and explanation, the phenomenological method can be reformulated in a manner that absolves it of this problematic bias and retains its usefulness as an interpretive tool for mystical experience. Eliade already indicates the purview within which phenomenology of religion is an appropriate method: disclosure of the "meanings of religious data."[10] In interpretation, the "reduction" of religious or mystical experience to social, psychological, or historical causes is illegitimate and misleading; as Proudfoot suggests, such reduction leads to the misconstrual, if not the replacement, of the experience under consideration. Insofar as a given experience is described by a mystic with reference to supernatural causes or religious entities, that aspect of the experience must be retained in the descriptive or interpretive phase of analysis. To describe such an experience with reference to social, psychological, or other naturalistic causes would radically alter the meaning of the experience under consideration. In Eliade's terms, this would represent a failure to interpret religious data "on their own plane of reference."

That warning is synonymous with Proudfoot's directive to identify or describe an experience "under the description employed by the subject and with reference to his concepts and beliefs" (73). Proudfoot thereby endorses an interpretive approach that coincides with the phenomenological method that Eliade prescribes; however, Proudfoot's bifurcation can be used to suggest a revision of Eliade's phenomenological approach by limiting its scope only to the descriptive or interpretive phase of analysis. In this formulation, phenomenology of religion is the appropriate method for interpretation, but its employment as an explanatory delimitation is illegitimate. Thus revised, phenomenology of religion, as the attempt to disclose the "meanings of religious data," fulfills the interpretive role called for by Proudfoot's method.

In seeking to disclose the meaning of religious data "on their own plane of reference," phenomenology of religion inevitably refers to the context of a religious phenomenon or, in this case, an experiential account. As I suggested in chapter 1, Katz's method of incorporating context into interpretation is problematic because it presumes a heavy explanatory dependence of the nature of mystical experience on context prior to interpretation, thereby conflating the interpretive and explanatory tasks. Another method of incorporating context into interpretation, without presuming such an explanatory relation or neo-Kantian contextualist epistemology, is needed. Recent philosophical work on interpretation offers a way forward. Based largely on Donald Davidson's work on radical interpretation, a number of scholars have identified the principle of holism as the basic tenet of interpretation.[11] Nancy Frankenberry and Hans Penner define holism in the following terms:

> [Holism] states that the value or significance of an element, unit, or object in a system stems not from some intrinsic value that it possesses in itself, but from its relations with other elements. Thus, our propositional attitudes, that is to say, our beliefs, desires, intentions, hopes, fears and memories are logically related to perception, learning and language. They are constituted by their simultaneous interdependence, forming a network. Given the principle of holism, there is no hierarchical priority. The principle also tells us that we cannot ascribe beliefs, for example, to others independently of additional beliefs and attitudes. It follows, then, that no single belief is in itself rational or irrational. From a holistic point of view, rationality is not an intrinsic property of an object or a propositional attitude.[12]

Holism provides a model for the interpretation of mystic experiential accounts that fulfills the phenomenological principle. Within fields such as philosophy of language and science, numerous versions of holism obtain; here, it is specifically semantic holism that is relevant, which suggests that linguistic content or meaning is not derived from individual sentences but rather arises from the relationships of sentences and propositions with other "elements"—related beliefs, desires, emotions, and attitudes in a network or system. In the context of this project, the relevant system is the set of theological and experiential assumptions within which a mystic's experiential account—or a specific claim or sentence in such an account—is situated: the broad set of related beliefs, notions, and assumptions that constitute the notional context of a described mystical experience.

According to holism, the statements contained within a mystic experiential account derive their meaning from their relations with other units that together constitute a matrix of meaning, including both discursive concepts and more ambiguous elements such as "desires, hopes, and fears." Significantly, as Penner and Frankenberry note, "there is no hierarchical priority" that would privilege certain elements or epistemological functions over others; meaning arises holistically from the system as a whole. This suggests that holism conceptualizes experience in a more "egalitarian" fashion than the mediation thesis does. The epistemological structure that Katz employs features contextual influence as the primary determinative factor; context sets limits that constrain or restrict other possible dimensions of experience within distinct boundaries. By contrast, holism construes all dimensions of experience as existing in "simultaneous interdependence"; while various elements are related to one another, none necessarily has superior or delimiting influence over others. In this perspective, context, while relevant, does not delimit the possible forms in which experience may manifest.

As Davidson rightly notes, holism, as a "constraint" on radical interpretation, recognizes a hermeneutic circle between single elements of a subject's psychic world and the larger web of his beliefs, concepts, and desires.[13] Interpretation therefore involves a continual dialectic between particular beliefs and propositions and other elements that constitute and inform the subject's discourse. This suggests that, rather than analyzing a mystic's utterance in isolation, a full understanding of it requires consideration of other elements with which it is related. Holism thus achieves the same end as Katz's contextualism: it suggests that particular elements of an experiential account cannot be interpreted in isolation from other elements, the text as a whole, and other relevant beliefs, notions, and concepts related to the mystic's experience and description thereof.

Unlike contextualism, however, holism does not depend on the epistemological assumption that a subject's experiences are delimited by filters derived from the subject's historical background and context. Rather than formulating itself as a psychological or epistemological principle, holism is a *semantic* guideline. Katz's single epistemological assumption presumes knowledge of the functionality of the mystic's experience or consciousness—a phenomenon to which the interpreter does not have access. Holism, by contrast, focuses on the experiential *account* and related contextual elements, to which the interpreter does have access. Holism operates as a semantic guide to disclosing the meaning of an experiential account, rather than as an epistemological principle that claims to describe the nature and functionality of experience. Interpretation thus becomes a matter of discerning meaning in a historically informed fashion, rather than presuming a certain kind of psychological causality. In effect, holism acknowledges Katz's own observation that all an interpreter has access to are *accounts* of experience, rather than experiences themselves: "The main legacy we have of the great mystics is their *writings* and related *linguistic* creations. We have no access to their special experience independently of these texts. What we call the great historical mystical traditions of the world are in fact a series of documents of differing sorts. No one has any privileged access here to the original mystics' experience outside its textual incorporation. And it is these documents that are the data for all analytical decipherment and scholarly reconstructions."[14] Even in the case of an interview performed with a living mystic, an interpreter has access only to the subject's verbal account of the experience, rather than to the experience itself.[15] This suggests that Katz's single epistemological assumption—precisely because it is an *epistemological* assumption—is inappropriate. As Katz himself implies, a more appropriate method will focus on the mystic's *account* of his experience rather than make claims about the experience itself. Holism does so by focusing the interpretive endeavor on the attempt to disclose the meaning of an experiential account, rather than by presuming a particular structure of experience or consciousness.

In contextualizing particular experiential claims within the web of attitudes and beliefs with which they are related, holism discloses the rationality of those claims, understood in a coherentist fashion: "The principle of holism places constraints on our interpretive tasks. It tells us that we cannot ascribe beliefs to others independently of other beliefs and other propositional attitudes. This interconnectedness, which entails logical consistency and coherence, constitutes rationality."[16] In this fashion, holism entails the principle of charity, the notion that interpretation depends upon the assumption of the general rational consistency of a subject's claims and beliefs with one another.[17] As Frankenberry and Penner emphasize, this "rationality" does not denote the truth of either any one of the subject's claims or the subject's larger perspective; the interpreter need not affirm the truth of any claims on the part of the subject or the text he interprets. The principle of charity is not a call for tolerance or sympathy with regard to the subject. Rather, the principle of charity makes interpretation possible by suggesting that within the context of the subject's beliefs, desires, statements, and attitudes, there will be a sufficient degree of corroborative consistency such that the subject's claims can be recognized as meaningful, or as not demonstrating such a high degree of internal inconsistency that meaning cannot be recognized.

Note that the principle of charity assumes a "relatively high" degree of "general" consistency; it does not assume that any subject's beliefs, attitudes, and ideas are all always entirely consistent. While almost all persons (excluding the most deeply deranged or mentally ill) exhibit the minimal degree of internal consistency that the principle of charity assumes, almost no one ever exhibits complete consistency. The principle of charity thereby suggests that interpretation be guided by the rather modest presupposition that a subject's behavior and language *are interpretable*. Without such a presumption, the task of deriving meaning from the subject's speech and/or writing becomes impossible. The principle of charity, therefore, is not just an aid to interpretation but the basic presumption that a subject's language and behavior have meaning that can be discerned by the interpreter. It is not merely a tool of interpretation but a foundational assumption that makes interpretation possible.[18]

In the context of this project, holism directs the interpreter to the contextual sources harnessed in chapters 3, 4, and 5 to interpret the experiential claims of Ibn al-'Arabi, Meister Eckhart, and Hui-neng. These sources represent the notional context with which the mystics' experiential claims are assumed to demonstrate a minimal degree of consistency. Holism does not assume, however, that these or other sources inscribe absolute boundaries to the possible experiences available to a mystic, or that they operate

(consciously or subconsciously) as discursive concepts that delimit consciousness. Rather, holism regards these contextual sources as semantic
lexicons through which terms, notions, and qualities in a mystic experiential account may be understood. The principle of charity, concurrently,
suggests that there will be a recognizable degree of consistency between
the subject's experiential account and related contextual sources. The
meaning of an experiential account thereby arises out of the logical relations between it and the other sources of information—historical context,
theology, etc.—with which it is related. As chapters 3 through 5 reveal, this
assumption can be demonstrably substantiated; mystic experiential accounts
reflect basic assumptions about the functionality of experience and the
metaphysical nature of encounters with ultimacy that can be identified in
related texts. However, rather than constitute context as the delimiting
function of consciousness or the primary explanation for the nature of
mystical experience, holism regards context as the best available resource
for semantic correlates to the elements of an experiential account. Under
these circumstances, the interpreter does not begin with context and then
deduce the possibilities for mystical experience from it—a procedure that
the mediation thesis suggests. Rather, holism suggests that the meaning of
a mystic experiential account arises in relation to, *but not in subservience to*,
contextual elements.

For example, Katz compares the Jewish term *ayin* to the Buddhist term
sunyata. He argues that, despite the fact that both terms are commonly
translated into English as "nothingness," the meanings of these terms are
quite different.[19] Since this difference is only recognizable through consideration of context, Katz suggests that the respective experiences of "nothingness" must not be comparable. Based on their immersion in different
traditions, Katz argues, Jewish and Buddhist mystics *necessarily* experience
different types of "nothingness." Holism is equally capable of acknowledging this important distinction, but without prescribing, prior to inquiry,
that the experience of either *ayin* or *sunyata* is necessarily the result of
contextually prefigured limitations to consciousness, or assuming that
the two are necessarily incompatible. Having encountered these terms in
two separate mystical reports, holism guides the interpreter to relevant
sources—in this case, the rest of the mystics' experiential accounts, their
other writings, and relevant sources of kabbalist and Buddhist teaching,
respectively—in order to derive the meanings of the terms as used in the
individual accounts. Rather than assume that the kabbalist's and Buddhist's

experiential possibilities are limited by their contextual backgrounds, the holist simply acknowledges that when it comes to interpreting a mystic's experiential description, it is first the account itself, and then related texts and teachings, that represent the best guides to meaning. Ensuing comparison can then reveal whether any similarities between *ayin* and *sunyata* obtain.

Because holism does not assume that context preemptively determines experience, it is also better equipped to recognize innovation and idiosyncratic uses of terms in mystical texts. Holism focuses interpretation on the experiential account itself and its relation to related sources of information; it does not assume, prior to inquiry, that an experiential account will necessarily be in complete accordance with contextual sources. Rather, because it compares an experiential account and contextual sources on an equal footing, holism highlights those instances in which divergence, if present, arises.

Hans-Georg Gadamer provides a description of the process by which such assumptions of conformity can be checked. Citing Heidegger, Gadamer writes, "All correct interpretation must be on guard against the arbitrary fancies and the limitations imposed by imperceptible habits of thought, and it must direct its gaze 'on the things themselves.' . . . For the interpreter to let himself be guided by the things themselves is obviously not a matter of a single, 'conscientious' decision, but is 'the first, last, and constant task.' For it is necessary to keep one's gaze fixed on the thing throughout all the constant distractions that originate in the interpreter himself."[20] This could seem to be a naïve call for pure objectivity on the interpreter's part.[21] However, Gadamer recognizes the impossibility of such an ideal. In encountering a text, Gadamer writes, the interpreter will inevitably "project" a meaning for it—an assumed interpretation that, while arising from the interpreter's encounter with the text, also inevitably includes presuppositions on the interpreter's part. This is unavoidable. However, Gadamer writes, such "projections" or "fore-conceptions" are under constant revision, evoked by further engagement with the text. This, in fact, constitutes the process of interpretation:

> Interpretation begins with fore-conceptions that are replaced by more suitable ones. This constant process of new projection constitutes the movement of understanding and interpretation. A person who is trying to understand is exposed to distraction from fore-meanings that

are not borne out by the things themselves. Working out appropriate projections, anticipatory in nature, to be confirmed "by the things" themselves, is the constant task of understanding. The only "objectivity" here is the confirmation of a fore-meaning in its being worked out. Indeed, what characterizes the arbitrariness of inappropriate fore-meanings if not that they come to nothing in being worked out?[22]

Rather than strive for a completely objective perspective, the interpreter, in Gadamer's formula, acknowledges the "fore-meanings" he projects for the text. In this case, such fore-meanings would probably represent aspects of context, which the interpreter assumes will define the experiential account under consideration. In cases where the account diverges from those expectations, however, such fore-meanings will be revised in light of the meaning that gradually emerges from the account itself. Thus the interpreter is able to check his fore-conceptions—prior assumptions about the meaning of the text—by comparing and contrasting them with the emerging meaning of the account itself. This is an ongoing process wherein assumed fore-meanings are constantly revised in light of further engagement with the text. The identification of apparent divergences from context can spur either the search for other contextual influences or the recognition of innovation on the mystic's part. The importance of this capability is underscored by both the radical hermeneutics performed by mystics, discussed in chapter 1, and the function of mystical epistemologies, to be discussed later.

To summarize the difference between contextualism and holism: Katz constructs the issue of analyzing mystical experience as an epistemological one, based on an assumed epistemological structure wherein all experience is necessarily mediated. Holism addresses this as an interpretive question of meaning and makes no assumptions about either the functionality of consciousness or the nature of the experience itself. Whereas Katz deploys a prescriptive epistemology to explain the relation between the subject's experience and context, holism places the experiential *account* within concentric systems of reference that act as lexicons for deriving meaning.[23] Figure 1 represents the contrast between contextualism and semantic holism.

Holism seeks to foreground the mystic's own assumptions about experience, rather than those of the scholar, in the act of interpretation. As de Certeau argued, if we are to understand mystical experience—especially given the tendency of mystical literature to confound rationalistic

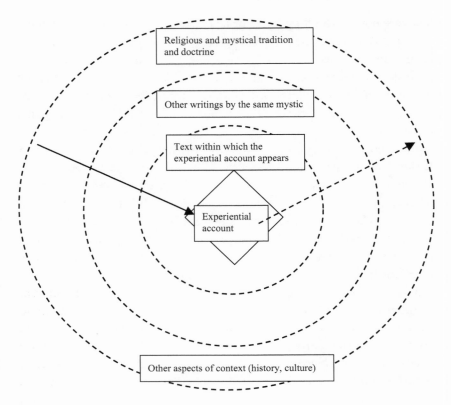

FIGURE 1

Semantic holism (phenomenological interpretation): dotted line
Interpretation begins with the experiential account and moves outward through expanding systems of reference; increasing distance from the account signals a decreasing degree of relational proximity. The lines of the concentric circles are dotted, rather than solid, to signal that the boundaries between the systems of reference are not absolute. During the process of interpretation, certain aspects of context may prove to be more relevant than others. Interpretation always begins, however, with the account itself.

The dotted line indicates a relation of semantics rather than epistemological causality. In interpreting an account in relation to these sources, divergences may be discovered.

Epistemological contextualism: solid line
By contrast, the contextualist method begins with context and determines the meaning of experience in a deductive fashion that moves inward. The solid line indicates an assumed relation of epistemological causality; this is Katz's "single epistemological assumption" that experience is always mediated by context.

analysis—"we must return to what the mystic says of his or her own experience," rather than relying on our own assumptions about what experience "must be" like.[24]

This procedure is compatible with the bifurcation that Proudfoot draws between descriptive and explanatory reduction. If Proudfoot's bifurcation restricts the validity of the phenomenological approach strictly to the descriptive or interpretive phase of analysis, it also suggests a delimitation to the valid employment of the analyst's own explanatory theory. In order to foreground the concepts and beliefs of the subject or experiential account for interpretation, a second interpretive maneuver is implied: the bracketing or heuristic suspension of the analyst's own philosophical commitments. Charles Long, following Eliade, defines this practice in the following terms: "The phenomenological epoché is the restraint we exercise on the level of thought—a restraint that allows the phenomenon, the other, to appear."[25]

Phenomenology of religion has sometimes been criticized for a kind of methodological naïveté that too easily assumes the interpreter's ability to step outside her historical conditioning in order to encounter, in a pure fashion, "the given." Phenomenology of religion need not, however, claim so abstract a goal. Gadamer writes of the necessity for a kind of intellectual restraint in interpretation: "This is the first condition of hermeneutics . . . namely the fundamental suspension of our own prejudices."[26] For Gadamer, this suspension does not consist simply of the interpreter's setting aside his own prejudices en masse in order to accept those of the text as valid. Rather, Gadamer construes this suspension as allowing a prejudice to be "brought into play by being put at risk" when confronted by the text.[27] Gadamer's understanding of the suspension enacted by the interpreter is informed by the conversational manner in which he depicts the encounter with a text. His description of this aspect of the hermeneutical process is commensurate with that advocated by phenomenological *epoché*: the unseating or destabilization of the interpreter's assumptions as truths or filters through which a text is to be read.

As Gadamer acknowledges, however, this suspension is a difficult task. The prejudices of the interpreter are insidious; they tend to operate subconsciously and therefore resist conscious restraint or suspension. The encounter with a text, however, provides the mechanism by which prejudices can be foregrounded and recognized, and thereby suspended: "It is impossible to make ourselves aware of a prejudice while it is constantly operating unnoticed, but only when it is, so to speak, provoked. The encounter with a . . . text can provide this provocation."[28] In the encounter with a text, the interpreter's prejudices are challenged by those aspects of it that contradict her presuppositions. In this manner, the interpreter becomes aware of a philosophical tension or disagreement between herself and the text she interprets. This facilitates acknowledgment of presuppositions on the interpreter's part that had formerly gone unnoticed. It then becomes possible, for purposes of interpretation, to suspend those presuppositions temporarily. *Epoché*, in this formulation, does not denote the interpreter's negation of her entire philosophical perspective or historical worldview, but more plausibly indicates the temporary suspension of those specific presuppositions that are contradicted by the text under interpretation.

With regard to this project, such provocation is facilitated by the interrogative categories of ontology and epistemology employed in the next three chapters. In asking what the ontological and epistemological presuppositions of mystical experience are, the contemporary interpreter comes upon answers that probably contravene his own assumptions, such as the incontrovertible distinction between subject and object, the mediated nature of consciousness, the fundamentally linguistic character of experience, and so on. This disjunction demonstrates the necessity for *epoché*. In this scenario, the interpreter realizes both the basic assumptions of the experiential account and his own, contrary presuppositions, the latter of which can then be bracketed for purposes of interpretation. In this manner, the interpreter acknowledges the historicity of both his own philosophical perspective and that of the subject or text he seeks to interpret.

This procedure makes no claims concerning the truthfulness of either set of philosophical commitments; rather, it acknowledges that the subject or text is immersed within and employs basic assumptions that differ from those of the interpreter. *Epoché* acknowledges that the meaning of a subject's or text's own claims and beliefs becomes manifest in relation to other commitments and beliefs on the part of the subject or embedded in the text that the interpreter need not—and, especially in the case of medieval and ancient mystics, probably does not—share. With regard to Katz, *epoché* would bracket his single epistemological assumption, which underlies both his assumption of the necessary delimitation of experience by context and his consequent claim that mystical experiences arising in different traditions will necessarily be different. Reflexively, *epoché* also restrains the explanatory limitations of phenomenology of religion to which Proudfoot objects. If an analyst assumes that an experience cannot be explained by naturalistic causes, that assumption as well must be suspended for purposes of interpretation. *Epoché* thereby buttresses the distinction between interpretation and explanation called for by Proudfoot's bifurcation.

Proudfoot's distinction between descriptive and explanatory tasks implicitly recognizes the necessity for this bracketing on the part of the interpreter: "In the study of religion considerable confusion has resulted from the failure to distinguish the requisite conditions for the identification of an experience under a certain description from those for explaining the experience. The analyst must cite, but need not endorse, the concepts, beliefs, and judgments that enter into the subject's identification of his experience" (196). In seeking to counter the protective interpretive program he critiques, Proudfoot emphasizes the necessity of the independence of the scholar's explanation from the "concepts, beliefs, and judgments" of the subject. In reciprocal fashion, concepts and beliefs on the part of the subject must be acknowledged and incorporated into interpretation independently of those of the analyst. The distinction thereby upheld retains the integrity of both the interpreter's description of an experience as an interpretation *of the subject's reported experience* and the interpreter's own ability to explain (in the latter phase of analysis) the experience in terms and concepts distinct from those of the subject.

After delineating the proper scope of the descriptive phase of Proudfoot's analytical method (what I expand and refer to as "interpretation"), explanation of an experiential account may be attempted. Here, Proudfoot argues that reduction is appropriate: "*Explanatory reduction* consists in offering an explanation of an experience in terms that are not those of the subject and that might not meet with his approval. This is perfectly justifiable and is, in fact, normal procedure" (197). Proudfoot claims that "[in] general, what we want is historical or cultural explanation," thereby endorsing an explanatory paradigm that assumes a naturalistic worldview (223). This preference for naturalistic explanation reflects his own particular beliefs and philosophical perspective. While I do not necessarily share this preference, the method of interpretation I recommend does not invalidate such a procedure prima facie. The viability of such an explanation—or of any other type, including those that refer to supernatural realities—would be assessed by the extent to which it can satisfactorily account for the experience under consideration (210). This explanatory endeavor, however, must follow interpretation, rather than precede or replace it.

To summarize, the method I recommend for analysis of an experiential account may be broken down into the following principles:

(1) *Bifurcation between interpretation and explanation.* In drawing a strict bifurcation between description and explanation, Proudfoot provides a method that distinguishes between two separate tasks that preserves the integrity of both. In relating description to the subject's own beliefs or the concepts implicit in a text, Proudfoot encourages a kind of analysis wherein emic assumptions about experience may be incorporated into interpretation, while simultaneously preserving room for the analyst's own explanation.

(2) *Epoché.* Epoché reinforces this bifurcation by directing that the analyst suspend his own philosophical assumptions—including his explanatory theory—until the second phase of analysis. For purposes of interpretation, the analyst's own philosophical perspective and assumptions play no role.

(3) *Phenomenological interpretation.* Proudfoot's method retains the necessary theoretical space for interpretation. A phenomenological approach, revised in light of the analytical bifurcation between interpretation and explanation, fulfills this task. While Proudfoot focuses on the subject's belief that his experience is inexplicable in purely naturalistic terms, I suggest that interpretation is better guided by a broader incorporation of the subject's (sometimes implicit) philosophical assumptions and worldview, particularly as they relate to experience.

(4) *Holism.* Holism is the mechanism by which phenomenological interpretation may be performed. Holism acknowledges a hermeneutic circle between an experiential account and its notional context, including contextual sources and texts, with which it is related. It acknowledges that meaning arises from the relations between individual beliefs and statements and other elements, including discursive beliefs and other, nondiscursive emotions, attitudes, etc. Context is incorporated into interpretation semantically rather than epistemologically.

(5) *Principle of charity.* The principle of charity grounds this interpretive process by assuming a basic, minimal degree of rational consistency between the subject's concepts, desires, and statements. However,

divergences between the experiential account and contextual sources may arise and are acknowledged. The experiential account itself remains the focal point of interpretation.

(6) *Explanation*. Here, the analyst's perspective, philosophical assumptions, and/or explanatory theory (such as naturalism, or Katz's single epistemological assumption) may be employed. A given explanation stands or falls according to the degree to which it can account for the experiential account. This procedure is separate from, and must be performed after, interpretation.

In the following three chapters, I employ this approach to interpreting mystic experiential accounts. Specifically, I examine the experiential claims of three mystics (Ibn al-ʿArabi, Meister Eckhart, and Hui-neng) in light of contextual sources, following the structure mapped out here. These analyses demonstrate the utility of analyzing mystic experiential accounts in semantic relation to their contexts, independently of any explanatory hypothesis. They also reinforce the necessity of *epoché*, given the drastic differences between the philosophical assumptions of these mystics and those of contemporary academics. I organize these interpretations through the categories of ontology and epistemology, with intriguing results.

3

IBN AL-ʿARABI AND THE
NAMES OF GOD

Abu Bakr Muhammad Ibn al-ʿArabi was born in Murcia, in southeastern Spain, in 1165. The son of a family that appears to have been both pious and politically well positioned, Ibn al-ʿArabi is said to have displayed an inclination for the life of a mystic early on, purportedly attaining considerable spiritual insight in his teens before being officially initiated into Sufism at the age of twenty.[1] Beginning in the early 1190s and for the next thirty years of his life, Ibn al-ʿArabi traveled widely in the Middle East and North Africa, seeking tutelage at the feet of Sufi masters throughout those regions of the Islamic world. As often as not, however, it is said that Ibn al-ʿArabi played the role of teacher rather than that of student. From an early age, Ibn al-ʿArabi was quite confident in his spiritual authority, a factor that sometimes led to conflicts with those teachers whom he sought out during his travels (3).

This period was seminal in the Sufi master's life. During this time, he had numerous mystical experiences, some of them serving to guide him in his journeys. He also acquired a far-reaching reputation during this period, which often preceded him in some of the most significant centers of Islamic learning. One of the most influential Sufi thinkers in history, his vast influence is indicated by the nicknames he accumulated: "Animator of the Religion," "Doctor Maximus," "The Son of Plato."[2] Ibn al-ʿArabi came to Mecca in 1200 and was received with honors by some of the holy city's most learned citizens (7). He remained in the city for approximately four years, during which time—inspired by numerous trips to the Kʿaaba, in addition to visions and mystical experiences—he began composing *The*

Meccan Revelations, a monumental work that would remain uncompleted for decades to come.

Despite (or perhaps because of) his popularity in certain quarters, Ibn al-ʿArabi managed to make more than a few enemies during his career, and his reputation did not always ensure pleasant travels for the wandering Sufi. One prevalent theme of Ibn al-ʿArabi's writing is the contrast between the mystical path of Sufism and the rationalism and legalism of more orthodox Islamic thinkers; the master's language and tone leave little doubt as to which path is preferable in his estimation. It was opinions such as these that led to his having to leave Cairo in 1206, after threats to his life were made by Qurʾanic scholars in the city. No doubt, it was like-minded members of the *ulema* who bestowed upon Ibn al-ʿArabi another of his monikers: *Mumītuddīn*, or "he who kills the religion."[3]

By 1223—at the age of fifty-eight—Ibn al-ʿArabi's nomadic lifestyle appears to have taken its toll on him, and, at the invitation of the city's ruler, he settled in Damascus. He was to stay there until the end of his life, seventeen years later. Although this period marked an end to Ibn al-ʿArabi's travels, it by no means marked an end to either his spiritual life or his writing. During this time he completed *The Meccan Revelations*—which contains a passage describing what appears to be a culminating experience in the sheikh's own mystical path—and *The Bezels of Wisdom*, intended as a summary of his mystical thought and reflections. These two texts are arguably the most important works of the Sufi master, and two of the most influential in Sufi history.

As most if not all translators and commentators on the work of Ibn al-ʿArabi note, the man's work is immensely challenging to interpret. The profusion of topics addressed in any one text, the density of the symbolism employed, the extent of often specialized knowledge to which he alludes (in fields such as alchemy and astronomy), and the complexity of Ibn al-ʿArabi's own theological thought are more than sufficient to render his work difficult, to say the least. In addition to all of this, however, is the fact that Ibn al-ʿArabi's writing is meant to challenge the reader not only in terms of content but also in its very structure. Often, the reader is unsure whether the perspective from which the text speaks is intended to be that of God, Ibn al-ʿArabi, or one of the numerous prophets whom he takes as models of the spiritual path. The confusion thereby created is intentional, and it reflects some of the author's central mystical beliefs and insights.

For these reasons, a full exposition of the entirety of Ibn al-'Arabi's mysticism is not possible within the constraints of a single chapter. In order both to control the current exploration and to facilitate comparison with other accounts of mystical experience, I therefore limit my inquiry to two specific questions: (1) what is the ontology presumed in Ibn al-'Arabi's understanding of mystical experience (what is the metaphysical relationship between mystic and ultimacy)?, and (2) what is the epistemology presumed in Ibn al-'Arabi's understanding of mystical experience (what is the mode of knowing or experience that obtains in the encounter with ultimacy)? Given the challenges in interpreting Ibn al-'Arabi's work, some hermeneutic method is clearly necessary, and the temptation to rely on a contextual approach such as Katz's is understandable. The basic tenets of mainstream Muslim thought are well known, and Ibn al-'Arabi was thoroughly educated in Islamic teaching and tradition. This might suggest that one could approach the sheikh's writing from the outside, as it were, beginning with the well-known canons of Islamic theology and attempting to derive the nature of Ibn al-'Arabi's own experience from them. As I will show, however, the Sufi master's description of his mystical experience is steeped not in the central doctrines of mainstream Islamic thought but in his own particular set of epistemological and ontological assumptions. Therefore, interpreting Ibn al-'Arabi according to any exterior hermeneutic—either mainstream Islamic theology or the central philosophical tenets of modern Western thought—would misconstrue his writing in fundamental ways.[4] Instead, it is necessary to interpret Ibn al-'Arabi's experiential text through a semantic matrix that takes account of the particular philosophical assumptions through which the mystic himself describes it.

First, I identify the passage in which Ibn al-'Arabi relates what appears to be the culmination of his own mystical path. Following the interpretive method described in chapter 2, this passage can be envisioned as sitting at the center of the diagram in that chapter. Moving outward from the center, I interpret it first with reference to other aspects of the text in which it appears (*The Meccan Revelations*), then with reference to other aspects of the author's work (primarily *The Bezels of Wisdom*), and finally with reference to other dimensions of the religious and mystical traditions within which the author stands (Islam and Sufism). This hermeneutic serves to reveal the lineaments of mystical experience as described by Ibn al-'Arabi, while minimizing interference from ulterior philosophical assumptions.

Key Passage

The Meccan Revelations is an immense work, only parts of which have become available in translation owing to the efforts of a number of scholars working for more than a decade. Embedded within the text is a report of what appears to be the culmination of Ibn al-'Arabi's own spiritual journey, in which he attains the apex of his mystical path. The key passage reads as follows:

> I received the good tidings that I had (been granted) the "Muhammadan station," that I was among the heirs of Muhammad's comprehensiveness. . . . Now when that happened to me I exclaimed: "Enough, enough!' My (bodily) elements are filled up, and my place cannot contain me!," and through that (inspiration) God removed from me my contingent dimension. Thus I attained in this nocturnal journey the inner realities (*ma'ani*) of all the Names, and I saw them all returning to One Subject and One Entity: that Subject was what I witnessed, and that Entity was my Being. For my voyage was only in myself and only pointed to myself, and through this I came to know that I was a pure "servant," without a trace of lordship in me at all. Then the treasures of this station were opened up (for me).[5]

The first-person perspective employed here is common in mystical literature, both within and outside the Islamic tradition. As numerous commentators on his corpus note, however, the autobiographical tone appears to be more than merely a literary conceit. Throughout Ibn al-'Arabi's life, he is reported to have had numerous distinct mystical experiences that played a significant role in his maturation as a religious thinker. Moreover, this experiential account assumes or refers to many of the central features of the sheikh's mystical thought. Ibn al-'Arabi himself claims that his voluminous writings are the product of his own spiritual edification and experiences, rather than solely of a discursive process of reflection and intellection.

In describing himself during the process of composing *The Meccan Revelations*, Ibn al-'Arabi writes that he was nothing more than a "heart prostrate before the door of the Divine Presence," "indigent," and "devoid of any knowledge," emphasizing that he saw himself as playing a largely passive role with regard to these experiences.[6] Additionally, Ibn al-'Arabi began composing the *Revelations* while he was in Mecca, a location that certainly would have lent itself to powerful experiences for a devout follower of Islam. James Winston Morris refers to this passage as "a decisive personal revelation, a compelling spiritual experience," and the language of the passage clearly suggests that the traveling Sufi is referring to a powerful personal event.

The passage is replete with references and allusions to various aspects of Ibn al-'Arabi's complex mystical theology, some of which are common to Sufi thought and others of which are more idiosyncratic. These peculiar usages and common allusions provide a foundation from which to begin analyzing the mystic's experience. For example, the term "nocturnal journey" is, of course, used intentionally. For Ibn al-'Arabi, as for many others in the Sufi tradition, Muhammad's own nocturnal journey—the *m'iraj*—serves as a kind of model or prototype for the spiritual journey of the mystic. In the traditional version, Muhammad mounts a winged steed known as the *burraq*, which carries him from Mecca to the Al-Aqsa Mosque in Jerusalem, at which point he ascends into a series of heavenly realms, encountering and conversing with various prophets along the way. In *The Meccan Revelations*, just before the passage cited above, Ibn al-'Arabi details a similar progression, during which he meets prophets such as Adam, Joseph, and Idris, from whom he receives instruction on certain Qur'anic passages and teachings. For Ibn al-'Arabi, although the exact nature of each mystic's own spiritual journey differs according to the character of the individual mystic, Muhammad's *m'iraj* serves as a symbol of the highest, culminating stage of that spiritual development.[7]

Other terms and allusions in the passage above, however, refer specifically to dimensions of his own thought. For example, the term "Muhammadan station" refers to Ibn al-'Arabi's belief that he had attained a unique spiritual status, which he refers to as the "the Seal of Muhammadan Sainthood" (6). While indicating Ibn al-'Arabi's belief that his own spiritual attainment was of an especially exalted kind (although certainly still inferior to that of Muhammad himself), this title seems to have suggested to the Sufi a responsibility to teach, and to help guide others on their own spiritual journey to more intimate knowledge of God.

The language of servant and lordship, as well, has special meaning in Ibn al-'Arabi's lexicon. Certainly, the seemingly innocuous claim that Ibn al-'Arabi "came to know that [he] was a pure 'servant'" could seem merely to refer to every Muslim's duty to submit himself to the will of God. For

Ibn al-'Arabi, however, the terms servant and lord have specific connotations that become apparent only in light of other aspects of the master's writing. Consider the following passage, also from the *Revelations*, in which Ibn al-'Arabi discusses the teaching of Ibn 'Abbas:

> Ibn 'Abbas said, "the meaning of the words 'to serve Me' is 'to know Me.'" So he did not explain (*tafsir*) [this verse] in terms of what is given by the reality of the word's denotation (*dalala*). Its explanation can only be: "to be lowly toward Me"; but none is lowly toward Him unless he knows Him, so it is necessary first to know Him and then to know the fact that He is the Possessor of Mightiness ('*izza*) before which the mighty are lowly. Hence Ibn 'Abbas turned his explanation of "service" to knowledge. This is the opinion (*zann*) concerning him.[8]

Here, through his discussion of Ibn 'Abbas, Ibn al-'Arabi does invoke the literal meaning of the relationship between lord and servant; the servant is "lowly" relative to the lord, beneath him in terms of rank and power. To "serve," however, is also to "know" the lord. According to Ibn al-'Arabi's reading of Ibn 'Abbas, one cannot serve God unless one first knows him, and so the notion of being a servant vis-à-vis the lord, just as it implies subservience, also suggests knowledge of the lord on a deeper, more metaphorical level—and it is this level of meaning with which Ibn al-'Arabi is primarily concerned.

Morris relates that the term "servant" has a second technical meaning for Ibn al-'Arabi throughout his mystical corpus, reflecting its use in certain Qur'anic passages. In these cases, the term describes those individuals among the saints and prophets who have fully realized their special, inner relationship to the creator, and who therefore have no illusions concerning other beings to whom they may think themselves subject.[9] This relationship is partially explained in another passage of the *Revelations*: "Hence throughout this journey the servant remains God and not-God. And since he remains God and not-God, He makes (the servant) travel—with respect to Him, not with respect to (what is) not-Him—in Him, in a subtle spiritual (*ma'nawi*) journey."[10] In describing the servant as "not-God," Ibn al-'Arabi refers to the typical understanding of the human self as part of the mundane, temporal world, conceived in opposition to or as radically different from the divine. In truth, however, the human individual is not merely an aspect of the physical world, radically distinct from God; rather, he has a unique spiritual potential to actualize himself as "the Perfect Man," whose being reflects that of the divine in a uniquely comprehensive fashion. The "subtle spiritual journey" therefore refers to the mystic's increasing realization that his being more accurately reflects that of God rather than the world. According to Michael Sells, the knowledge of the lord that the servant realizes is precisely the fact of unity between the two; to know one's lord is, in this case, to know that oneself and one's lord are one and the same.[11] Hence the servant is also God.

Ibn al-'Arabi's own realization of being a "pure servant," then, does not indicate primarily (if at all) a relation of subservience to God, at least not in the usual sense of the word. Rather, it indicates, first of all, knowledge; through his discussion of Ibn 'Abbas, Ibn al-'Arabi suggests that servant-hood actually indicates a type of knowledge that obtains in the relation-ship between a mystic and God. "Pure servanthood," then, would seem to suggest a more perfect or complete knowledge of God. Drawing on another passage in the *Revelations*, that knowledge appears to be of a specific sort: the realization that one is not in fact distinct from the lord (God), and that a certain kind of union or unity between the self and God obtains.

These brief discussions indicate something of the complexity and inter-laced nature of Ibn al-'Arabi's writing and thought. In many ways, the Sufi master works within and through a lexicon of his own devising, employing allusions and references that are explicable only within the context of his own corpus. And just as the Sufi master often relies on his own language and terminology, he also employs epistemological and ontological assump-tions that are distinct to his work. Having canvassed some of the specific religious terms and ideas alluded to in this passage, and in order to achieve an accurate understanding of Ibn al-'Arabi's culminating mystical experi-ence, it is now necessary to explore the metaphysical and epistemological theories through which he explicates his experience.

Ibn al-'Arabi's Ontology of Mystical Experience

The Sufi master's ontology provides an essential framework for under-standing his experience. For Ibn al-'Arabi, it is not merely the mind or the soul that undergoes mystical experience; the entirety of the mystic's being is affected by it. Therefore, the especially intimate relationship with God afforded by mystical experience can be grasped properly only through an understanding of the metaphysical nature of the mystic, God, and the relationship between them.

In the key passage quoted above, the Sufi states that "God removed from me my contingent dimension." This line appears to refer to something about Ibn al-'Arabi's being, rather than his knowledge, but the passage itself does not offer any explanation of what he might mean by his "contingent dimension," or what might be the effect of God's "removing" it from him. Another passage from the *Revelations*, however, provides some guidance:

> Now this journey (in God) involves the "dissolving" of their compos-
> ite nature. Through this journey God (first of all) acquaints them
> with what corresponds to them in each world (of being), by passing
> with them through the different sorts of worlds, both composite and
> simple. Then (the spiritual traveler) leaves behind in each world that
> part of himself which corresponds to it: the form of his leaving it
> behind is that God sends a barrier between that person and that part
> of himself he left behind in that sort of world, so that he is not aware
> of it. But he still has the awareness of what remains with him, until
> eventually he remains (alone) with the divine Mystery which is the
> "specific aspect" extending from God to him. So when he alone
> remains (without any of those other attachments to the world), then
> God removes from him the barrier of the veil and he remains with
> God, just as everything else in him remained with (the world) cor-
> responding to it.[12]

Ibn al-'Arabi refers in the first line to the "dissolving" of the composite nature of other mystics who have achieved special knowledge of God. In further describing the nature of this dissolution, distinct similarities to the notion of being removed from his "contingent dimension" become apparent.

The mystical journey to God involves passage through a number of spiritual worlds, culminating in the divine realm wherein one encounters God himself. The human being, apparently, consists of a number of differ-ent ontological dimensions (his "composite nature"), each of which corre-sponds to one of the "worlds" through which the mystic aspirant passes. In journeying toward God, the mystic sheds different layers of himself, leav-ing behind those contingent aspects of himself that are not essentially part of his true nature. The process is facilitated by God himself, who effects this shedding of layers by sending "barriers," each of which functions to separate one of the mystic's contingent dimensions from himself.

The human being, then—or at least a substantial portion of him—can be spiritually disassembled. There are dimensions of the human person that can be divided from him or provisionally eliminated in order to achieve a more intimate encounter with God. A very similar understanding of the metaphysical nature of the human mystic appears in this selection from a poem by Ibn al-'Arabi, in which he cites another famous Sufi, Junayd:

> And Junayd said in the same regard
>> When the originated is related to the eternal
>> no trace remains of the originated
> When the heart encompasses the eternal
>> how can it feel the existence of the originated?

Sells relates the poem to the classic Sufi notions of *fanā'* and *baqā'*, and these provide perhaps the most helpful insight into understanding this aspect of Ibn al-'Arabi's mystical experience.[13] The former term refers to the annihilation of the self in mystical experience, and the latter to the subsequent manifestation of divine attributes in the person of the mystic. In essence, the pair *fanā'* and *baqā'* describe a process wherein the human mystic is temporarily annihilated—the created, contingent dimensions of his being are eliminated—and replaced, if only temporarily, with attributes of the divine.[14]

This infilling of the human mystic with divine attributes in the encounter with God has radical implications for understanding that encounter itself: who, then, is meeting whom, under these conditions? In fact, in this scenario, it is no longer Ibn al-'Arabi who encounters God but God who reveals himself to God, through the being of the mystic himself.[15] The human mystic becomes the site of a theophany in which God reveals himself in an act of what is essentially self-contemplation. This conception of the encounter with God is apparent in another of Ibn al-'Arabi's texts, the *Kitab-al 'Isra*, in which the master includes another description of his own encounter with God. In this version of the experience, God separates Ibn al-'Arabi into two halves, each of which then comes to experience a deep sense of love and longing for the other.[16] The passage actually, however, describes the sundering of a human-divine unity in which the love and desire experienced are actually the longing of the self for the self. Interestingly, Morris notes that the term the sheikh employs in this text, *hanna*, has numerous meanings, including not only love and desire but also "homesickness."[17] Given that Ibn al-ʿArabi is known for his wordplay, the polysemy of the term is probably intentional. The homesickness of the one half for the other, then, signals a desire to return to that place and state from which one originated, to return to a state of original unity.

Returning to a state of unity, in fact, may more accurately capture the ontological dimension of mystical experience than the notion of God's possessing the human mystic or manifesting divine attributes in him. Recall that Ibn al-ʿArabi writes that in the midst of this experience, God removed from him his "contingent dimension," suggesting that there may be another, noncontingent dimension of the mystic that is not removed in this process. And in the other passage from the *Revelations* quoted above, Ibn al-ʿArabi describes the mystic as being divested of his composite nature until only "the 'specific aspect' extending from God to him" remains. Taken together, these passages suggest that rather than the human mystic's being newly filled or infused with aspects of the divine, that dimension of the mystic was already present and is merely revealed once his contingent or nonessential aspects have been dissolved.

This notion of the human person containing or instantiating some aspect of God would seem to depart radically from mainstream Islamic theology, which emphasizes the radical distinction between human and divine and categorically rejects the idea that anything can be equal to God. A straightforward reading of mainstream Islamic doctrine, if taken as the basis on which to determine the nature of mystical experience in Islam, would never suggest that an experience like that which Ibn al-ʿArabi describes is possible. To the contrary, however, Ibn al-ʿArabi does suggest that there is an intimate ontological relationship between man and God that prefigures mystical experience proper. That relationship appears to involve some degree of shared ontology between the two, despite the implications that one might deduce from mainstream Islamic thought.

Other Sufis, also on the basis of the doctrine of *fanāʾ* and *baqāʾ*, suggest a similarly intimate metaphysical relationship between man and God. *Shathiyat*, or "theopathic locutions," are exclamations made by Sufis in the midst of mystical experience. Schimmel defines them simply as moments in which "the mystic utters words that he should not say."[18] These statements, interpreted in the absence of the semantics of Muslim mysticism and the kind of ontology Ibn al-ʿArabi invokes, often seem to be blatantly blasphemous. The two most famous *shathiyat* are *'Anā al-haqq* and *subhānī*. The former translates as "I am the real" and was uttered by the famous Sufi Abu al-Mughith al-Husayn ibn Mansur ibn Muhammad al-Hallaj, a Persian mystic who was martyred in 922 for heresy. The charge was certainly based in part on this statement, in which al-Hallaj appears to equate himself with God, one of whose Qur'anic names is *al-Haqq*, "the Real." Assertions of unity with divinity, in fact, can be found throughout al-Hallaj's writings.[19]

Similarly, the declaration of Abu Yazid al-Bistami (a ninth-century Persian Sufi)—*subhānī*, or "glory to me"—also seems to be a claim to godhood. However, to interpret these statements as the literal pronouncements of men speaking out of a normal epistemological mode is misleading. Al-Bistami and al-Hallaj are speaking out of an abnormal modality of experience wherein it is God himself—"the Real"—who announces his own glory through them. Rather than blasphemous declarations of their own equality to God or their usurpation of his unique status, al-Bistami's and al-Hallaj's exclamations signal their personal obliteration and God's infusion of their beings. Considered in light of the ontology to which Ibn al-'Arabi refers in discussing the loss of his "contingent dimension," their exclamations shift from radically heretical to acceptably orthodox statements of Islamic teaching. A theologian adhering strictly to literal Islamic doctrine would transgress one of the most fundamental tenets of Islam by claiming to be "the Real." But the Sufi doctrines of *fanā'* and *baqā'* establish that neither al-Hallaj nor al-Bistami is truly speaking here. Although Ibn al-'Arabi is not known for his own *shathiyat*, his discussion of the dissolution of the mystic's being is clarified in light of the notions of *fanā'* and *baqā'* exemplified by these mystics.

In other sections of the *Revelations*, Ibn al-'Arabi suggests that God's relationship, not only to the aspiring mystic but to the whole of creation, is closer than one might suspect. For example, he writes, "The beauty of His Making (*sun'*) permeates His creation, while the world is His loci of manifestation (*mazahir*). So the love of the different parts of the world for each other derives from God's love for Himself."[20] Here, the sheikh suggests that God is in some sense immanent in creation—"the world is His loci of manifestation." Those who truly understand the nature of God, according to Ibn al-'Arabi, understand that his being cannot be limited in any way, shape, or form. Therefore, to posit the world as separate from God—as outside his being—is incorrect, because this would suggest that God's being is limited by that of the world. In fact, in acknowledging the unlimited scope of the ontology of God, one must realize that the world itself is also a manifestation of God. This is why, according to Ibn al-'Arabi, "The gnostics see Him as the essential identity of all things."[21]

This theme of God's immanence in the created world also appears throughout *The Bezels of Wisdom*, stated in various ways. At times, Ibn al-'Arabi's language in the *Bezels* is direct and unequivocal on this point: "He is Being itself, the Essence of Being. . . . He is the observer in the observer and the observed in the observed" (135). Here, the sheikh leaves no room for doubt concerning the relationship between God and creation. As the "Essence of Being," God is manifest as the fundamental metaphysical substratum of existence, the ontological basis of all that can be said to exist. God's immanence in this fashion, however, is also personal; he is both the subject that perceives the object and the object that is perceived by the subject. As suggested earlier, rather than Ibn al-'Arabi's mystical experience consisting of his being filled with divine attributes, these attributes are merely disclosed through the removal of the contingent dimensions of the sheikh's being.

This being the case, one might wonder why and how this divine immanence is not generally recognized. Why is it that this supremely important fact remains to be discovered by mystics, and seemingly by mystics alone? The Sufi master suggests that this is because God conceals himself in existents. Although he stands as the essential nature of being—and therefore as the central ontological dimension of all individual entities in existence—he does so in a subtle or hidden way that is not obvious to mundane perception. Therefore, it is only spiritual adepts who realize this aspect of God's being. In fact, Ibn al-'Arabi suggests that differences in the "spiritual rank" between different men can be discerned according to whether or not they realize this divine immanence (133).

Of course, God is not merely immanent from the Sufi master's perspective. Although this aspect of Ibn al-'Arabi's thought has garnered significant attention and has sometimes led to charges that he is a kind of pantheist, to pigeonhole the sheikh as such would distort his thought. While God is immanent in a certain fashion, he also, of course, transcends the world, standing beyond it in a way that more closely reflects traditional mainstream Islamic thought. Ibn al-'Arabi's writing probably focuses more on the immanental dimension of the divine partly because its transcendent dimension can be taken as a given. Intriguingly, the multidimensional ontological character of God requires a similarly multidimensional mode of apprehension on the part of the human being. In the *Bezels*, Ibn al-'Arabi says that the prophet Elias divested himself of lust and purged himself of the urgings of his "lower soul" (230). While such a procedure might sound appropriate as a type of self-purification, it actually resulted in limiting Elias's ability to know God: "In him [Elias] God was transcendent, so that he had half the gnosis of God. That is because the intellect, by itself, absorbing knowledge in its own way, knows only according to the transcendental and nothing of the immanental. It is only when God acquaints it with His Self-manifestation that its knowledge of God becomes complete, seeing Him as transcendent when appropriate, and as immanent when appropriate, and perceiving the diffusion of God in natural and elemental forms" (230). The intellect grasps God in his transcendental aspect, as a deity beyond physical reality and distinct from the mundane world. This is not an incorrect description, and it is this modality of God's existence that is most commonly asserted by the Islamic scholars whom Ibn al-'Arabi often criticizes.

It is, however, an incomplete description of God's ontology. In response to orthodox theologians who maintain only God's transcendence, Ibn al-'Arabi states that the deity "puts Himself beyond their insistence on His transcendence, because such insistence [in fact] limits Him by reason of the inadequacy of the intellect to grasp such things" (230–31). Here, Ibn al-'Arabi castigates Islamic theologians for presuming to limit the being of God according to the limitations of their own conceptual capacities. Since they approach him through the intellect alone, Ibn al-'Arabi claims, theologians inappropriately conclude that God is only transcendent. For Ibn al-'Arabi, this conclusion erroneously transfers the epistemological limits of the human mind to the ontological being of God. Seen in this fashion, Ibn al-'Arabi's more all-encompassing vision of the being of God renders his view, ironically, more orthodox than that of the theologians with whom he spars. Given the divine nature of God, it is entirely unsurprising that the individual human—precisely because of its creaturely limitations—cannot perceive him fully. The assumption that human limitations of conception represent or reflect limitations in the divine being, Ibn al-'Arabi suggests, is nothing other than hubris, which leads to a flawed and incomplete understanding of God.

Those who assert only God's transcendence are either fools or rogues, in Ibn al-'Arabi's estimation, because they impose a limitation on the divine (73). To describe God as only or entirely transcendent implies that that which is not transcendent—the mundane, created world—stands outside God and thereby constitutes a limitation to him. This perspective fails to acknowledge the truly unlimited ontological scope of God's being, the fact that his reality is all-encompassing and incorporates every aspect of reality. Insofar as the metaphysical status of God can be described, therefore, it is necessary to attribute to him both immanence and transcendence:

> If you insist only on His transcendence, you restrict Him,
> And if you insist only on His immanence, you limit Him.
> If you maintain both aspects you are right,
> An Imam and a master in the spiritual sciences.
> Whoso would say He is two things is a polytheist,
> While the one who isolates Him tries to regulate Him.
> Beware of comparing Him if you profess duality,
> And, if unity, beware of making Him transcendent.
> You are not He and you are He and
> You see Him in the essences of things both boundless
> And limited. (75)

Neither transcendence nor immanence, Ibn al-'Arabi writes, sufficiently describes God. To attribute only one or the other quality to the divine constitutes a drastic error, an artificial restriction or limitation of that which is neither restricted nor limited. Holding both features as true independently of each other is also incorrect, as that implies the existence of two distinct entities, one transcendent and one immanent. Ibn al-'Arabi rejects that implied polytheism as well. Ultimately, the only proper description must retain both transcendence and immanence simultaneously, despite the apparent contradiction that this entails. The clear implication is that language—as long as it functions within the semantic boundaries of logic—is inherently incapable of capturing divinity. Insofar as language must be employed, it can be done only by eschewing those strictures that govern language spoken in a state of normal consciousness. It is necessary to move beyond the epistemological limitations of the human mind and the semantic limitations of language in order to grasp the ontologically unlimited nature of God.

While God's transcendence may be taken as a given, Ibn al-'Arabi naturally must spend some time explaining the modality of God's immanence in the world. This is achieved through the divine "names," providing another key to understanding the culminating experiential passage from the *Revelations*. Although God is immanent in creation, he is not present in his entirety in each created entity. Rather, according to Ibn al-'Arabi's ontology, individual aspects of creation are sites or instantiations of particular, limited aspects of the divine. Each individual entity represents merely one dimension of God, manifested in a particular, limited fashion. Ibn al-'Arabi uses the well-known Islamic notion of God's names in articulating this aspect of his ontology. Although God is traditionally said to have ninety-nine names, Ibn al-'Arabi suggests that each individual entity in existence is a manifestation of one of God's names:

> So when He becomes manifest to Himself in the entity of a possible thing through one of the Divine Names, the preparedness of the entity bestows upon Him a temporally originated Name (*'ism hadith*) by which He is then called. It is said that this is a Throne, this an Intellect, this a Pen, a Tablet, a Footstool, a celestial sphere, an angel, fire, air, water, earth, an inanimate thing, a plant, an animal, and a man, in all kinds and species. Then this Reality permeates the individuals and it is said that this is Zayd, 'Amr, this horse, this stone, this tree. All of this is bestowed by the preparedness of the entities of the possible things.[22]

God manifests himself through individual entities. The list the master offers in this passage is basically inclusive of all possible dimensions of existence. God manifests himself in entities as uninteresting and mundane as a pen or a footstool, and as abstract and exalted as celestial spheres and angels.

In fact, it is only through the perdurance of the divine names that existence continues to subsist at all. In another passage of the *Revelations*, Ibn al-'Arabi describes the divine names as "veils," emphasizing the role they play in concealing the reality of the divine nature behind the appearance of a mundane object or being. These veils, however, do not merely serve to hide the true, divine essence; in doing so, they retain the existence of mundane entities. Were the veils to be lifted, the sheikh writes, then the true unity of God and the world would become fully manifest. Individual entities would cease to be qualified by existence and would return to complete unity with the divine—the world, in essence, would cease to exist, swallowed up and collapsed into complete and utter unity with God.[23] The divine names, while "veiling" the true nature of things, also facilitate their individual existence.

God went about this entire process—creating a world through the instantiation of his names—because he wanted to see the glory of himself. He does so through the names rather than by contemplating himself directly. In the *Bezels*, Ibn al-ʿArabi relates that seeing a thing in its own self is not the same as seeing one's self in another, or "in a mirror." Although God was obviously capable of contemplating himself, to manifest himself through his names, and then to contemplate himself through the world thus manifested, provides a different experience and quality of self-knowledge (50). The world, therefore, serves as a mode of self-disclosure and self-contemplation for God, allowing him to encounter or know himself through the medium of existence. Ibn al-ʿArabi therefore comments that humanity and God are, in a fascinating way, mutually dependent (127). Human individuals depend on God for their very existence, while God depends on human beings as a mode of self-revelation.

In fact, the human being plays a distinctive and very significant role in manifesting the divine names of God in the world. While each and every existent entity manifests one or another specific divine name, the human person uniquely manifests all the divine names at once, and therefore represents a more complete instantiation of the divine presence in the world. Ibn al-ʿArabi draws on the Qurʾanic account of creation in describing this special ontological function of the human being. According to the relevant passages, the angels initially questioned God's decision to place a regent (Adam) on earth, suggesting that he would sully God's creation with violence while they continued to sing God's praises. In response, God teaches Adam "the names," which Ibn al-ʿArabi interprets as the divine names. Realizing that they are ignorant of the names God teaches Adam, the angels are then made to prostrate themselves before him.[24]

Another passage in the *Bezels* further clarifies the reason for Adam's apparent superiority over the angels. The angels are like other aspects of creation, in that each one represents an instantiation of only one divine name. Therefore, while they can praise God, they can do so only in a limited fashion, according to the individual names that each of them instantiates. Adam, by contrast, comprehends all the divine names in his being; he is therefore a more inclusive and complete instantiation of the divine manifestation in the world and is able to praise God in ways unavailable to the angels (52). In all of creation, no other being enjoys this special status, and it is this "Synthesis [of divine realities] possessed by the Regent" that renders him superior to all other beings (56).

Ibn al-ʿArabi goes on to clarify that Adam is the "single spiritual essence" from which all of humankind was created (57). This, then, clarifies the precise relationship that the human person has with God, as the complete manifestation of all of God's divine names, which are the modality through which he reveals himself to himself in the world. While the entire world may be described as a reflective manifestation of God on a macrocosmic scale, the human person functions in the same way on a microcosmic scale.[25] This ontology also sheds light on the reference to the names in the key passage describing Ibn al-ʿArabi's own mystical journey as reported in the *Revelations*: "Thus I attained in this nocturnal journey the inner realities (*maʿani*) of all the Names, and I saw them all returning to One Subject and One Entity: that Subject was what I witnessed, and that Entity was my Being." In stating that he "attained" the inner realities of all the names, the sheikh is not claiming that they were infused into him for the first time during the nocturnal journey. As we know from the exegesis above, the divine names are already instantiated in Ibn al-ʿArabi, merely by virtue of the fact that he is a human being and a spiritual descendant of Adam. What the passage would appear to be describing, then, is his personal realization of those names as dimensions of his own being, the fundamental recognition of them as already inscribed in himself. As he emphasizes, the entity in which he witnesses all the names is his own being.

This aspect of the mystical journey is even more clearly indicated by the line "For my voyage was only in myself and only pointed to myself." Ultimately, the mystical path that Ibn al-ʿArabi follows is not from one physical place to another, nor is it even a movement toward God. It is a sojourn within himself, through the depths of his own spiritual nature. In another passage of the *Revelations*, God suggests that it is illogical to describe the mystical ascension as the mystic's coming to him because God is already with the mystic wherever he is.[26] Similarly, in the *Bezels*, Ibn al-ʿArabi compares the relationship between man and God to that between the spirit and the body, suggesting that God resides within the human person much as the spirit resides within the human body (74). Therefore, Ibn al-ʿArabi's spiritual journey—while modeled on the prophet's *miʿraj*—is really a self-contained exploration of his own spiritual nature, at the heart of which is God.

This is not a journey of self-realization only for Ibn al-ʿArabi, however; as the sheikh's ontology implies, it is just as much a path to self-discovery for God. Ibn al-ʿArabi's reflexive recognition of the names in himself is also God's experience of seeing and knowing himself, as in a "clear mirror."[27] The human being, through his unique instantiation of the divine names, is the theophany through which God most directly comes to know himself. As should be apparent, however, this mode of (self-)knowledge must operate differently from the kind of knowledge human beings typically employ vis-à-vis the physical world.

Ibn al-ʿArabi's Epistemology of Mystical Experience

Fortunately, Ibn al-ʿArabi discusses his epistemological framework explicitly in *The Meccan Revelations* and invokes it frequently in other texts, such as *The Bezels of Wisdom*. In the introduction to the former, the sheikh writes:

> If the properly prepared person persists in remembrance of God (*dhikr*)[28] and spiritual retreat, if they empty the place (of their heart) of all mental chatter, and sit at the doorstep of their Lord like a poor beggar who has nothing—then God will bestow upon them and give them some of that knowledge of Him, of those divine secrets and supernal understandings which He granted to His servant al-Khadir. . . . So the person with focused spiritual intention, during their retreat with God, may realise through Him—how exalted are His gifts and how prodigious His grace!—(forms of spiritual) knowledge that are concealed from every theologian on the face of the earth, and indeed from anyone relying on purely intellectual inquiry and proofs who lacks that spiritual state. For such knowledge is beyond (the grasp of) inquiry through the discursive intellect.[29]

Here, Ibn al-ʿArabi lays out one of the basic principles of his mystical epistemology: a strict bifurcation between mystical knowledge of God and knowledge that can be obtained through intellection and discursive reasoning. Indeed, the language of the first line recalls the manner in which Ibn al-ʿArabi describes the mental comportment that he claims to take up with regard to all of his written work. As discussed earlier, the Sufi master describes himself as "indigent" and "devoid of any knowledge" when writing the *Revelations*; his language here is nearly identical, exhorting his reader to become "like a poor beggar" who is emptied of "all mental chatter." Echoing himself, Ibn al-'Arabi clearly means to suggest that in order to achieve the kind of spiritual knowledge that he describes in the *Revelations*, one must forego or overcome theological learning and education, and achieve a state of mind that is open to alternative forms of edification.

The last two sentences of the passage confirm this sentiment, further underscoring the apparently obstructive role of the intellect in achieving the kind of spiritual knowledge that Ibn al-'Arabi endorses. In fact, the spiritual knowledge of which he writes is concealed "from every theologian on the face of the earth." Elsewhere, he suggests that the human race could be divided into three categories: disciples of the "science of the heart" (mystics), disciples of the rational intellect (philosophers and Scholastic theologians), and simple believers. Under normal circumstances, it is possible for simple believers to ascend into the first group, mystics. Philosophers and theologians, however, are permanently barred from that category.[30] Michael Sells relates a similar tale of the Sufi master's in which a philosopher (*sāhib al-nazar*) and a follower (*tābiʿ*) ascend to the heavens in a manner reminiscent of the *mʿiraj*. The philosopher can reach only a certain level and must be content with interrogating spirit entities (*rūhāniyyāt*). The follower, however, gains greater access to the divine mysteries and eventually leaves the philosopher behind.[31]

Clearly, for Ibn al-'Arabi, there is a distinct and apparently insurmountable chasm between intellectuals and mystics. Mystical enlightenment is barred to every theologian on the planet; while simple believers may become mystics, philosophers and theologians cannot. And while the unsophisticated follower of Islam can ascend to the highest heaven, the philosopher must be satisfied with a lesser degree of access to the divine. The message is clear: something about theological learning and the rational, philosophical mind-set is antithetical to mystical enlightenment.

Note the contrast here between the epistemology with which Ibn al-'Arabi operates and that presumed by Katz and other like-minded scholars. The predominant assumption of contemporary academic epistemology is that learning and experience provide an inescapable screen or framework through which all experience is inevitably filtered; for Katz, this structure of consciousness is a given, and it provides the basic principle on which his interpretive method is based. Ibn al-'Arabi adopts a diametrically opposed epistemological stance. From the Sufi master's perspective, it is precisely education and discursive thought that cannot grasp the spiritual knowledge of which he writes. This is because such spiritual knowledge transcends the discursive mind, rendering the intellect impotent with regard to it.

This principle—that discursive thought is inherently limited with regard to spiritual knowledge and cannot grasp the higher, more valuable forms of mystical knowing—forms the basis of Ibn al-'Arabi's entire epistemology. This is clear at another point in the *Revelations*, where Ibn al-'Arabi lays out his epistemology in greater detail. Here, he proposes three levels of knowing, of which discursive intellection is the most basic: "For there are three levels of knowledge. Knowledge through the discursive intellect (*'ilm al-'aql*) is whatever knowledge you obtain either immediately or as a result of inquiry concerning an 'indicator,' provided that you discover the probative aspect of that indicator. And mistakes with regard to this kind of knowledge (come about) in the realm of that discursive thinking which is linked together and typifies this type of knowledge. That is why they say about purely intellectual inquiry that some of it is sound, while some is invalid."[32] This is the most mundane form of knowing, commonly employed by human beings in daily contexts. Whether a man is tallying the weekly profits from his business, identifying the shortest route from his home to his workplace, or determining Islamic law based on rational interpretation of the Qur'an, he is using his discursive intellect. As Ibn al-'Arabi notes, this mental function is liable to err, and so some of its deductions can be regarded as reliable, while others cannot.

Echoing the same theme, in *The Bezels of Wisdom* Ibn al-'Arabi castigates those thinkers, especially Scholastic philosophers, who attempt to know God through rational thought. It is through the "soul" that God may be known, and only after eschewing "speculation": "As for the theorists and thinkers among the ancients, as also the scholastic theologians, in their talk about the soul and its quiddity, none of them have grasped its true reality, and speculation will never grasp it. He who seeks to know it by theoretical speculation is flogging a dead horse. Such are certainly of those whose endeavor is awry in this world, but who consider that they do well. He who seeks to know this matter other than by its proper course will never grasp its truth" (153). Seeking to know God through intellectual speculation is likened to flogging a dead horse. The message here is clear: the intellect is precisely the wrong route by which to achieve intimate knowledge of God. Throughout the *Bezels*, one of Ibn al-'Arabi's main concerns is to explicate the nature of mystical knowledge of ultimacy, which Austin translates as "gnosis." The following is one of the definitions

Austin offers for Ibn al-ʿArabi's notion of mystical knowledge: "in its perfection, [gnosis] is nothing other than immediate knowledge and experience of the All-synthesizing Oneness of Being. To be a true Gnostic,
therefore, it is not enough . . . to concentrate exclusively on the intellect,
purged of its vital urges and susceptibilities, but to experience also, as fully
as possible, the inarticulate urge of animal life, devoid of thought and
precept, which is after all nothing other [than] the divine life of His Form"
(229). Austin's definition unequivocally distinguishes Ibn al-ʿArabi's understanding of gnosis from normal intellectual knowledge; it is "not enough"
to know God merely through one's intellectual capacities. In the chapter of
The Bezels of Wisdom on which Austin is commenting, Ibn al-ʿArabi explicitly states that this was precisely the error of the prophet Elias's approach to
knowing God. Recall his interpretation of Elias: Elias had purged himself of
lust, thereby eliminating the passions of the "lower soul" and, in Elias's
estimation, making him more worthy of knowing God. However, Ibn al-
ʿArabi claims, having excised this portion of his spiritual being, Elias was
able to have only "half the gnosis of God" (230). By restricting himself solely
to the intellect, Elias ultimately sabotages his ability to know God fully.

This theme is confirmed by a tradition of Sufi thought regarding the
prophet Muhammad, who is traditionally said to have been illiterate. Islamic
mystics hypothesize that the prophet's inability to read implies that he was
especially well suited to receive divine revelation. Because his "heart was not
spoiled by outward intellectual achievement and learning," he was able to
receive the word of God in an especially pure fashion.[33] Thus a traditional
tenet of Islam is given a mystical spin that confirms a central theme of Ibn
al-ʿArabi's mystical theology.

Ibn al-ʿArabi takes this theme of the problematic nature of the intellect
further, going so far as to suggest that belief in God itself constitutes a
hindrance to mystical communion with him. Every specific image and
definition of God is ultimately inadequate, because they are all merely
products of the intellect. Therefore, belief in God often has far more to do
with the personal preferences of individuals rather than with the actuality
of the deity himself:

> In general, most men have, perforce, an individual concept [belief] of
> their Lord, which they ascribe to Him and in which they seek Him.
> So long as the Reality is presented to them according to it they recog-
> nize Him and affirm Him, whereas if presented in any other form,

they deny Him, flee from Him and treat Him improperly, while at the same time imagining that they are acting toward Him fittingly. One who believes [in the ordinary way] believes only in a deity he has created in himself, since a deity in "beliefs" is a [mental] construction. Therefore, be completely and utterly receptive to all doctrinal forms, for God, Most High, is too All-embracing and Great to be confined within one creed rather than another. (137)

"Belief" in God—in the intellectual and therefore restrictive sense that Ibn al-ʿArabi intends—is contrary not only to progress toward mystical encounter with him but to knowing him at all. Beliefs are derived from finite human minds, and are therefore images or idols borne of individual expectations and the inherent limitations of creaturely consciousness. They are "constructions." The intellect, because of its limited functionality, creates an image of God only by demarcating that image from other images, which are thereby declared wrong and either dismissed or condemned as heretical. Such behavior ultimately only severs one from the "true knowledge" of God.

Accurate knowledge of God results only when one ceases to depend upon belief: "When however the knot [of belief] is loosened, belief ceases [to bind his heart] and he knows once more by [direct] contemplation. After his sight has been sharpened, his weak-sightedness does not recur" (152). By abandoning one's own limited notions of God, one transcends the particular constructions of the intellect and is able to encounter God authentically. In an ironic twist, the "belief" of which Ibn al-ʿArabi writes functions in a manner quite similar to the mediation on which contextualism insists; it is a perceptual filter brought to experience by the mind of the knower that then structures or colors—and hence delimits—the experience itself. Ibn al-ʿArabi, however, clearly states that this mediation must be overcome in order to encounter ultimacy authentically. One's own images and beliefs about God must be disrupted. Otherwise, one's experience of God is limited, if not falsified, by the interference of one's own mediating mind. Here, experience is not facilitated by one's perceptual filters (as in the neo-Kantian model of perception), but sabotaged by them.

Ibn al-ʿArabi's devaluation of the intellect in the *Revelations* is corroborated by numerous passages in the *Bezels*, and it resonates with other aspects of Sufi thought. Having established the insufficiency of the intellect, Ibn al-ʿArabi goes on to discuss the second stage in his epistemological hierarchy, that of "immediate experience": "The second (level of) knowledge is the knowledge of 'states.' The only way to that is through immediate experience: it can't be defined intellectually, and no proof can ever establish that knowing. (It includes things) like knowledge of the sweetness of honey, the bitterness of aloes, the pleasure of intercourse, love, ecstasy, or passionate longing, and other examples of this sort of knowledge. It is impossible for someone to know this kind of knowledge without directly experiencing it and participating in it."[34] Here, Ibn al-'Arabi provides a number of illuminating comparisons by which to understand the type of knowledge he intends. Two qualities in particular seem to characterize this modality of knowing. The first is direct sensory input. While one may describe or read about the taste and texture of honey, one does not actually know the taste of honey unless one has actually had the experience of placing a drop of it on one's tongue. In many ways, Ibn al-'Arabi's discussion here is similar to William James's distinction between knowledge-by-acquaintance and knowledge-about. Only direct personal experience (knowledge-by-acquaintance) can provide this second type of knowledge; anything else is secondary and incomplete.

In addition to emphasizing this direct, sensory quality, Ibn al-'Arabi also appears to underscore the emotional power of knowledge in this second tier. Love, ecstasy, and passionate longing, while they are not sensory stimuli like the sweetness of honey or the bitterness of aloes, are also types of knowledge that cannot be said to be truly known until they are directly experienced. While this may be said of nearly all emotions, it may be especially true of those emotions to which the Sufi master refers—those particularly strong, sometimes overwhelming emotional states that are well known to poets and lovers.

Ibn al-'Arabi does not draw a distinction between these two types of knowing: sensory knowledge or knowledge-by-acquaintance, on one hand, and what we might call emotional knowledge, on the other. In both cases, the essential factor is that only direct experience provides the relevant kind of knowledge. In describing this type of experiential modality, Ibn al-'Arabi tellingly employs the term *dhawq*, which means "to taste." In Ibn al-'Arabi's lexicon, however, the verb *dhawq* also means "to have immediate/direct experience," and this usage is revealing of the type of knowledge the sheikh wishes to describe at this stage of spiritual discernment. The language of sensory perception is employed to draw a sharp contrast between intellectual knowledge or discursive deduction, and direct experience without the intervention of the rational mind. Ibn al-'Arabi returns to this theme numerous times in the *Revelations*, consistently underscoring the importance of this modality of experience and its difference from intellectual knowledge.

For instance, during his own nocturnal journey as recounted in *The Meccan Revelations*, Ibn al-'Arabi encounters Moses and thanks him for persuading Muhammad to negotiate the number of prayers required of the Muslim community during his own ascension into heaven. According to a number of *hadith*, God had originally demanded fifty prayers per day of Muslims; Moses persuades Muhammad to return to God, who eventually agrees to reduce the number to five.[35] During his own exchange with Moses, Ibn al-'Arabi asks what sets him apart from other men. Moses answers, "By an immediate personal experience (*dhawq*) in that regard, which can only be known by the person who actually experiences it."[36] Here, Ibn al-'Arabi clearly explicates the type of knowing he intends with the term; it cannot be related through description or education, because it can be acquired only through direct personal experience. Like tasting honey or all-consuming passion, Moses experienced a type of knowledge of God that can be known only through personal experience of it. During this same encounter, Moses describes *dhawq* as a "(spiritual) condition that can only be perceived through immediate contact," again emphasizing the intimacy and lack of intellectual processing during this modality of experience.[37] Morris notes that the same theme arises at another point in the *Revelations*, when Ibn al-'Arabi encounters Joseph, who insists on the "indispensable, irreducible character of direct personal experience, as opposed to what can be gained by mental reflection or purely imaginative participation." Morris bases this comparison on his translation of the term *mubashara*, or "hands-on experience," which suggests something very similar to *dhawq*.[38]

At another point in the *Revelations*, Ibn al-'Arabi draws a direct relation between his notion of experience and the sense of taste: "There is a specific gustative knowledge (*dhawq*), unknown to the others. . . . Now experience (*khubr*) means gustative knowledge, which is a 'state of knowledge' ('*ilm hal*)."[39] Here, Ibn al-'Arabi explicitly equates experience with "gustative knowledge," leaving no doubt about the direct, sensory nature of the type of knowing he is describing.

Ibn al-ʿArabi also mentions "immediate" or "direct" experience numerous times in *The Bezels of Wisdom* (238). In his chapter on the prophet Ezra, he writes:

> Since, therefore, the prophets derive their knowledge only from a particular divine revelation, their hearts are simple from the intellectual point of view, knowing as they do the deficiency of the intellect, in its discursive aspect, when it comes to the understanding of things as they really are [essentially]. Similarly, [verbal] communication is also deficient in conveying what is only accessible to direct experience. Thus, perfect knowledge is to be had only through a divine Self-revelation or only when God draws back the veils from Hearts and eyes so that they might perceive things, eternal and ephemeral, non-existent and existent, impossible, necessary, or permissible, as they are in their eternal reality and essentiality. (166)

Here, Ibn al-ʿArabi is unequivocal about the nature of mystical experience. The prophets, he states, were not qualified for their vocation because they had greater intellectual understanding of either God or scripture. In fact, the prophets were "simple from the intellectual point of view." This, however, was no obstacle for knowledge of God because the intellect is inadequate for such knowledge anyway. Similarly, verbal communication is "deficient" with regard to knowledge of divine things. Only "direct experience" was sufficient to allow the prophets authentic gnosis of God. As Ibn al-ʿArabi notes, that experience was only possible if God chose to reveal himself. In fact, Ibn al-ʿArabi could be read as claiming that this "direct experience" was possible only because the mediating intellectual structures that usually filter experience had been disabled. This is one possible interpretation of his statement that God "draws back the veils from Hearts and eyes so that they might perceive things . . . as they are in their eternal reality and essentiality."

Ibn al-ʿArabi returns to the theme of the primacy of experience over intellection in chapter 22 of *The Bezels of Wisdom*:

> An indication of the weakness of intellectual speculation is the notion that a cause cannot be [also] the effect of that to which it is a cause. Such is the judgment of the intellect, while in the science of divine Self-revelation it is known that a cause may be the effect of

that for which it is a cause . . . the intellect is not capable of grasping, things the intellect declares to be absurd, except in the case of one who has had an immediate experience of divine manifestation; afterwards, left to himself, he is confused as to what he has seen. If he is a servant of his Lord, he refers his intelligence to Him, but if he is a servant of reason, he reduces God to his yardstick. This happens only so long as he is in this worldly state, being veiled from his otherworldly state in this world. (234)

The weakness of the intellect is demonstrated by its insistence that a phenomenon cannot be both its own cause and effect simultaneously. For Ibn al-'Arabi, this perspective is irrelevant with regard to ultimacy; the illogicality of the statement is simply evidence of the intellect's inability to understand ultimacy. While the judgment that an effect and its cause must be distinct may be correct with regard to worldly things, it is incorrect with regard to the "science of divine Self-revelation." Its application to God represents a presumptuous and mistaken assumption that creaturely logic is applicable to the divine being. Left to itself, the intellect will disregard that which appears irrational and thereby "reduce God to its yardstick." But he who has had an "immediate experience" of the divine knows that the limitations of the intellect are just that. He therefore "refers his intelligence to [God]"; he defers allegiance to logic in favor of acknowledging that God supersedes rational strictures. The mystic thereby avoids fragmenting God in accord with the intellect's categories and instead adheres only to what experience reveals.

This theme is echoed throughout Sufi literature, and especially in the different schemes Sufis developed to describe their collections of mystical states: gnosis, or mystical knowledge, is radically different from 'ilm, or discursive knowledge. Schimmel relates the story of a seventeenth-century Sufi who refers to a *hadith* that calls 'ilm "the 'greatest veil' separating man from God." He likens the intellect to a "lame ass" that carries books, whereas love is likened to "the winged *burāq* that brought Muhammad into the presence of God."[40] Carl Ernst suggests that this debate represents a fundamental disagreement between Islamic theologians, who were influenced by the intellectualism of Aristotelian philosophy, and Sufi mystics, who insisted on achieving a state of awareness beyond reason.[41]

In discussing this notion of immediacy and the second tier of knowledge, Ibn al-'Arabi invokes another term with special relevance to Sufi thought: state (*hal*). In the introduction to the *Revelations*, he clearly places the experience of states in the middle position of his three-tier hierarchy of knowledge:

> And as for the "knowledge of states," that is between this knowledge of secrets and knowledge (gained by discursive) intellects. Most of those who have faith in the knowledge of states are people who rely on their own spiritual experiences (*'ahl al-tajārib*). And the knowledge of states is closer to the knowledge of secrets than it is to the intellective knowledge gained by inquiry. . . . Therefore you should know that if this (kind of report concerning spiritual knowledge) seems good to you, and you accept it and have faith in it—then rejoice (in your good fortune)! For you are necessarily in a state of direct spiritual "unveiling" (*kashf*) concerning that, even if you aren't aware of it.[42]

The knowledge of states—defined by direct experience, or *dhawq*—is closer in character to the "knowledge of secrets" (Ibn al-'Arabi's third stage of knowing) than to discursive knowledge (the first, least perfect stage). This again emphasizes the significant difference between intellectual, rational knowledge and the kind of experience Ibn al-'Arabi emphasizes at the second tier of his epistemological hierarchy.

The paired notions of state (*hal*) and station (*maqam*) are central to Sufi attempts to organize the hierarchy of spiritual stages through which a mystic progresses on his way to a more intimate encounter with God. Ibn al-'Arabi describes his own conception of the meaning of these terms, and their relationship to each other, in the *Revelations*:

> For each station there is a corresponding state (*hal*) and a certain kind of knowledge (*'ilm*), or rather a set of spiritual sciences. It is possible to experience the state characteristic of a station without having reached the station and, conversely, it is possible to reach a station without experiencing its corresponding *hal*. Only the *'ilm* is important to the true *salik* ("traveler"), the celestial nomad who cannot be turned away from his goal by the temptation of spiritual joys. But the *'ilm* itself should be gone beyond: in the individual who is no longer closed in by the stations, it is followed by *hayra*—perplexity, a dazzled stupefaction, an absence of knowledge that transcends all

knowledge in the same way that the Divine Essence transcends all perfection.[43]

Within Sufism, there was a widespread desire to systematize the hierarchy of stages available to the aspiring mystic. As a result, distinct categorizations and entire vocabularies were developed, the purpose of which was the arrangement of the various states of consciousness Islamic mystics report and describe. The Sufis' propensity for categorization is best represented in the distinction and relationship between the terms *hal* and *maqam*, or "state" and "station." The former, according to Sufi tradition, is a state of consciousness or experience that descends upon a Sufi from God; it cannot be brought about through one's own doing, and it cannot be resisted when imposed. These states seem to be mystical experiences in the sense of the term used today. They include, for instance, *bast*, which is derived from the root meaning "to get wider and enlarge." Schimmel defines it as "an extension of enthusiastic feeling, a perfect joy and ease that may develop, in some cases, into true 'cosmic consciousness,' into the feeling of partaking of the life of everything created, into that rapture of which the intoxicated poets of Iran and Turkey have sung so often."[44]

Maqam, by contrast, is a lasting stage of spiritual development that a mystic achieves, at least to some extent, through his own striving. As the mystic progresses through his ascetic and moral discipline, he achieves higher stations (*maqamat*). These stations bring with them specific responsibilities concerning the ethical and religious quality of life the mystic leads.[45] Sufis disagreed among themselves as to the precise arrangement of the states and stations, and over their exact nature. Common *maqamat* include *tauba* (repentance, the turning away from sins and the abandonment of worldly concerns), *tawakkul* (trust in God and absolute surrender to him), and *sabr* (a type of patience in which the Sufi bears any and all afflictions—which ultimately come from God—with quiet acceptance).[46] Theoretically, the station in which a Sufi lives defines the states to which he may be prone. In other words, although a Sufi cannot bring about a given state (*hal*) himself, through moral and religious observance he can achieve higher stations (*maqamat*) and thereby make himself deserving of higher states.

This background of Sufi thought—basically a framework of mystical epistemology—sheds light on the key passage describing Ibn al-'Arabi's experience. While interpreting this passage in light of Sufi thought makes sense of it, it also underscores subtle ways in which Ibn al-'Arabi revises Sufi thought, tweaking it so as to reveal his own epistemological assumptions. Generally speaking, states and stations are related in a rough correspondence; certain states are likely to be experienced once the Sufi has achieved a certain station. Ibn al-'Arabi, however, argues for a less consistent relationship between the two. He claims that one may experience a state without achieving its corresponding station, or reach a given station without undergoing the state or states that are associated with it. Clearly, the Sufi master is not centrally concerned with the hierarchy itself. He first says that it is the 'ilm ("knowledge") derived from or associated with the states and stations that is important. He immediately contradicts this assertion, however, when he says that this knowledge also must be surpassed: "But the 'ilm itself should be gone beyond: in the individual who is no longer closed in by the stations, it is followed by hayra—perplexity, a dazzled stupefaction, an absence of knowledge that transcends all knowledge in the same way that the Divine Essence transcends all perfection."[47]

The states and stations of the mystical path may lead to certain spiritual insights; ultimately, however, even the knowledge garnered from these experiences, Ibn al-'Arabi writes, must be surpassed in favor of "an absence of knowledge." This exhortation suggests another, third stage of knowledge. This is the last stage in Ibn al-'Arabi's epistemological hierarchy:

> The third (level of) knowledge is knowledge of (divine) secrets: this is the knowledge that is beyond the stage of the discursive intellect. It is knowledge of "the inbreathing of the Holy Spirit in the heart," and it is peculiar to the prophets and the friends (of God). This knowledge is of two kinds. One kind is perceived by the intellect, just like the first (category of purely discursive) knowledge, except that the person who knows in this (inspired) way does not acquire their knowledge through discursive "inquiry" (nazar). Instead, the (divine) "level" of this knowledge bestows it upon them. The second kind (of divinely inspired knowledge) is of two sorts. The first sort is connected with the second (above-mentioned level of) knowledge (i.e., of inner "states"), except that this knower's state is more exalted. And the other sort is knowledge through (divine) "informing."[48]

Following the culmination of his spiritual journey quoted at the beginning of this chapter, Ibn al-'Arabi relates that he received sixty-nine different kinds of knowledge after reaching this point in his mystical ascension. This suggestion that he received different kinds of knowledge, and the fact that they can be enumerated and distinguished from one another, could seem to suggest that, having passed through the second, experiential and nondiscursive tier of mystical experience, the third level returns one to a more discursive, rational form of knowledge. But this is not quite the case. Commenting on this passage, Morris points out that Ibn al-'Arabi repeats the phrase "I saw in it" before each of the sixty-nine insights he enumerates. The repetition of this phrase, Morris argues, is intended to emphasize the direct and experiential form of knowing that takes place at this stage.[49] The reference to vision is reminiscent of Ibn al-'Arabi's use of the verb *dhawq* (to taste), and the reference to sensory perception seems to perpetuate the distinction between experiential knowing and discursive or deductive knowing.

This is confirmed by Ibn al-'Arabi's own description of the third stage of knowledge in his three-tier hierarchy, where he explicitly writes that the knowledge of secrets is "beyond . . . the discursive intellect." The distinction he seeks to draw here is subtle but significant. In this third stage of knowledge, one can be said to gain some sort of insight—not insight that can be deduced or inferred through rational processes but insight that is impressed into the mind through divine inspiration. One is reminded of James's claim that mystical experiences are "states of insight into depths of truth unplumbed by the discursive intellect."[50]

Ibn al-'Arabi goes on to suggest that this final stage of mystical knowing can itself be broken down into further subcategories, and this subdivision is difficult to follow. On one hand, there is the knowledge that is received by the mind but cannot be obtained other than by divine inspiration. Presumably, this constitutes the sixty-nine insights, which are not reached by inquiry. In addition to these, however, Ibn al-'Arabi mentions a second kind of divinely inspired knowledge, which is further subdivided into two sorts. The first sort resembles the experiential states that characterize the second tier of his epistemology, while the latter is "knowledge through divine informing." The discussion of these subdivisions does not offer much clarification of the nature of this third, final tier in Ibn al-'Arabi's mystical epistemology.

Some clarity on this third level of mystical knowledge can be afforded by adverting to other passages in the sheikh's writing. For instance, elsewhere in the *Revelations*, Ibn al-'Arabi again takes up the topic of epistemology, offering a condensed list of types of mystical knowledge. He describes the last—and therefore presumably the highest—entry in this brief list in the following words: "and some [insights] are considered impossible by reflection, while the intellect accepts from reflection that they cannot exist. The intellect cannot accept them because of the proof of their impossibility, so it comes to know them from God through a sound Incident (waqi'a), which is not impossible. But the name and property of impossibility do not disappear from them in respect to the intellect."[51] This passage goes some distance in explaining how and why the intellect comes to receive knowledge through divine inspiration that cannot be obtained otherwise. If subjected to reflection, the intellect will determine this knowledge to be impossible, and therefore is likely to reject it. However, the mystic who has reached this stage of spiritual insight, if he is wise, will realize that this would be inappropriate. Divine secrets, inspired by God, are not untrue merely because they appear to be impossible from the perspective of the human intellect. Rather, demonstrating a kind of epistemic humility, the mystic ought to accept this secret knowledge despite its appearance of illogicality. The fact of divine inspiration trumps the violation of logic or rationality.

This is why knowledge that is attained at the culmination of the spiritual ascent can be attained only by divine inspiration. Violating the laws of logic, the human intellect cannot reach it through its own deliberative processes. In fact, Ibn al-'Arabi seems to suggest that once these divine secrets are received, they should not be subjected to reflection, which will predictably find them problematic. Another passage of the Revelations discusses what appears to be the same epistemological modality:

> Those who know God come to know concerning Him through His knowledge of His own Essence that which intellects cannot know in respect of their own sound reflections. This is the knowledge about which the Tribe says that it lies beyond the stage of the intellect (wara tawr al-'aql). God says concerning His servant Khidr, "We taught him a knowledge from us" (Qur'an 18:64); and He says, "[He created man] and taught him the explanation" (Qur'an 55:4); so He attributed the teaching to Himself, not to reflection (al-fikr). Hence we know that there is a station beyond reflection that bestows upon the servant knowledge of various things.[52]

Interestingly, in his description of the culmination of his spiritual journey, Ibn al-'Arabi does not offer a great deal of information about the experience itself beyond the key passage quoted earlier. In both the *Revelations* and the *Bezels*, he offers substantial commentary on his understanding of mystical epistemology, and the culminating passage itself does offer some intriguing comments about the ontological relationship between Ibn al-'Arabi and God, but there is not a great deal of description of the quality of the experience itself. This apparent lacuna can be explained by further consideration of Ibn al-'Arabi's own beliefs about mystical experience, and by comparisons with other aspects of Sufi thought.

According to the Sufi master, "not every knowledge can be expressed."[53] He repeats this theme in the *Bezels* on numerous occasions. For instance: "Some of us there are who profess ignorance as part of their knowledge, maintaining [with Abu Bakr] that 'To realize that one cannot know God is to know.' There are others from among us, however, who know, but who do not say such things, their knowledge instilling in them silence rather than [professions] of ignorance. This is the highest knowledge of God, possessed only by the Seal of the Apostles and the Seal of the Saints" (66). The realization that God is beyond the capacity of the mind to know him is evidence of spiritual insight, according to Ibn al-'Arabi. But while that realization is accurate, the master seems to imply that even stating that realization is to attempt to capture something of God in language and is therefore foolish. So it may in fact be better to remain silent, refusing to give voice to even the impossibility of describing God. According to Ibn al-'Arabi, this was known to the prophets, who realized that, just as the intellect was "deficient" when it comes to understanding divine revelation, language was also unable to convey what is accessible only to "direct experience" (166).

In an unusually succinct passage, Ibn al-'Arabi states that "the intellect restricts and seeks to define the truth within a particular qualification, while in fact the Reality does not admit of such limitation" (150). The intellect, in Ibn al-'Arabi's view, functions through a process of categorization and analysis; it understands what it encounters by classifying and delimiting it. A thing is known by determining what it is not, by qualifying it in relation to other, limited phenomena. Such a process cannot be performed with relation to God simply because God is unlimited. There is nothing against which to contrast him and no boundary by which to conceptually delimit him. The usual procedure by which the intellect produces knowledge simply cannot be applied to ultimacy.

Michael Sells, in commenting on this dimension of Ibn al-'Arabi's thought, places the sheikh in the apophatic tradition of negative theology. From this perspective, language fails with regard to God because language, like the intellect, inevitably functions in a delimiting fashion. To name a thing is to limit it, to posit it as an entity distinct and separate from other entities that are not named as such. That hypostatization unavoidably suggests that the object named is delimited; otherwise, it could not be identified as distinct from that which is excluded by the act of naming. This fundamental failure of language, Sells points out, cannot be avoided in the act of acknowledging the failure. To say of a thing that "language cannot contain or describe it" is still to refer to the putative object as "it," and therefore to delimit it in some (albeit minimal) fashion.[54] This is the logic behind Ibn al-ʿArabi's statement that even the term "God" is "in reality, [but] a verbal expression" and therefore has no intrinsic value (231).

This kind of attitude concerning language pervades Sufi thought. Consider, for example, the following poem by Ibn ʿAta:

> When men of common parlance question us,
> we answer them with signs mysterious
> and dark enigmas; for the tongue of man
> cannot express so high a truth, whose span
> surpasses human measure. But my heart
> has known it, and has known of it a rapture
> that thrilled and filled my body, every part.
> Seest thou not, these mystic feelings capture
> the very art of speech, as men who know
> vanquish and silence their unlettered foe.[55]

Ibn ʿAta states that the motivation behind the dark sayings of Sufi mystics is not mere obfuscation. Their recondite language is not a ruse to preserve an air of mystery, as some scholars have suggested.[56] Rather, their motivation arises from the fact that human language is simply incapable of expressing mystical experience. In fact, it is not the mind at all that undergoes the experience, but the heart. The failure of language therefore arises directly from the nature of the experience itself. As Ibn al-ʿArabi notes, the rational strictures of language render it incapable of capturing an experience that the heart undergoes. The rapture of which Ibn ʿAta writes is far more a bodily than a mental experience, which paradoxically captures the "very essence" of speech while simultaneously surpassing speech itself. The rather brief account of mystical experience that Ibn al-ʿArabi offers in the *Revelations* may therefore be all that one can reasonably be expected to say about an experience that by its very nature exceeds the ability of the mind to conceptualize it and the capacity of language to articulate it.

Conclusion

I have argued here for a particular understanding of Ibn al-ʿArabi's mystical experience, based on a hermeneutic method that interprets Ibn al-ʿArabi's account of his mystical experience against, first, the background of his own epistemological and ontological assumptions, garnered from his own writings, and, second, broader consideration of Sufi and Muslim sources. This approach stands in contrast to other methods, most particularly contextualism. Katz employs an epistemology in which the interpreter begins with contextual sources and mainstream doctrines, and then deduces the nature and limitations of mystical experience for any particular tradition based on the assumption that all consciousness and experience is necessarily shaped and filtered by context. As I have shown here, such a procedure runs the risk of misconstruing mystical experience.

First, the hermeneutic I deploy, rather than resting on its own set of epistemological assumptions, seeks instead to disclose those assumptions already embedded in the mystical text. The case of Ibn al-ʿArabi illustrates one of the reasons why this approach is preferable. As I have shown, the epistemology embedded in the sheikh's text and expressed in his description of his mystical experience contradicts that employed by Katz on a number of points. Consider some of the primary epistemological assumptions revealed by this analysis of Ibn al-ʿArabi's work: (1) the intellect is fundamentally incapable of achieving mystical experience; (2) experience independent of the intervention of the discursive mind is not only possible but is the preferable mode of spiritual apprehension; (3) this type of experience, because of its fundamental violation of the laws of logic and rationality, cannot be captured in language. These are fundamental aspects of Ibn al-ʿArabi's epistemology, and each of them runs contrary to the epistemology on which contextualism is based. This is not to suggest that an interpreter must adopt Ibn al-ʿArabi's own epistemology in order to understand it; but it does suggest that insofar as Katz's interpretive method is based on these assumptions and adopts them categorically, it very well may obscure or ignore those aspects of the text with which it disagrees. The imposition of an ulterior epistemology runs the risk of obfuscating those aspects of the mystic's own epistemology that it contradicts.

Consider, also, the radical ontological assumption at the heart of Ibn al-'Arabi's mystical experience—that an essential and eternal dimension of the human being is in fact an aspect of the self-manifestation of God. This metaphysical notion flies in the face of orthodox Islamic teaching. Katz's interpretive method, presuming as it does that mystical experience will necessarily accord with the basic tenets of mainstream religious doctrine, would predict that this type of mystical experience would be entirely absent from Islam. But this would be a radical misrepresentation of Ibn al-'Arabi's mystical experience. In fact, it would be a misrepresentation of a good number of Muslim mystics—among them Junayd, al-Hallaj, and al-Bistami— and ignores the implications of one of the most common themes of Sufism, *fanā'* and *baqā'*. In short, neither Ibn al-'Arabi's mystical experiences nor those of any other mystic can be predicted on the basis of the lineaments of the mainstream doctrines of the religious traditions in which they are situated, nor can they best be understood through the imposition of an ulterior epistemology, or in absence of consideration of the mystic's own embedded assumptions concerning the experiential modality and ontological underpinnings of mystical experience.

4

MEISTER ECKHART AND THE BREAKING-THROUGH INTO THE QUIET DESERT

Meister Eckhart was probably born sometime in the year 1260, in Thuringia, Germany. Sources suggest that his first name was probably John, but he is remembered by the appellation "Meister" (master), which reflects the extent of his influence on Christian mystical thought and writing. Eckhart was a friar of the Dominican order and showed promise early in his career. He was sent to the University of Paris for training in the teacher's program, an honor the Dominican order bestowed upon only their most promising members.[1] Shortly thereafter, Eckhart traveled to Cologne to study theology, returning to Paris in 1293 or 1294 to earn his master's degree. After completing the degree, he returned to Germany, and for the next ten to fifteen years enjoyed a number of promotions in recognition of his ability as an administrator. Eckhart once again transferred to Paris in 1311, where he began work on his magnum opus, the *Opus Tripartitum*, or *Three-Part Work*, a project that was never to be completed. Upon returning to Germany for good in 1313, Eckhart's time and energy seem to have been dedicated mostly to his public sermons and, later, to defending himself against charges of heresy (10).

Throughout his career, Eckhart was concerned primarily with public preaching. This is not to say that his academic works or aspirations were at all lacking in quality or depth; his theological reflections are profound, complex, and challenging. He was, however, deeply invested in his calling as a preacher, an emphasis that was shared by the Dominican order in general. At the same time, Eckhart's approach appears to have been his own. Theologically, there is substantial continuity between his formal academic works and the themes that he preached to his congregation. His sermons, however, clearly indicate—in both content and form—that rather than merely relating doctrine to his parishioners or even seeking to deepen their religious and moral commitment through exhortation, he sought to surprise and shock them into a deeper relationship with God (24–26). Through heterodox interpretations of doctrine and intentionally edgy language, Eckhart sought to provoke his audience, to wake them up from any easy or complacent kind of religion and to push them toward a profound encounter with the Christian faith and a deeper, more personal relationship with God. Throughout both his Latin treatises and vernacular sermons, the need for a deeply personal relationship with God—indeed, one might say, for a powerful appropriation of God—is a continuous theme. One is tempted to see Eckhart as a precursor to today's megachurch pastor: a preacher with both impressive rhetorical skill and deep commitment, who seeks to drive his congregation to a knowledge of God deeper than they might have imagined.

It is at least in part due to his provocative language and willingness to push the envelope of orthodox theology that he eventually came under investigation by the church. The first signs of trouble appeared during a period that Eckhart spent in Cologne, to which he came, at the earliest, in 1323. At that time he was investigated by Nicholas of Strassburg, an agent of the pope. Although Eckhart's teachings were determined initially to be free of heresy, the archbishop of Cologne ordered a full inquisitorial investigation (10). Twenty-eight propositions—essentially statements of doctrine excerpted from Eckhart's sermons and academic works—were examined in the course of the investigation; ultimately, seventeen of them were condemned as heretical, and the remaining eleven were deemed offensive but, with "many explanations and additions," could be construed as in conformity with church doctrine (12).

It is significant that of the twenty-eight propositions, Eckhart willingly admitted to having taught all but two (although it has been suggested that even these can be traced to Eckhart's work). This should not be interpreted merely as evidence of Eckhart's integrity. Eckhart held fast to the argument that these teachings were squarely within the bounds of Christian orthodoxy. In fact, in his written defense Eckhart argues that it is impossible that he could be guilty of heresy. "I can be in error," Eckhart writes, "but I cannot be a heretic, because the first belongs to the intellect, and the second to the will" (72). Heresy, Eckhart argues, is a sin of the will; it arises from the intention to contravene the teaching of the church. Of this, Eckhart claims, he could never be guilty, because his intention was always to preach the true Christian message, even if he might have been mistaken in his understanding of it.

It is unfortunate that the investigation and ultimate condemnation of Eckhart's work came so late in his life. He died circa 1327, and sources suggest that by the end of his life his intellectual powers were beginning to wane (14). His defense against the inquisitorial charges, therefore, may not have been as effective as it might have been otherwise. Neither this nor his papal condemnation appears to have had much effect on his legacy, however. In theory at least, the finding of heresy should have outlawed Christians from reading or commenting on Eckhart's work, let alone defending his teachings. This, however, was precisely what happened. Eckhart's works continued to be popular, and two of his students, John Tauler and Henry Suso, themselves luminaries of the Christian mystical tradition, continued to teach many of Eckhart's central themes after his death. By 1440, the papal condemnation appears to have lost much of its bite (21).

It is recorded that Eckhart recanted on his deathbed, and it has been claimed that this confession represents an unequivocal repudiation of his problematic teachings. The record of his recantation, however, is not quite so clear: "the aforesaid Eckhart . . . at the end of his life . . . revoked and also deplored the twenty-six articles which he admitted that he had preached, and also any others, written and taught by him . . . insofar as they could generate in the minds of the faithful a heretical opinion, or one erroneous and hostile to the true faith" (14–15). The phrase "insofar as" is crucial and bespeaks not only a spiritual resilience on Eckhart's part but a final flicker of the agile mind that so vexed the papal authorities. Apologizing for his teachings "insofar as" they may have inspired his listeners to ideas and theological opinions that were contrary to the teachings of the church is not quite the same as admitting that the actual content and meaning of his teachings were problematic. The subtlety of the wording, one suspects, is intentional. As will be seen, this careful nuance in expression not only marks Eckhart's deathbed confession but plays a significant role throughout his complex and multilayered theology.

That theology—and the core mystical themes that will be emphasized here—is expressed in both Eckhart's vernacular sermons and his learned treatises. Although the former are marked by more provocative terminology and seemingly heterodox claims, similar themes are explored in both, and a full understanding of the preacher's mystical thought must consider both the German and Latin works. The dynamic and creative nature of his discourse presents certain interpretive challenges (24, 25, 30), but two guiding themes to reading the master's work can be identified. First, the Dominican's thought on the nature of God and his relationship to creation—and specifically the human mystic's ability to come to know God more intimately—is consistently rooted in experience.[2] Despite the often abstract nature of Eckhart's reflections on the nature of God and reality, he is consistently concerned to bring these observations back to the experience of God, rather than merely to offer theoretical disquisitions. The master's exposition of the nature of God and the human soul, in other words, is designed not only to inform but—especially in the case of his vernacular sermons—to guide the religious practitioner to a personal experience of the doctrine he expounds.

Second, Eckhart does not promote what may be thought of as distinct, ecstatic encounters with divinity. The experience of God with which he is concerned is a more permanent state of being that would infuse the everyday life of the religious individual.[3] It is for this reason that Eckhart reverses the traditional preference of Christian mystics for Mary over Martha. In this iconic biblical scene, related in the Gospel of Luke, Jesus visits two sisters, one of whom, Mary, sits in quiet reception and apparent contemplation of Jesus's words while her sister, Martha, busies herself about the house. The scene is often interpreted as an allegory for two paths of religious practice, the first quiet, introspective, and contemplative, the other active and outwardly engaged, and a majority of mystics in the Christian tradition evince a preference for the path symbolized by Mary. Eckhart, however, prefers Martha, whose active life, he holds, suggests not an incomplete immersion in God but a more sustained and profound kind of union that can obtain simultaneously with engaged living. Eckhart thereby seeks to promote what Bernard McGinn calls a "totally God-centered life" in which the presence of God is intimately felt even as an individual goes about his daily business.[4]

This is not to suggest that the encounter with God that Eckhart describes is any less radical or complete than that of any of the boldest mystical thinkers in the Christian tradition. In fact, as will be seen, it may very well be that Eckhart's encounter with God is more radical than that of many of his brethren. In order to explore his understanding of the mystical encounter with God, I focus on a key passage from his German Sermon 5b, in which Eckhart makes one of his most iconic claims concerning the relationship

between the soul and God. I then explore his understanding of this encounter through the lenses of ontology and epistemology, disclosing both the
metaphysical nature of the encounter he envisions and the mode of knowing by which that encounter is realized.

Key Passage

One of Meister Eckhart's most famous and controversial teachings is that
the human soul and God share the same "ground" (German: *grunt*). The
exact meaning of this claim, and the manner in which the aspiring Christian mystic is to realize it, are themes to which he returns again and again
in both his sermons and theological treatises. His clearest statement of this
doctrine is found in Sermon 5b: "This is what the text means with which I
began: 'God has sent his Only-Begotten Son into the World.' You must not
by this understand the external world in which the Son ate and drank with
us, but understand it to apply to the inner world. As truly as the Father in
his simple nature gives his Son birth naturally, so truly does he give him
birth in the most inward part of the spirit, and that is the inner world. Here
God's ground is my ground, and my ground is God's ground" (183). The
birth of the Son in the soul is one of Eckhart's favorite tropes for describing
this relationship, and I address it below. First, however, it is important to
note the emphasis on inwardness. In claiming that his listeners should not
understand this statement to refer to the "external world," Eckhart does
not mean to deny that Jesus was the Son of God or that he lived an earthly
existence in the physical world that human beings inhabit. He does, however, wish to focus his attention—and that of his congregation—on
another, deeper and more personal meaning of this phrase.[5] In that sense,
the birth of the Son refers to a spiritual truth having to do with the inner
self of the human person. This truth is simply that God's ground is also the
ground of the self.

　　Unpacking Eckhart's reasons for this claim, and its implications, requires
exploration of his thought on the ontology of divine reality and the nature
of the human self. Before such an exploration can be conducted, however,
it is necessary to note another aspect of Eckhart's writing: the *in quantum*
(roughly, "insofar as") principle. This is a central philosophical and termi-
nological tool of Eckhart's writing, and its repeated use reflects both the
complexity of his theological thinking and his consistent awareness that

the use of human language to speak of divine realities is an inherently problematic endeavor. In general, the *in quantum* principle is based on Eckhart's belief that the attribution of descriptive terms—including the attribute of existence itself—necessarily functions differently depending on whether these terms are being applied to created things or to aspects of the divine reality. For example, when existence (*esse*) is predicated of creatures, it must be denied of God, and when existence is predicated of God, it must be denied of creatures (33). This, in a sense, reflects a standard tenet of Christian thought: there is an essential difference between the ontological nature of the creator and that which he creates. To attribute existence to God and creation simultaneously would be to imply that both exist in the same manner, and Eckhart clearly does not believe this (nor do most Christian theologians). The *in quantum* principle therefore suggests that whenever any claim is made concerning the nature of God, the soul, or any other object, one must consider the perspective from which the claim is made.

From one perspective, it may certainly be said that those things that populate the universe exist, insofar as they have physical properties and come to be and pass away in this world. From another perspective, however, the furniture of the world does not exist, insofar as the type of existence it enjoys pales fundamentally in comparison to God's mode of existence. The distinction Eckhart suggests here is dialectical in nature; it involves a dynamic and continuous shift in meaning between two poles that are interrelated and dependent on each other but at the same time radically different from each other in nature. The apparent paradox of this claim signals the complexities of Eckhart's metaphysical thought.

Eckhart's Ontology of Mystical Experience

Sermon 5b includes a few other short statements in this ontological key. For instance, after the key passage quoted above, Eckhart encourages his listeners to "let God be God in you." Exhortations such as this are suggestive in both metaphysical and epistemological terms. Metaphysically, the implication that God can be God "in" the human individual indicates a relationship of great intimacy, while the verb "let" suggests that realizing this intimacy requires a certain passivity on the part of Christians. These themes appear throughout Eckhart's writing. The sermon itself is a brief text, and in order to disclose the full implications of these themes, and to reveal the role they play in Eckhart's understanding of mystical experience, it is necessary to reflect on the overarching metaphysical ideas that pervade his thought concerning matters such as the creation of the universe and the ongoing relationship between creation and God.

The act of creation, for Eckhart, is not the simple and singular act of God's giving rise to creation and then remaining at a distance from it. In discussing God's creation of the universe, Eckhart draws a distinction between the divine mode of creation and its human counterpart. An architect, for example, creates a house that comes to exist outside himself; once it is created, its continued existence is no longer essentially tied to the architect. God, by contrast, creates things "in principle," according to Eckhart ("Commentary on Genesis," 89). This mode of production or procreation, Eckhart argues, is distinctly different in kind from the modality of creation that may be attributed to human artificers. First, it does not result in an end product that is "outside the producer." Rather, what is produced remains within the producer, and Eckhart therefore denies that what God produces may be described as an "effect":

> Everything that the One produces that is not an effect, or something made on the outside, is necessarily one inasmuch as it remains in the One. It is not an effect, or something made on the outside, but it is before what is made, prior in nature to what is made, not divided from the One, but one with the One, from the One, through the One and in the One—one, I say, in unity, entity, wisdom and in all similar immanent things. It is produced indeed, but it is not made, or something different or created. (Ibid., 97)

Terms such as "made" suggest a division between that which is produced and the producer, and Eckhart takes pains to reject this understanding of the divine mode of creation. In fact, he suggests that what is ultimately produced "is before what is made, prior in nature to what is made." In other words, creation "in principle" seems to involve two dimensions or aspects: on one hand, there is the physical creation of material objects in the universe, those things that may be directly perceived with the human senses. On the other, there is the divine act of conceptualizing an entity, and this may more directly represent what Eckhart has in mind when he claims that the divine creates "in principle."[6] The priority of which Eckhart writes in this passage is probably logical rather than temporal, meaning that God's conception of a thing represents a more significant or basic instantiation of its being than its material reality in the physical universe.

This explains how the act of divine production involves the retention of a thing's being within God himself. A thing's existence "in principle"—roughly, the conception of it that is necessary to its physical manifestation—is rooted in the divine reality. Therefore, the divine modality of creation does not really involve a distinction between creature and creator; what is created remains within the creator (in principle). This signals that ultimately there is a way in which all of creation remains continuously rooted in the divine: "Even though some things are produced and come about from other things that are secondary causes, each and every being whether it be produced by nature or by art possesses its existence or the fact that it is immediately from God alone, so that the text can be read, 'All things made exist through him.' The whole of existence and the existence of all things is from God alone, as was said above" ("Commentary on John," 141). Both natural and man-made things have their tangible, physical causes; the oak tree grows from the acorn and the table is built by the carpenter. But these, in Eckhart's language, are "secondary causes." While we may perceive the acorn and the carpenter as the proximate causes of the oak tree and the table, they are not the ultimate causes of these things. Rather, these and all other things in the created world derive their existence, in the final analysis, from God.

This might be taken to mean that Eckhart regards God as the "first cause," in the sense that in explaining the chain of causality that ultimately gives rise to any existent, we must ultimately come to rest at some basic, self-caused entity whose existence is not dependent on or caused by anything else. But this does not seem to be the sense Eckhart intends in suggesting that "all things made exist through him." Rather, he means to say that *the fact that a thing is* is ultimately rooted in God. This is not some temporal chain of causality that finally comes to end in the being of God. Rather, the very fact that a thing exists is only possible because existence itself is rooted in the nature of God, and to the extent that anything at all exists, it does so through partaking in the essence of God. The relationship that Eckhart suggests here is very much reminiscent of the Platonic doctrine of the forms; existence, in this sense, is like a kind of divine form in which existents participate. Created things exist "through" God, therefore, not in the sense that their secondary causes can ultimately be traced back to God temporally or causally, but in the sense that the fact of their existence is an incomplete reflection of the kind of true existence enjoyed by God.

Existence, in this sense, is a quality that precedes the being of any existents in the created universe. Robert Dobie, in analyzing the ontological dimension of Eckhart's thought, uses the example of a rose. When we claim that a rose exists, we are not suggesting that there is such a thing as a rose to which we then attach the predicate "existence." To the contrary, we can only mean that the predicate itself (existence) precedes the subject (rose); the rose, in this sense, inheres or participates in existence.[7] This is because God *is* existence; his essence involves existence to such an intimate degree, and the being of all other things is derivative from him in such a way, that the divine being itself is existence.

This demonstrates the necessity of the *in quantum* principle: creatures can be said to exist only insofar as their existence is understood as secondary to and derivative from God. However, insofar as we understand created things like roses to be independent of God, we must regard them as lacking existence. Therefore, insofar as created things have no independent, self-sufficient being, they are utterly different from God. Because God clearly and necessarily exists in and of himself, he is radically distinct from all other things in the universe, which have existence only indirectly. However, because all existents have existence—to the degree that they do—through him, they are thus intimately related to God, and to that degree are indistinct from him.[8]

Eckhart describes this indirect ontological nature of all existents in various ways. In his commentary on the Gospel of John, he likens it to the notion of life: "one must know that everything that is moved by itself or by a principle within and in itself is said to be alive or living. What is moved only by something outside itself is neither alive nor said to be living. From this it is clear that nothing that has a maker prior to it or above it, or an end that is beyond it or different from it, is alive in the proper sense. Everything created fits that description. God alone, insofar as he is Final End and First Mover, lives and is life." We have already seen that Eckhart acknowledges the "secondary causes" of all things in this world, including those produced "by nature." Given the statement here, however, that "nothing that has a maker prior to it or above it . . . is alive in the proper sense," he would seem to be claiming that no natural thing in this world is actually alive "in the proper sense." Clearly, Eckhart does not mean to suggest that this world is populated by zombies or automatons that merely mimic actually living things. Rather, he uses the terms "life" and "living" here as stand-ins for existence. Natural beings in this world do live, but their life is dependent upon and derivative from God in the same manner that existence is ultimately derived from God. God and God alone, Eckhart writes, "lives and is life." Life is instantiated in its truest and most real form only in the being of God, and all other living things are alive in a lesser, derivative sense.

This notion may be further understood in light of Eckhart's Neoplatonic take on the act of creation. Like Augustine and many others, Eckhart endorses the doctrine of *creatio ex nihilo*—that the universe was created out of nothing. However, he also regards all things as having a virtual existence through their idea, a nonphysical ideal that is "more real" than the physical instantiation of the created phenomenon that exists through or participates in that idea (40). Of course, the ideas themselves do not exist independently of God. More significantly, however, Eckhart suggests that there is an important sense in which creation was (or "is") not a temporally limited event. The act of creation effected through God's speaking is, for Eckhart, an eternal act. This is not to suggest that the universe itself is eternal (a point of confusion that was to cause problems for Eckhart at trial); rather, all of God's acts occur in an "eternal now," a single ongoing moment that embraces all of time and is therefore not bounded by either a beginning or an ending (41). This indicates not only that all of creation owes its existence to God but that all of creation is rooted in a continual, ongoing act of creation that is always in process. God's relationship to the universe is therefore not that of an artisan who creates a thing that then perdures independently of its creator; rather, God is the fundamental, ongoing source of creation, implicated in each and every moment of the continuing perdurance of created things.

While Eckhart describes all of creation through this derivative relationship with God, he points out specifically that this is also the manner of existence of the human soul. "When the Father begot all created things," he writes, "then he begot me, and I flowed out with all created things, and yet I remained within, in the Father" (Sermon 22, 193). Like all other inhabitants of creation, Eckhart himself is an aspect of creation, a product of the activity of God the Father. However, in being created, he was not thus sundered completely from God; he still remains "within" the Father. Eckhart likens this act of creation to a burning fire: "Fire as fire does not burn; it is so pure and so fine that it does not burn; but it is fire's nature that burns and pours its nature and its brightness according to its highest perfection into the dry wood. God has acted like this. He created the soul according to the highest perfection, and poured into it in its first purity all his brightness and yet he has remained unmixed" (ibid., 194). Fire, in burning a piece of wood, neither loses any aspect of its being nor mingles with the being of the wood; the fire remains pure flame. It pours something of its nature into the wood without itself being diminished. Similarly, God, in creating the human soul, pours his own divine nature into it.[9] In doing so, God, like the fire, loses nothing of his own nature and self ("he has remained unmixed").

Eckhart uses another metaphor to explicate the deep intimacy that is retained even though human persons are the creations of God. His own human father is his father in only a certain sense; while his earthly father may be regarded as the cause of Eckhart's existence, once that act of creation is completed (i.e., after Eckhart is conceived and born), he exists independently of his father. As Eckhart points out, his earthly father may die and Eckhart will still live. This is in stark contrast to the mode in which God is his father (Sermon 6, 188). The implication of the distinction is that Eckhart's being is continually rooted in and dependent on his "heavenly Father." The relationship between them is thus much closer—much more ontologically intertwined—than Eckhart's relationship to his human father.

This understanding of creation is not unique to Eckhart, of course. The theory of divine creation as an act of emanation that detracts nothing from the divine originary source is a familiar Neoplatonic theme, and the Neoplatonic character of Eckhart's thought is well documented (30). Its implications for the relationship between God and creation are apparent. The human soul, just like other existents (insofar as they are all creatures), is unlike God and therefore distinct from him. But the soul is also intimately linked to God insofar as it is that aspect of the human person into which God has poured his essential nature. In fact, Eckhart may be read as claiming that there is a perspective from which the soul—or at least one aspect of it—is uncreated, and is therefore identical with God (42).

This would seem to suggest that there is no greater unity with God to be sought; if creation already enjoys a kind of continued existence within the divine reality, and if the soul itself is uncreated or is actually already one with God, what kind of further development in the relationship with God is possible? Eckhart seems to address this question when he writes, "note that God, although he is everywhere and in all things as existence, and is also everywhere and in all things through his essence, is still said to 'come' when his presence is evident through some new effect" ("Commentary on

John," 158). Even though God is always already present within or through all aspects of creation by virtue of the simple fact of their existence, his presence may be more powerfully or fully realized in "new effects." This suggests that despite the already intimate relationship between the human soul and God, a more direct encounter with ultimacy is still possible.

This more direct encounter can be brought about through human means; in fact, Eckhart seems to suggest that if a man manifests the correct behavior and disposition, he may nearly be said to force God to come to him.

> The man who has annihilated himself in himself and in God and in all created things; this man has taken possession of the lowest place, and God must pour the whole of himself into this man, or else he is not God. I say in the truth, which is good and eternal and enduring, that God must pour out the whole of himself with all his might so totally into every man who has utterly abandoned himself that God withholds nothing of his being or his nature or his entire divinity, but he must pour all of it fruitfully into the man who has abandoned himself for God and has occupied the lowest place. (197)

The language and implications of this dramatic passage are striking. First, Eckhart seems to suggest that God has no choice but to "pour himself" into the being of the man who "has annihilated himself."[10] If he does not do so, Eckhart startlingly claims, then "he is not God." The notion of a human person's ability to compel God into any behavior is suspect, to say the least, from the perspective of mainstream Christian theology. Although a man may cleanse himself and make himself worthy to receive grace, the dispensation of grace is finally and entirely a question of God's uncompromised volition; one cannot bring grace upon oneself or force God's hand. Here, however, Eckhart makes the striking claim that God has no choice but to pour himself into the man who comports himself appropriately. Eckhart's language in the passage—his repeated use of the term "must"— suggests that this is not merely a matter of ill-chosen words.

Second, it is also clear that the "inpouring" of God that the self-annihilated man experiences is nothing short of God's entire being. Again, Eckhart's repeated use of extreme terminology—"God must pour the whole of himself" (twice), "with all his might," "so totally," "God withholds nothing of his being"—clearly signals that he means the claim to sound as drastic as it does. When God possesses a man in this way, he does so in a manner that is complete, without a hint of reservation or residue.

Both claims are extreme, and this willingness to make extreme claims in unequivocal language played a role in Eckhart's being subjected to papal investigation. Given other aspects of Eckhart's thought, however, these claims are not so shocking. The key passage quoted above states, in clear and equally unequivocal language, that God's ground and the ground of the soul are identical. And although the human person is one aspect of the created universe, we have seen that creation—even though it is distinct from God in important ways—is also characterized by an essential, ongoing ontological dependence on God, that its existence "in principle" always remains rooted within God. And, if anything, that dimension of the human soul that is uncreated or divine in nature enjoys an even more intimate and ongoing relationship with the deity. Given this notional context, it is unsurprising that Eckhart would make such powerful claims about God's pouring himself into the human person. Such a claim is scarcely more radical than the claim that God's ground is the human soul's ground, and vice versa.

It is also worthwhile here to note a point of contact with Ibn al-ʿArabi's thought. Both thinkers describe a prior ontological connection between human and ultimacy that makes possible the more intimate metaphysical encounter that both mystics seek. Both also suggest that the self must be somehow negated—or "annihilated"—in order for that encounter to take place. These are both significant similarities between the two. The only question that remains, in ontological terms, is what this more powerful and intimate encounter consists of.

Eckhart readily uses the most extreme language in describing the manner of this encounter. And he can be surprisingly succinct in doing so: "What is changed into something else becomes one with it. I am so changed into him that he produces his being in me as one, not just similar. By the living God, this is true! There is no distinction" (188). Eckhart employs language of this sort in various sermons and treatises, and one can sense his struggle to find or devise new language with which to capture the melding between human and divine. This struggle on Eckhart's part seems to arise from the fact that, while he asserts that God and man can and do in fact become one, they do so not by virtue of this trait or that quality but rather by virtue of the bare and essential fact of existence itself. It is not just

God's love or his wisdom or his mercy with which the human person may attain unity; it is, rather, God's "is-ness" (German: *isticheit*) that is central here (187). This leads Eckhart to make such forthright statements as: "But if I am to perceive God so, without a medium, then I must just become him, and he must become me. I say more: God must just become me, and I must just become God, so completely one that this 'he' and this 'I' become and are one 'is'" (208).

Here, God is known "without a medium." Such an encounter, however, ultimately turns out to be nothing other than an encounter with the self, which is one with God. At this point, there is no distinction between God and man. In his "Counsels on Discernment," Eckhart deploys a number of descriptive metaphors and comparisons by which to underscore the nature of this union. Here, even the angels cannot tell the difference between the divine being and the human, the two are so closely intertwined. The body and soul, Eckhart claims, were never as closely linked as the soul is to God (272). This description merits special consideration. The body and soul are the two basic constituents of the human person; they are the entirety of an individual's identity. To claim, therefore, that the soul is actually more closely linked to God than to the body with which it is paired is to suggest that the human person himself—or at least that aspect of him that is of the greatest importance soteriologically—is in its nature ultimately more divine than temporal.

The union achieved between soul and God, Eckhart writes, is also far closer than that created when a drop of water is added to a cask of wine. Even then, Eckhart writes, one may still speak of "water" and "wine," whereas in the other case no distinction whatsoever can be discerned (272). The wine and water metaphor is a common one in Christian mysticism, and Eckhart's claim that the union achieved between soul and God is closer than that may signal an attempt on his part to assert a kind of union that goes beyond that deemed acceptable by some of his Christian brethren.

In discussing this kind of union in "On Detachment," Eckhart again suggests that the human person may in fact compel God to come to him in order to experience this deeper union. Here, however, he suggests a number of other elements to this union:

> Now it is far greater for me to compel God to come to me than to compel myself to come to God; and that is because God is able to conform himself, far better and with more suppleness, and to unite

himself with me than I could unite myself with God. And I prove
that detachment compels God to come to me in this way; it is because
everything longs to achieve its own natural place. Now God's own
natural place is unity and purity, and that comes from detachment.
Therefore God must of necessity give himself to a heart that has
detachment. (286)

Not only is it possible to compel God to come to oneself through proper
religious practice; it is, in fact, preferable to the human self's going out to
God in order to achieve union. This is because God is far more capable of
conforming himself to unite with the human soul than the soul is of conforming itself to unite with God. Union is more perfectly achieved, therefore, to the degree that God comes to the human self.

Eckhart also seems to imply that this union is actually God's most natural state of being. Drawing on the Aristotelian notion that all things are
inherently drawn to their proper place, Eckhart suggests that God's natural
place is "unity and purity," which comes from detachment. Detachment, as
I discuss below, describes a human spiritual state in which the self has been
divested of all concerns and thoughts that stand between one and God, and
that therefore obstruct a more intimate relationship with him. Since detachment is a state of the human self, this passage seems to suggest that it is the
(detached) human self that is the natural resting place of God. If this is the
case, then the union achieved between the soul and God is nothing extraordinary; it is, rather, the natural state of affairs being restored.

Eckhart deploys two well-known metaphors to represent this union
between the self and God. Unsurprisingly, both metaphors draw on the
ontological resonance between the soul and God that Eckhart returns to
throughout his treatises, commentaries, and sermons. The first—which is
the central image quoted in the key passage above—is the birth of the Son
in the soul. Given the Trinitarian distinction between the Son and the
Father and the soul's identity with the Father—who is identical with the
Son—this notion gives rise to some of Eckhart's most challenging and
seemingly circular claims concerning the encounter with divinity:

"The Word was with God and God was the Word." (Jn. 1:1); it was the
same in the same nature. Yet I say more: He has given birth to him in
my soul. Not only is the soul with him, and he equal with it, but he is
in it, and the Father gives his Son birth in the soul in the same way as

he gives him birth in eternity, and not otherwise. He must do it whether he likes it or not. The Father gives birth to his Son without ceasing; and I say more: He gives me birth, me, his Son, but he gives birth to me as himself and himself as me and to me as his being and nature. (Sermon 6, 187)

To unravel the implications of this passage, one must first recall that God exists outside space and time. Therefore, while Jesus did enjoy a physical existence in the created world, the act of birth by which God produces the Son is an act that takes place outside time; God is giving birth to the Son eternally, continually ("without ceasing"). So there is a sense in which God is always already producing the Son.

Second, although God, the Son, and the Holy Spirit are three different persons, they are one in being. Therefore, in the act of giving birth to the Son, God is also giving birth to himself. This particular act of production is, therefore, circular. Third, Eckhart also holds that he is one with the Father, and this is true for all aspects of divinity. Therefore, the human person is identical not only with the Father who gives birth to the Son, but with the Son who is thereby birthed. Therefore, the implications of the last line of the passage follow logically: "He (God) gives me (Eckhart) birth, me, his Son (because Eckhart is identical with the Son), but he gives birth to me as himself (because Eckhart—who is identical with the Son—and the Son are both identical to God) and himself as me (for the same reason) and to me as his being and nature."

The birth of the Son in the soul is therefore nothing less than God's continual act of self-creation, which is nothing more or less than the continual act of the creation of the human soul. Colledge and McGinn note that Eckhart repeats this notion in numerous sermons (including Sermons 6, 5b, and 22). Eckhart thereby borrows a central and unique Christian doctrine and interprets it as a metaphor for one of his most radical mystical teachings. This interpretation brings a new meaning to the key passage quoted above. The "inner world" to which Eckhart refers there is the human soul, and the shared ground of the soul and God is, paradoxically, both the precondition and the effect of that birth. Because God and the soul share the same ground, the birth of the Son is an act that occurs within the human soul. Simultaneously, because that to which God gives birth is nothing other than himself, that which is produced in this birth (whether it be understood as "the Son" or the human soul, which are ultimately identical anyway) shares the same ground as God.

The second metaphor Eckhart uses to capture this radical unity of the self and God is articulated in terms that seem on their surface to be even more heterodox. This is the "breaking-through" of the soul into the divine ground. Here, the soul, fervently desiring the most intimate possible encounter with ultimacy, refuses to be satisfied with knowing the Son, the Father, or the Holy Spirit: "this same light [the divinely originated soul] is not content with the simple divine essence . . . but it wants to know the source of this essence, it wants to go into the simple ground, into the quiet desert, into which distinction never gazed, not the Father, nor the Son, nor the Holy Spirit" (Sermon 48, 198). Even the three persons of the Trinity will not suffice for the union that the soul craves. It insists on going beyond them and breaking through into another place, the "quiet desert, into which distinction never gazed." The denial of distinction here indicates that the unity sought by the soul is without medium or remainder; it is a complete and all-consuming encounter in which neither the divisions of the three divine persons nor that between God and the human self may be detected.

Again, however, Eckhart emphasizes that the realization of this unity is not the establishment of a new state of affairs but the recognition of an ontological resonance that already was and always will be. In Eckhart's words, here "man achieves what he has been eternally and will evermore remain" (Sermon 52, 203). The encounter with ultimacy that is the breaking-through, therefore, is not any change in metaphysical relations between the human self and God; it is, rather, the realization of that which has been and always will be true—the unity of the soul and God.

In Sermon 52, Eckhart goes on to describe this breaking-through in even more striking language: "But in the breaking-through when I come to be free of will of myself and of God's will and of all his works and of God himself, then I am above all created things, and I am neither God nor creature, but I am what I was and what I shall remain, now and eternally" (203). The notion is repeated here that the human soul realizes only what always already was. In addition, however, Eckhart seems to suggest that, at the height of this union, he is "neither God nor creature." A simplistic reading of this passage would seem to suggest that Eckhart claims to achieve unity with something beyond and other than the deity. A more dramatic and dangerous claim would be difficult to imagine. This, however, would be a misreading of the preacher's thought. In order to understand how he intends such a claim, it is necessary to consider the epistemological dimensions of the encounter with ultimacy as Eckhart understands it.

Before doing so, however, it will be beneficial to consider whether other mystics in the Christian tradition suggest a similar kind of relationship with God. In fact, similar examples are not difficult to find. Pseudo-Dionysius, the influential Neoplatonic writer of the fifth and sixth centuries C.E., argues that "the most divine knowledge of God, that which comes through unknowing, is achieved in a union far beyond mind."[11] For him as well, the most intimate knowledge of God is achieved in the midst of union with him. As numerous commentators have pointed out, Pseudo-Dionysius exerted a clear influence on Eckhart's writing. They shared a mutual willingness to put forth dramatic experiential claims concerning the ontological resonance between the self and God.

Another significant thinker in the Christian mystical tradition, probably writing shortly after Eckhart's death, also endorses a similar understanding of the metaphysics of the encounter with ultimacy. *The Cloud of Unknowing* is an anonymous work, probably written by an English priest in the latter half of the fourteenth century. The author of the *Cloud* writes, in a related work, that the "perfection of man's soul" consists of "nothing but the union effected between God and the soul." According to the author, this union utterly transcends human understanding, and so cannot be "seen" as it really is from the perspective of the discursive intellect.[12]

The author of *The Cloud of Unknowing* was also influenced by the works of Pseudo-Dionysius, and his work reflects similar general themes in Christian mysticism during the medieval period. Both thinkers advocate an understanding of the encounter with ultimacy as a kind of union wherein God and the human self experience an intimate and profound kind of ontological merger. Eckhart's own language is clear enough to establish the dramatic notion of union that he endorses. Pseudo-Dionysius and the *Cloud of Unknowing* author may be seen as providing corroborating evidence. One of them precedes Eckhart by more than five centuries, while the other was writing near the end of Eckhart's lifetime or shortly thereafter; both are influential figures in the history of Christian mysticism, as is Eckhart. All three of them construe the goal of mystical practice as an encounter with ultimacy wherein a deep ontological resonance—in this case, union between the self and God—is realized. As will be seen, many of Eckhart's epistemological ideas concerning this encounter are also corroborated by these and other mystical Christian thinkers.

Eckhart's Epistemology of Mystical Experience

Given that the ontological relationship between the soul and God is not that between subject and object as normally conceived, it would be reasonable to expect that the mode by which the aspiring mystic comes to know God would be different from the modality of knowledge operative in other kinds of experience. Eckhart is consistent in this regard. In order to come to know God, the individual must achieve a particular epistemological comportment that is distinctly keyed to this realization. The inward manner in which Eckhart exhorts his congregation to understand the biblical excerpt he quotes in the key passage above turns out to be a very particular kind of knowing. That comportment begins, according to Eckhart, with "detachment," which the master regards as the highest virtue that a human person can attain ("On Detachment," 285).

Eckhart's conception of detachment builds on his understanding of the general faculty of human knowing. Any "receptive potency," Eckhart argues, "must always be naked." He points to our ability to perceive color as an example: the power to perceive color must be colorless in itself; otherwise, it would not be able to receive colors other than itself. Similarly, the master concludes, the soul's "receptive powers"—its ability to receive perceptual input or to gain knowledge—must themselves be "naked" or empty ("Commentary on Genesis," 104). The ability to know God follows logically from this functionality of the soul; the soul can know God only after it has emptied itself of all obstructions (48).

Following as it does from the general theory of knowledge that Eckhart proposes, one might expect that pursuit of this state of detachment would be relatively unremarkable. Once the full implications of this claim are revealed, however, it becomes apparent that detachment requires extraordinary effort on the mystic's part. For instance, this epistemology leads Eckhart to argue for the ultimate inadequacy of external religious practice. This is a recurrent theme in the thought of Christian mystics, and the majority of them walk a thin line in this regard. On one hand, the suggestion that religious works and observation of basic Christian doctrine are meaningless could provoke retaliation from church authorities. At times, such teachings led to extreme views that all moral strictures endorsed by the church were unnecessary. This resulted in sometimes shocking heretical practices on the part of some sects, and church authorities were eager to resist such trends.

On the other hand, mystics like Eckhart who emphasize the importance of an internal, spiritual state or mode of experience were committed to the belief that one's own internal experience of God is of the highest importance. Like many of his fellows in the Christian mystical tradition, Eckhart's thought in this regard consists of a balancing act. The author of *The Cloud of Unknowing* also walks a fine line in this respect. He does offer an explicit endorsement of conventional religious practices, lauding, for example, "delightful meditations" on such familiar and orthodox Christian themes as the passion and the kindness of God. Such practices are, he claims, necessary to achieve the spiritual purity that is a prerequisite to mystical encounter with God. "However," the author continues, just as these practices are necessary, they must also eventually be left behind when one travels the mystical path: "when we are engaged on this work it profits little or nothing to think even of God's kindness or worth, or of our Lady, or of the saints or angels, or of the joys of heaven, if you think thereby by such meditation to strengthen your purpose. In this particular matter it will not help at all."[13] Similarly, Eckhart does not dismiss entirely the worthiness of external religious practice. But he does remind his congregation that such practice is insufficient to achieve more intimate knowledge of God (47). He maintains that if one "tinkers with fasts, bodily mortification, abstinence, and penance," one has not sufficiently understood the problem of obstruction that must be overcome if one is to achieve union with God.[14]

The delicacy of this balancing act, however, is easily forgotten in the face of Eckhart's rather strong claims about detachment. Every attachment to every work, the preacher tells his listeners, "deprives one of the freedom to wait upon God in the present" (Sermon 2, 178). Here, Eckhart seems to suggest that the ability to know God depends, if anything, on the ability of the mystical practitioner to be "in the moment"—to be as free of distractions as possible in order to leave oneself spiritually and intellectually unencumbered and therefore entirely free to receive God. Echoing his theory that any receptive capacity must itself be empty in order to function, Eckhart likens the ability to know God to a cask of wine. Just as a cask of water must be emptied in order to be filled with wine, he argues, the human soul must be emptied of created things in order to receive God. The mystic is therefore obliged to "pour out created things" in order to leave himself open to the reception of the divine ("Book of Benedictus," 220). In this regard, Eckhart makes the intentionally startling claim that the faintest recollection of any worldly thing is as great as God, because it serves to completely block one from encounter with the fullness of divinity (Sermon 5b, 184).

To argue that attachment to worldly pleasures stands in the way of one's ability to know God more intimately was not exceptional. After all, a number of the cardinal sins, such as greed and gluttony, consist of excessive attachment to things of this world. In order to achieve the purity of heart that is required to know God in this intimate fashion, Eckhart claims that the individual must "annihilate" everything that is created—i.e., he must divest himself of attachment to any and all created things (182–83). Similar admonitions are found in *The Cloud of Unknowing*, whose readers are also directed to turn their attention entirely away from all created things. There, the first clear statement of the need to divest oneself of worldly concerns appears within the first three pages, signaling the importance of this procedure as a precursor to any kind of encounter with ultimacy.[15]

And, like Eckhart, *The Cloud of Unknowing* describes mystical practice in straightforward and unequivocal language. The "whole created world" must be hidden away behind a "cloud of forgetting," according to the author. It does not matter whether a thing is physical or spiritual, good or evil; every creature, state, or action connected with the created world must be forgotten, without exception.[16] Eckhart's admonitions to put the created world out of one's mind reflect broad trends in Christian mystical thought at the time. But Eckhart goes beyond these rather orthodox claims to press his position in more drastic terms. It is not merely attachment to the things of the world that stands in the way of knowing God. For instance, Eckhart argues that even meditation on orthodox religious themes such as the image of Christ is ultimately detrimental to one's mystical practice. And if meditation on Christ himself undercuts one's receptivity to God, he argues further, how much worse must be fascination with transient, worldly things ("On Detachment," 294).

Eckhart goes even further, suggesting that excessive attachment to any religious image or concept—including God himself—thwarts one's ability to encounter ultimacy. This is a more radical suggestion, and it indicates the dramatic nature of detachment as Eckhart understands it: "So when the soul with these powers contemplates what consists of images, whether that be an angel's image or its own, there is for the soul something lacking. Even if the soul contemplates God, either as God or as an image or as three, the soul lacks something. But if all images are detached from the soul, and it contemplates only the Simple One, then the soul's naked being finds the naked, formless being of the divine unity, which is there a being above being, accepting and reposing in itself" (Sermon 83, 206). Regardless of how one conceives God—either as one or as the Trinity—that conception ultimately stands in the way of one's realization of God. Here, the tension between orthodox religious practice and the mystical path is most clearly apparent. Paradoxically, even God himself—or at least human images of him—must finally be put aside if one is to know God authentically, as he is in himself.

This denial of the utility of human understandings of the divine suggests that the human capacity for knowledge itself is problematic. Ultimately, the mind must be purified in ways that go far beyond the mere dissolution of possible distractions such as worldly temptations and even religious imagery. In the final analysis, pursuit of a more intimate encounter with ultimacy can be achieved only when that pursuit is made without reliance on the human intellect at all. This is for the simple reason that God, as he is in himself, is beyond human understanding:

> And do not try to understand God, for God is beyond all understanding. One authority says: "If I had a God whom I could understand, I should never consider him God." If you can understand anything about him, it in no way belongs to him, and insofar as you understand anything about him, that brings you into incomprehension, and from incomprehension you arrive at a brute's stupidity; for when created beings do not understand, they resemble the brutes. So if you do not wish to be brutish, do not understand the God who is beyond words. (Sermon 83, 207)

Any "understanding of God" the human individual thinks he has grasped is necessarily flawed, and therefore reliance on that "knowledge" only stands in the way of authentic knowledge of ultimacy. Eckhart goes so far as to describe this mistaken intellectual comportment as brutish stupidity.

The modality of knowing God is therefore opposed to that modality of knowledge that characterizes all other types of knowledge. Knowledge of any other created object may function in a cumulative fashion: the addition of further predicates represents increasing knowledge of a thing. In this case, however, addition of predicates only distances one further from knowledge of the divine. Here, predicates must be stripped away, eliminated from the intellect in order to clear the way for authentic knowledge of God. While such a process could be effected gradually by the consistent elimination of one predicate after another, Eckhart suggests a more radical approach: the subversion of that modality of knowledge itself. By circumventing discursive knowledge altogether, one avoids in one fell swoop all predicates that can obscure the mystical encounter with ultimacy. Insofar as God is "understood" in a manner that is in any way derived from the human intellect, that understanding hinders one's actual progress toward God.[17]

The "last end" of the mystical path, according to Eckhart, is the "hidden darkness of the external divinity." Ultimacy "is unknown, and it was never known, and it will never be known" (Sermon 22, 196). Dramatic language such as this could seem to suggest that God can never be known at all. In a sense, this is correct; insofar as "knowledge" is understood to mean the relationship of a distinct subject and object wherein the former grasps the latter through some sort of conceptual knowledge, it can never be achieved. If, however, this typical modality of knowledge is subverted fully, it clears the way for an entirely different approach to encountering ultimacy.

In order to subvert the mind sufficiently, every type of knowledge must ultimately be dissolved. As we have seen, this means at least the elimination of knowledge of worldly things, religious themes and images, and even human notions of God himself. Even this, however, is not sufficient. The final type of knowledge that must be eliminated is perhaps the most subtle and insidious kind: knowledge of the self. Once knowledge of all other things has been quashed, there may still remain the basic awareness of one's own self, and this too must go. Therefore, the mystic must also eliminate his own self-awareness—he must, in other words, know God without knowing that he knows God.

In addressing this final residue of awareness, Eckhart displays an impressive command of the epistemological nuances involved. The subtlety of Eckhart's thought in this regard requires that he be quoted at length:

> I say that as man, the soul, the spirit contemplates God, he also knows and perceives himself perceiving; that is, he perceives that he

is contemplating and perceiving God. Now some people have thought, and it seems quite plausible, that the flower and core of blessedness consists in knowledge, when the spirit knows that it knows God. For if I possessed all joy, and I did not know it, how could that help me and what joy would that be to me? Yet I say certainly that this is not so. It is only true that without that the soul would not be blessed; but blessedness does not consist in this, for the first thing in which blessedness consists is when the soul contemplates God directly. From there, out of God's ground, it takes all its being and its life and makes everything that it is, and it knows nothing about knowing or about love or about anything at all. It comes to rest completely and only in the being of God, and it knows nothing there except being and God. ("Book of Benedictus," 245)

The repeated reference to God's ground clearly echoes the key passage. Eckhart acknowledges the intuitive nature of supposing that blessedness consists in self-awareness of knowing God; to know that one knows God would surely be the height of joy. And what use is joy, Eckhart asks rhetorically, if one does not know that one feels joy? However, he argues, this self-reflective joy is not actually that in which blessedness consists. Rather, blessedness is "when the soul contemplates God directly." Here, Eckhart draws a subtle epistemological distinction. On one hand, there is the joy felt at knowing God; on the other is the knowing of God itself, minus the joyful self-awareness of the having of that knowledge. It is the latter, the preacher holds, that is of real value.

A moment's consideration reveals the logic underlying this distinction. If one experiences knowledge of ultimacy and simultaneously knows that one does so, this suggests that there is some aspect of the self, some residual dimension of meta-awareness, that is not subsumed in the knowing of ultimacy itself. Therefore, this type of knowledge is not completely absorptive, whereas knowledge of God without the attendant knowledge of having that knowledge represents a more consuming, and ultimately more perfect, modality of knowledge. Significantly, in discussing this mode of fully absorptive encounter with ultimacy, Eckhart recalls language from the key passage quoted earlier. He appears to suggest a connection between the fact that the soul draws its being "out of God's ground" and this kind of absorptive encounter with ultimacy. In this type of knowledge, he suggests, the soul "knows nothing about knowing . . . or about anything at all."

Self-awareness, therefore, is the final species of knowledge that must be eliminated. But because it is also the basis for any other kind of knowledge, an individual may take a more direct approach to eliminating the intellectual habits and contents that obscure knowledge of ultimacy, and that is to eliminate the self first and thereby simultaneously undercut all knowledge of created things. The man who wishes to know God intimately, Eckhart argues, ought to begin by "forsaking" himself, because in doing so he also forsakes everything else. To forsake everything created while holding on to oneself is ultimately fruitless, Eckhart argues, but if a man "renounces" himself directly, he thereby renounces "whatever else he retains, riches or honors or whatever it may be" ("Counsels on Discernment," 250). Self-awareness is, therefore, the most fundamental type of knowledge that must be eliminated.

Here, Eckhart's thinking is reflected especially closely by *The Cloud of Unknowing*. The anonymous author of that treatise also suggests that awareness of the self must ultimately be crushed in order to know God, and he also argues that such knowledge undergirds all other knowledge that stands between the self and God.[18] These themes are also apparent in the predecessor to both Eckhart and the author of *The Cloud of Unknowing*: "leave behind you everything perceived and understood, everything perceptible and understandable, all that is not and all that is, and, with your understanding laid aside, to strive upward as much as you can toward union with him who is beyond all being and knowledge. By an undivided and absolute abandonment of yourself and everything, shedding all and freed from all, you will be uplifted to the ray of the divine shadow which is above everything that is."[19] Pseudo-Dionysius emphasizes here that it is both the self and everything else that must be left behind in the mystical ascent. Eckhart was not alone in advocating such a radical emptying out of the mind—and ultimately of the self—in order to encounter ultimacy.

The elimination of self-awareness from the modality of knowledge that characterizes the encounter with ultimacy has important implications for this type of knowledge. Specifically, it suggests the absence of any subject/ object dichotomy. This is, after all, precisely the thrust of the ontological dimension of Eckhart's thought, as demonstrated earlier. In epistemological terms, this would suggest that—insofar as this encounter may be denoted "knowledge"—it is a kind of unmediated knowledge. Eckhart says as much in at least two of his sermons: "Sometimes I have spoken of a light that is uncreated and not capable of creation and that is in the soul. I always mention this light in my sermons; and this same light comprehends God without a medium, uncovered, naked, as he is in himself; and this comprehension is to be understood as happening when the birth takes place. Here I may truly say that this light may have more unity with God than it has with any power of the soul, with which, however, it is one in being" (Sermon 48, 198).[20] Note that Eckhart explicitly links this unmediated knowledge to the "birth"—i.e., the birth of the Son in the soul. He thereby establishes a direct link between the ontological relationship the mystic realizes and the mode of knowledge by which that realization is achieved. The ground of God and the ground of the self are identical; this fact is realized through the birth of the Son in the soul, and because that realization is precisely that of an identity between subject and object, that knowledge is unmediated.[21]

As discussed earlier, the notion of unmediated knowledge runs counter to dominant trends in scholarship on mystical experience. But this is irrelevant to the fact that Eckhart invokes the notion in describing the encounter with ultimacy. McGinn points out that this claim actually plays a central role throughout the history of Christian mystical discourse. Subjectively, the encounter with God is experienced as taking place at a level of the self that is deeper than that which characterizes knowledge obtained through usual processes of perception and conceptualization. And objectively, he writes, knowledge of ultimacy is often regarded by Christian mystics as unmediated, as taking place in a manner that subverts the kinds of mediation that usually characterize any kind of awareness. This claim, McGinn relates, may be found in "almost all mystical texts."[22]

That claim of immediacy plays a significant role in disclosing Eckhart's full understanding of this modality of knowledge. Discursive knowledge, clearly, is insufficient to the task of achieving this intimate relation with God. Because of the ontological identity of self and God, that intimate relation can only be realized experientially. The moment the soul attempts to separate itself from God in order to know him, the soul deceives itself, because the epistemological comportment it thereby seeks to adopt is already a misrepresentation of its relationship with ultimacy.[23] Knowledge conceived of in the discursive mode as the relationship between a distinct subject and object is by definition incapable of realizing this relationship; it can only be realized experientially.

This emphasis on an experiential rather than an intellectual encounter with ultimacy is also echoed by other Christian mystics, including both

Eckhart's predecessors and those who follow after him. Pseudo-Dionysius, for example, argues that reliance on the resources of one's own intellect disqualifies one from the mystical practice he endorses.[24] The *Cloud of Unknowing* makes similar claims,[25] and an identical stream of thought may be found in the work of John Tauler, a student of Eckhart's: "It is when a person with all his faculties and his soul turns within and goes into this Temple that he truly finds [*vindet*] God within living and working. He finds him in an experiential way [*in bevindender wisen*], not by sensation or by reason, or as something heard or read about, or as something that comes in from the senses, but by tasting in an experiential way [*in bevindender smackender wisen*], as something that wells up out of the ground as from its own source and spring."[26] Intriguingly, Tauler's use of the term *smackender*—"tasting"—echoes Ibn al-'Arabi's use of the term *dhawq*.

As suggested earlier, Eckhart does not endorse a notion of mystical experience as a distinct contemplative or ecstatic experience wherein one loses the ability to function in the physical world. Rather, this experience of unity with God appears to be a kind of ongoing experiential state constantly underlying awareness. Its lack of intellectual content, in fact, may suggest an easier merger with involvement in mundane affairs. This lack of intellectual content, however, has implications for one's ability—or lack thereof—to articulate the experience. Eckhart makes much of the ineffability of the encounter with ultimacy, exploiting it through both logical paradoxes and bold affirmations that would wake a complacent audience from its slumber.

It is not possible, he claims, to find a single name that might be attributed to God. However, he quickly adds, those names may be used that God has consecrated and "poured into" the hearts of the saints to be used in addressing him. Through these names, Eckhart says, one should learn how to pray to God. Immediately after affirming these names, however, Eckhart claims that one should learn not to give any name to God, because "God is 'above names' and ineffable" (Sermon 53, 204–5).

Here, Eckhart once again engages in a delicate balancing act, juxtaposing an endorsement of a thoroughly orthodox Christian practice with its simultaneous denial. This is a familiar pattern, apparent in both Pseudo-Dionysius's *Mystical Theology* and *The Cloud of Unknowing*. The former, for instance, first affirms appellations of God such as "cause of the ages," "ancient of days," and, simply, "powerful." These references to God, Pseudo-Dionysius writes, are derived from scripture and refer "unreservedly" to

God.[27] It is, however, "more appropriate" to deny these affirmations, because the nature of God's being puts God beyond all affirmations and human terms. As one ascends the mystical path, language becomes progressively more attenuated, until finally the intellect is entirely surpassed and language is rendered impossible.[28]

Charlotte Radler suggests that Eckhart's view of language in the mystical path is a three-step movement. Eckhart first endorses a cataphatic approach, affirming God in language; he then moves to an apophatic position and denies the utility of language, signaling that the cataphatic path must be superceded by the apophatic one. Finally, however, even the apophatic position must be transcended, as one moves to a position beyond either the affirmation or the denial of language altogether.[29] God is so far above names that even the denial of them does not sufficiently indicate the degree to which the divine surpasses the limits of language. Any attempt at all to capture ultimacy within the confines of language, Eckhart claims, is nothing more than "lies and sinning" (Sermon 83, 207). This argument reflects similar strains in *The Cloud of Unknowing*, where even the term God itself ought to be divested of any intellectual content one might associate with it.[30]

The indescribability of God is of a piece with the nonintellectual nature of the encounter with him, and is closely linked to the metaphysical unity that defines the relationship of the soul to God: "Therefore Moses said, 'He who is sent me' (Ex. 3:14), he who is without name, who is a denial of all names and who never acquired a name; and therefore the prophet said: 'Truly you are the hidden God' (Is. 45:15), in the ground of the soul, where God's ground and the soul's ground are one ground. The more one seeks you, the less one finds you. You should so seek him that you find him nowhere. If you do not seek him, then you will find him" (Sermon 15, 192). Eckhart repeats here that the ground of the soul and the ground of God are identical. The placement of this assertion—immediately after a denial that God can be named and before the paradoxical assertion that finding God requires that one not look for him—suggests that God's ineffability, his ontological connection to the self, and the nondiscursive modality of coming to know God are related to one another.

The logical connections between these claims are not difficult to discern. To seek God suggests attachment to a name or characterization of him; if one pursues a goal, one must necessarily have some image or understanding of what that goal is, however slight such an understanding might be. But this necessarily means envisioning God in some fashion—in other words, attempting to conceptualize that which is beyond conceptualization. So construed, the attempt can only succeed in misleading one. Therefore, the only way to achieve encounter with divinity is not to seek it.

Additionally, because God is ultimately identical with the self, he is impossible to know in any usual fashion (i.e., any way that presumes a subject/object structure of knowledge). Because the ground of the soul is the ground of God, knowing God consists of a radical turning inward that attempts to direct the knowing intellect toward an object that is not an object. The ineffability of God is directly linked to the nondiscursive nature of knowledge of him, which is a result of the ontological resonance between him and the soul. All of these themes, therefore, are closely linked.

In his sermons, Eckhart harnesses the paradoxes that result from God's ineffability and the impossibility of knowing him discursively. This allows him to put forth claims that would assuredly reverberate in the ears of the faithful:

> I can even say: "I am better than God," for whatever is good can become better, and whatever can become better can become best of all. But since God is not good, he cannot become better. And since he cannot become better, he cannot be best of all. For these three degrees are alien to God: "good," "better," and "best," for he is superior to them all. And if I say: "God is wise," that is not true. I am wiser than he. If I say: "God is a being," it is not true; he is a being transcending being and a transcending nothingness. (Sermon 83, 206–7)

In this passage Eckhart makes the stunning claim that he is "better than" and "wiser than" God. This is true insofar as terms such as "good" and "wise" apply more properly to Eckhart than they do to God. Such descriptions, because they are made in human language and rooted in human concepts, are fundamentally inapplicable to the divine nature. Therefore, Eckhart—or any human being—is in fact better and wiser than God, because the nature of God is such that terms like these are fundamentally inappropriate. God transcends such descriptions so completely that this transcendence can be best indicated by awed or overwhelmed silence. Ultimately, God is beyond language, and the encounter with him—because it is the unmediated encounter of the self with that with which it is identical—is beyond human conception.

Conclusion

Unlike some other Christian mystics, Meister Eckhart does not place great emphasis on the idea of a distinct, dateable experience of unity with God; rather, he endorses an experience of unity with ultimacy that can become a more permanent or at least ongoing state in which the mystic remains essentially unified with God while continuing to interact with the temporal world. Ibn al-'Arabi, by contrast, is more directly interested in special, distinct moments of experiential unity with ultimacy that stand apart from our activity in the physical world. Despite this difference, shared themes emerge in the writing of both mystics, and these commonalities also suggest the inadequacy of reliance on contemporary epistemology or mainstream religious doctrine as a guide for interpreting either.

In apparent contradistinction to basic Christian theology—but mirroring the metaphysical thought of Ibn al-'Arabi—Eckhart clearly suggests that there is a fundamental aspect of the nature of the human being that is identical with God. The ontological gulf between creator and creature, at least in this aspect, is not very great at all; it is, in fact, nonexistent. Eckhart deploys various metaphors to describe this divine dimension of the human soul, such as the birth of the Son in the soul mentioned in the key passage. Also reminiscent of Ibn al-'Arabi, this ontological resonance can be traced back to the original creation, in which God gave rise to existence; and although the manner through which God creates suggests that his presence is inherent (to some degree) in all aspects of creation, both Eckhart and Ibn al-'Arabi suggest that this is especially true of the human soul, with which God continues to have a unique metaphysical connection. Although Eckhart wishes to downplay the importance of ecstatic experience, he does suggest that this relationship of unity can be realized more directly or powerfully. His favored metaphors—the birth of the Son in the soul and the breaking-through into the quiet desert—represent this aspect of Eckhart's thought. They suggest that even though the soul is already, because of its original nature, part of the divine, this unity may be realized or experienced in a more direct, more intimate fashion.

Eckhart's understanding of the modality by which this unity is recognized also echoes the Sufi master in numerous ways. Both mystics argue that before this union with ultimacy may be realized, the mystic must first empty himself of psychic attachments to the mundane world. For both mystics, this involves not only a clearing away of materialistic thoughts and tendencies but putting aside even themes, images, and ideas central to their respective religious traditions. Following that, awareness of the self must also be eliminated. For both mystical thinkers, this achieves a mode of unknowing that is, in their terms, unmediated or direct. And for both Eckhart and Ibn al-'Arabi, this type of knowledge is nonconceptual and ineffable.

In many ways, this type of experience runs counter to the expectations of both contemporary Western epistemology—which generally construes knowledge as conceptual, linguistic, and structurally bifurcated into subject and object—and the basic tenets of Christianity and Islam, which hold that God and humanity are ontologically distinct. Reliance on assumptions derived from either religion therefore risks obscuring basic notions at work in the thought and writing of both mystics. As with Ibn al-'Arabi, only by focusing interpretation first and foremost on Eckhart himself, and then through corroborative reliance on related sources such as Pseudo-Dionysius and *The Cloud of Unknowing*, can the central ideas and experiential assumptions of Eckhart's mystical thought be unearthed.

It should be noted that many of the mystical themes in the work of both Meister Eckhart and Ibn al-'Arabi are common among mystics and religious thinkers influenced by the Neoplatonic tradition. Neoplatonic thought is characterized by the notion that creation is an act of emanation from a single, unified divine source, and therefore that all of creation is in some sense an extension of the being of the One. This line of theological speculation may be traced back to Plotinus, and because Eckhart and Ibn al-'Arabi were both influenced by this tradition, the similarities between them could theoretically be explained as evidence of shared textual-historical influence. As will be shown in the next chapter, however, very similar themes may be found in the work of Hui-neng, the fifth-century Zen Buddhist thinker, who knew nothing of Plotinus or his mystical speculations.

5

HUI-NENG AND THE STINK OF ZEN

Within the Abrahamic religions, the category of mysticism is applied with relative ease. Christianity has a well-developed tradition of thought, texts, and figures that are commonly identified as "mystical," and both Islam and Judaism have evolved distinct traditions (Sufism and Kabbalah, respectively) that encapsulate both mystic experiential accounts and reflection on them. Although the boundary between mystical and nonmystical religious thinkers and writers is porous, there is sufficient scholarly consensus to identify certain texts, traditions, and figures in the Abrahamic religions as "mystics," Meister Eckhart and Ibn al-'Arabi being two prominent examples.

Because the category of "mysticism" has developed primarily in discourse about the Abrahamic religions and is therefore tailored to them, application of the category to Buddhism is not unproblematic. Within Buddhism, however, certain streams of practice and thought have been identified as mystical, if with somewhat less consensus than typically found with regard to the Abrahamic traditions. One of the most popular scenes of Buddhist legend discussed by scholars researching mysticism is the enlightenment of Mahakasyapa. According to legend, Shakyamuni (the Buddha) once appeared before the assembled *sangha*, or Buddhist community, which expected to receive a sermon from the Buddha. Instead of speaking, however, the Buddha raised a small flower and twirled it lightly in his hand. The assembly was confused by this, except for Mahakasyapa, who smiled in understanding. Mahakasyapa thereby signaled his grasp of the Buddha's teaching and was designated the true heir of the enlightened one.[1] This scene is generally understood as the founding legend of Zen Buddhism, marking Mahakasyapa as the first patriarch of that tradition. Scholars commonly regard Zen as representative of the mystical trend within Buddhism.[2] This identification is sensible, given the emphasis that Zen training explicitly places on experience as necessary in addition to, if not in place of, doctrinal learning.

The character of a great deal of Zen thought and writing complies with the definition of mysticism I employ: a collection of practices, texts, and beliefs related to, and experiential reports of, an encounter between a mystic and ultimacy that is understood to be more intimate than that afforded by religious practice as performed by the general religious community. Buddhism appears in a wide variety of forms and has been adapted to various distinct cultures and indigenous religions. Zen Buddhism, however, constructs itself as a tradition that affords an especially intimate encounter with the form of ultimacy acknowledged in Buddhist thought, and places special emphasis on experience as the most important—and perhaps the only—mode of encountering that ultimacy.[3] It is therefore apposite to regard Zen as a mystical tradition and experiential accounts articulated within it as accounts of mystical experience. As an eminent representative of the Zen tradition, Hui-neng may be taken as a Buddhist mystic.

Legend surrounds the history of Hui-neng, and it is not possible to reliably separate fact from fiction in reconstructing his biography. He lived in the late seventh and early eighth centuries in China; best estimates suggest that he died circa 713.[4] Hui-neng is recognized as the thirty-third patriarch of the Zen tradition—a list that includes such figures as Mahakasyapa, Ananda, and Bodhidharma—and the sixth patriarch of Chan, the Chinese branch of Zen.[5] Hui-neng's membership in this august lineage and the recognition of his text as a sutra indicate the esteem with which he is regarded in the Zen tradition. *The Sutra of Hui-neng*, also called *The Platform Sutra*, is the only Chinese text to be acknowledged as a sutra, a term usually reserved for sermons attributed to Siddhartha Gautama (the historical Buddha) and writings of other great bodhisattvas.

Tales of Hui-neng's birth include the sorts of embellishments that are common in the legendary biographies of great religious figures. According to one source, at the moment of his birth, beams of light erupted in the air and a strange fragrance filled the room. At dawn, two mysterious monks appeared at the newborn's home and informed his father that the child deserved an auspicious name. They suggested "Hui-neng," explaining that "Hui" means "to bestow beneficence on sentient beings" and that "Neng" means "the capacity to carry out the affairs of the Buddha." The same source reports that the child refused to drink his mother's milk and that a "heavenly being" later delivered nectar for him.[6]

Such legends indicate the importance of the figure of Hui-neng within the Zen tradition. As his teachings spread through China and, later, the larger Buddhist world, details such as these proliferated, adding color and dimension to his originally rather sparse biography. *The Sutra of Hui-neng* itself contributes to this evolving biography, emphasizing details that conveniently echo central motifs of Hui-neng's own mystical experience and understanding of enlightenment. Although *The Sutra of Hui-neng* presents itself as a series of Hui-neng's sermons and teachings as delivered to various audiences, its early sections constitute a brief biography of the patriarch. We learn that Hui-neng's father passed away when Hui-neng was very young, leaving his mother to raise him. The two of them apparently lived in very straitened circumstances, eventually settling in Canton, where Hui-neng supported them as a manual laborer, selling firewood and pounding rice. Throughout the text, various characters describe the future patriarch as a "barbarian," often questioning how an individual from such humble and uncultured origins could deserve the title of a Zen patriarch.[7] This repeated theme adds an element of drama to the text, as parties who question his authenticity or ability are consistently brought around by displays of Hui-neng's wisdom.

Interestingly, Hui-neng is repeatedly described as illiterate. *The Sutra of Hui-neng*, both while recounting his background and throughout the later portions of the text, emphasizes that at the time of his enlightenment, Hui-neng could not read. According to the text, he never learned to read, even after being officially recognized as a leading authority on Zen teaching. As will be seen, this detail of Hui-neng's biography resonates not only with important aspects of his understanding of enlightenment and mystical experience but with broader themes that pervade Zen thought. In fact, it may be argued that *The Sutra of Hui-neng* is not an especially innovative text, instead drawing on and developing notions and themes that can be found in other sutras and Buddhist texts that predate it. Nor is the derivative nature of *The Sutra of Hui-neng* suppressed by the text; various passages have Hui-neng stating that his own teaching is consistent with the dharma as taught by Siddhartha Gautama and other Buddhist teachers before him.[8]

The apparent lack of originality in *The Sutra of Hui-neng* suggests that Hui-neng's work has been enshrined in the Zen tradition not because of the unique nature of its author's insights but because of the clarity and accuracy with which it encapsulates central themes of the Zen tradition. That *The Sutra of Hui-neng* was compiled in roughly 820—about a century after Hui-neng's death—further suggests that it should be regarded not only or primarily as a record of Hui-neng's individual teachings but as representing central Zen ideas of the time.[9] Therefore, even if questions may be raised concerning the historical accuracy of particular aspects of Hui-neng's biography or teaching, it is appropriate to regard the essential philosophical themes of the text as representing an understanding of experience and enlightenment that was widely influential in its time and that resonates broadly within Zen Buddhism.

Articulating the nature of mystical experience in this context, however, presents certain challenges. Often, both in Hui-neng's own writings and in those of Buddhist thinkers who influenced his thought, contradictions seem to be rampant; an assertion concerning enlightenment, the nature of reality, or the essence of the self is made, only to be refuted in the next breath. In the absence of an understanding of the nature of both the self and ultimacy according to Zen thought, these apparent contradictions can frustrate interpretation. Yet their frequency in Buddhist writings suggests that something more significant and telling than simple inconsistency or sloppiness is afoot.

Many Buddhist thinkers, including Hui-neng, evince a deep and abiding suspicion of language; they doubt its ability not only to capture the nature of mystical experience but to accurately describe the nature of anything at all. All language, from this perspective, is conventional; it can be helpful as far as it goes, but one must remember that all linguistic designations are heuristic. Language does serve certain purposes and is appropriate for certain ends. But once the terms used to denote phenomena are taken to have meaning in anything but a conventional, impermanent, ad hoc sense, they propagate fundamental misunderstandings that militate against the soteriological goal of Buddhism. This limitation of the effectiveness of language pertains to both the most mundane things (tables, chairs, ham sandwiches, etc.) and the most central and sublime values, teachings, and topics of Buddhism (enlightenment, nirvana, the nature of the self, etc.). All language is therefore in a constant state of dialectical instability in Zen Buddhist discourse. Insofar as a term is taken to refer only to a conventionally identified phenomenon or state of being that is itself understood as impermanent and lacking essential identity or meaning, the term is useful; but insofar as the same term is taken to refer to the same phenomenon in an absolute, permanent, or essential fashion, it fundamentally misconstrues Buddhist teaching and misrepresents the phenomenon itself. This persistent tension is the source of the unending contradictions in Hui-neng's writings, and it can be resolved only by considering terms in their proper context, which is rarely made explicitly clear. When terms are used in the first sense, they may be affirmed, but when used in the second sense, they must be denied.

This complicated interplay of language, ontology, and epistemology echoes tensions already discussed in the mystical writings of Ibn al-'Arabi and Meister Eckhart. However, this tension cannot be explained in the same manner as for either of the Abrahamic mystics; the apparent failures and recursive self-destruction of language for Hui-neng do not (indeed, cannot) result from the metaphysical transcendence of ultimacy, as they do for Eckhart and Ibn al-'Arabi. As will be seen, however, there are clear and distinct reasons for the unstable nature of language in Hui-neng's works, and these reasons signal fundamental beliefs about reality, the self, and the nature of knowledge that must be acknowledged in order to understand mystical experience as Hui-neng presents it.

Key Passage

The Sutra of Hui-neng actually appears to describe two experiences of enlightenment, or what may be taken as Hui-neng's own mystical experiences. The first, related in the early biographical portion of the sutra, reports that one day Hui-neng was in a marketplace to deliver firewood to a customer. While there, he happened to overhear the *Diamond Sutra* being recited and "at once became enlightened."[10]

The relevant passage includes few details about the nature of this experience or Hui-neng's understanding of it. Something of the nature of the experience can, however, be deduced from this spare description. As noted, Hui-neng's formal encounter with Buddhism did not come until later in his life. Prior to this moment, he is nothing other than an illiterate manual laborer, a "barbarian" from an unknown village with no formal training or education. Taken in this context, Hui-neng's initial experience of enlightenment actually reveals a number of significant facts about his understanding of the nature of mystical experience. First, it does not necessarily require long and arduous study of Buddhist doctrine or dedicated performance of iconic Buddhist practices such as meditation. Hui-neng's enlightenment is sudden, without premeditation, training, or precursor. In fact, the school of Zen thought to which Hui-neng belongs and that he was soon to lead is known as the "sudden school." This is an initial indication, at least, that mystical experience can happen independently of religious or mystical training.

Further, not only is Hui-neng ignorant of Buddhist doctrine, but he lacks formal education entirely—he is a manual laborer who is unable to read or write, a fact that is emphasized a number of times. It is worth noting that, according to Sufi tradition, the prophet Muhammad was also illiterate. This intriguing point of contact between the two figures seems to have similar implications in both cases: mystical experience is possible not only without prior immersion in specifically religious teaching but without any form of education or discursive learning whatsoever. In fact, both Ibn al-'Arabi and Hui-neng agree that textual learning and discursive thought can actually militate against having a mystical experience.

Later in *The Sutra of Hui-neng*, we find another account of Hui-neng's enlightenment, and this one provides more detail about the nature of the experience. According to the sutra, after experiencing enlightenment in the crowded marketplace, Hui-neng travels to the monastery of Hung-jen, the fifth Chan patriarch. Shortly after his arrival, Hung-jen challenges his students to write a short stanza about enlightenment. Shen-hsiu, generally acknowledged as the most talented of the patriarch's students, writes a stanza that evinces wisdom but not full enlightenment. Hui-neng submits his own stanza anonymously, which clearly suggests to Hung-jen Hui-neng's profound understanding of Buddhist teaching. Presently, he invites Hui-neng to his room for a private interview, during which the patriarch recognizes Hui-neng's insight and acknowledges him as his successor and the next patriarch. Both men, however, realize that the news that an uneducated outsider has succeeded where the monastery's star pupil has failed could cause considerable upset, and even place Hui-neng's life in danger. Hui-neng relates the scene of his meeting with the fifth patriarch in the following words: "Using the robe as a screen so that none could see us, he expounded the Diamond Sutra to me. When he came to the sentence, 'One should use one's mind in such a way that it will be free from any attachment,' I at once became thoroughly enlightened, and realized that all things in the universe are the essence of mind itself" (73). Again, the theme of sudden enlightenment is emphasized. Here, however, we are given some further detail about the content of this mystical experience. Through it, Hui-neng realizes that all the varied phenomena in the universe are of the same nature as the "essence of mind itself."

This brief description begs the obvious question, "what is the essence of mind?" Before answering this complicated question, it is significant to note that we are given another clue here concerning the philosophical background against which Hui-neng's mystical experience is to be understood: there is no essential difference between the nature of phenomena and the nature of mind. At the very least, this is a clear denial of any sort of metaphysical dualism that would view mental and physical objects as distinct types of entities. The universe is not made up of radically different phenomena, some of which are physical and some of which are mental. Rather, all things—persons, objects, and thoughts—are of a single, shared nature, whatever that may be. Determining the nature of that shared essence requires exploration of the ontology implicit in Hui-neng's work.

Hui-neng's Ontology of Mystical Experience

In many ways, the "essence of mind" as described in *The Sutra of Hui-neng* echoes other religious traditions' assertions that the most essential aspect of the human person is something inherently special and distinct from the world, and that this element of the self is the key to mystical experience. For instance, the sutra relates that the fifth patriarch states that the attainment of enlightenment depends on the spontaneous realization of one's own essence of mind, which is "neither created nor can it be annihilated" (71).

Hui-neng heartily embraces this notion, and *The Sutra of Hui-neng* depicts him reveling in its truth: "'Who would have thought,' I said to the patriarch, 'that the essence of mind is intrinsically pure! Who would have thought that the essence of mind is intrinsically free from becoming or annihilation! Who would have thought that the essence of mind is intrinsically self-sufficient! Who would have thought that the essence of mind is intrinsically free from change!'" (73). This realization of the essence of mind is clearly a celebratory moment, signaling its importance to Hui-neng's mystical path. Described as such, the essence of mind appears to be of a uniquely special nature: it is neither created nor destroyed, its existence is not dependent on another reality or substance, and it never changes. In many ways, this brief description seems to suggest that the essence of mind is similar in structure to the soul that Meister Eckhart and Ibn al-'Arabi describe—something eternal and more metaphysically significant than all the various phenomena of the material world.

According to Hui-neng, this essence of mind is the "seed or kernel of enlightenment," and it is by the use of "mind alone" that one reaches buddhahood (67). In stating that buddhahood is achieved by mind alone, Hui-neng seems to suggest that other, external types of Buddhist practice and learning are irrelevant in attaining the experience that signals enlightenment. The essence of mind thus plays a central role in achieving enlightenment.

The nature of that essence, however, is somewhat surprising given the central, salvific role it plays in Hui-neng's thought: "Intrinsically our transcendental nature is void. . . . It is the same with the essence of mind, which is a state of absolute void" (80). The essence of mind is in fact void—emptiness. This might seem to contradict Hui-neng's other, rather exuberant declarations about the essence of mind. Upon inspection, however, it becomes apparent that they are actually commensurable. In stating that the essence of mind is "absolute void," Hui-neng does not mean that there is some essence or fundamental thing called "void" that stands at the center of the mind and defines the human person. Rather, he means to say, quite literally, that mind itself is nothing; to define the essence of mind as void is to suggest that there actually is no essence that can be called the fundamental nature of mind.

And insofar as voidness can be characterized, it is reasonable to describe it as "intrinsically free from becoming or annihilation." To "become," an object would have to exist in some fashion—it would have to have some sort of created being or nature that was not present prior to its becoming and that ceases to exist after it is annihilated. How could such alterations be said of voidness? Because voidness is not any kind of object, substance, or activity at all, it cannot be said to either come into or pass out of existence. Voidness cannot be created or destroyed, because these qualities can be attributed only to phenomena that can be said to exist at some point in time. Voidness, properly understood, does not meet this criterion. Similarly, voidness is "intrinsically self-sufficient" in the sense that it is not dependent on some more fundamental substrate. There is nothing that serves as the metaphysical ground or foundation for voidness because there is nothing to be grounded. In the same way, the essence of mind is free from change because voidness has no attributes that can be said to alter. As mere emptiness, voidness is without characteristics or traits, and so cannot be said to change in any way.

The implications of the voidness of the essence of mind for understanding the self are apparent and dramatic. Put simply, Hui-neng asserts the familiar Buddhist doctrine of *anatman*—the denial of the self. To believe in a self, the patriarch claims, is "the source of sin" (111). Clearly, the term "sin" cannot be understood here as synonymous with Christian uses of the term.[11] The term, however, is not problematic insofar as it is taken to name some kind of error or mistake that undermines one's soteriological aspirations. Rather than suggest that such belief is sinful in the sense of being morally objectionable, Hui-neng means to say that such belief militates against the possibility of enlightenment. Belief in the self represents a fundamental stumbling block on the mystical path that leads to the enlightenment experience that ultimately frees one from the suffering that arises from "grasping" phenomena, i.e., taking things, including the self, to have some sort of deeper rootedness in reality than the phenomenal characteristics apparent in daily experience. In poetic form, Hui-neng propounds the truth of *anatman* in the following words:

> The self is nothing but a phantasm created by the union of five
> *skandhas*,
> And a phantasm can have nothing to do with absolute reality.
> To hold that there is *tathata* [suchness] for us to aim at or to
> return to
> Is another example of impure dharma. (132)

The denial of the self goes hand in hand with the assertion that the essence of mind is emptiness. These are, in fact, two ways of asserting the same essential notion; the nonexistence of the self is identical to the emptiness of the essence of mind in that both statements assert that the human person is possessed of no essential reality.

Hui-neng's experience of enlightenment therefore entails the realization of the essential emptiness of all persons. Such a claim appears to fly in the face of experience; human persons do have thoughts, feelings, and sensations, and they generally experience themselves and others *as* selves.

In this sense, the lack of self or essential emptiness of the mind seems to deny Descartes's fundamental insight that questioning the existence of one's own self is logically impossible, because in the very act of posing the question one thereby proves the existence of a self of some sort. How, then, can Hui-neng assert the doctrine of *anatman*, or the emptiness of the essence of mind?

In his commentary on *The Diamond Sutra*, the text that plays the pivotal role in Hui-neng's own enlightenment experience, Hui-neng addresses this issue. In order to facilitate the teaching of the dharma, Hui-neng claims, the self is "provisionally defined" (125). This provisional definition is a prime example of the difficulty that Hui-neng and other Buddhist thinkers constantly encounter in relating the content of Buddhist thought, especially as it regards mystical experience. In asserting the nonexistence of the self, Hui-neng states the Buddhist understanding of the human person in the strongest possible terms. The language, in fact, may be intentionally drastic in order to counter an instinctual resistance to the doctrine. This is not to say that Hui-neng or other Buddhist thinkers intentionally overstate their case, but rather that it is often put forth in this unapologetically counterintuitive fashion because of a pedagogical need to overcome the contrary notion (the existence of the self) that seems incontrovertibly intuitive.

In his commentary, Hui-neng offers further guidance on how to understand his straightforward denial of the self without denying the apparently incorrigible fact that there are experiences and subjects who undergo those experiences. "No person," Hui-neng claims, "means understanding the gross elements are not substantial and ultimately disintegrate. No being means no mind being born and dying. No liver of life means our bodies are originally nonexistent—how can there be a liver of life?" (100).

The elements that make up the supposed self are impermanent; they arise, perdure for a limited time, and then pass out of existence. Hui-neng refers here specifically to the "gross elements" that constitute the self, and this could be interpreted as the limited claim that the specifically physical aspects of a person have no essential reality, leaving open the possibility that the nonmaterial aspects—such as mind or soul—may exist in a more permanent fashion. The stanza quoted earlier from *The Sutra of Hui-neng*, however, asserts that the self is "nothing but a phantasm created by the union of five *skandhas*." Traditionally, the *skandhas* are understood in Buddhist literature as the various elements that make up the human person.

Significantly, they include—in addition to the body—other factors such as mind and perception. In stating that the self is nothing but the aggregation of the *skandhas*, which include both material and nonmaterial elements, Hui-neng suggests that the impermanence of the self includes both its physical and nonphysical dimensions. Therefore, Hui-neng must be understood not as denying the essential reality of just the subject's physical form, but as denying the reality of all aspects of the self, both material and nonmaterial.

The "provisional definition" of the self, therefore, may be interpreted as the self as constituted by the five impermanent *skandhas*. In this sense, the existence of the self may be asserted. It is of the utmost importance, however, that this understanding of the self—as impermanent and lacking any fundamental essence—is the only appropriate understanding possible. This provisional definition of the self allows Hui-neng to heuristically adopt the language of the unenlightened in order to address—and ultimately undercut—their mistaken conceptions of the self. The self can be defined only provisionally because the self has only provisional or contingent existence.

Both this understanding of the self and the acknowledgment of this heuristic use of language are found in *The Diamond Sutra* as well: "the World-Honored One [Siddhartha Gautama] declares that notions of selfhood, personality, entity and separate individuality, as really existing, are erroneous—these terms are merely figures of speech."[12] Just as Hui-neng insists that the self, if it is to be defined at all, must be defined only provisionally, *The Diamond Sutra* represents the Buddha asserting the same about any notion of selfhood, personality, or individuality. Beyond the merely contingent understanding of these terms, *The Diamond Sutra* repeats the erroneousness of holding to any of these ideas, charging that "no bodhisattva who is a real bodhisattva" maintains the existence of any of these.[13]

Hui-neng uses one other significant phrase in discussing the nature of the self, and its meaning could be misunderstood in the absence of this assertion of selflessness. "Our very nature," he claims, "is buddha, and apart from this nature there is no other buddha" (79). In appearing to assert the existence of some sort of fundamental personal nature or essence, this claim could seem to be a direct contradiction of Hui-neng's insistence on the essential emptiness of mind and the nonexistence of the self. But Hui-neng's further discussion of the nature of buddha suggests an interpretation of it that accords handily with these other notions. Quoting the *Mahaparinirvana Sutra*, Hui-neng states that buddha-nature is neither eternal nor noneternal (77). Logically, the statement is deeply problematic;

anything that exists either does so eternally or noneternally, since the two categories are logically exhaustive and mutually exclusive. However, if we parse the apparently paradoxical nature of the claim, its solution presents itself: eternality and noneternality must be attributes of all things *that exist*. If buddha-nature is recognized as nonexistent, then it becomes clear how it can be said to be neither eternal nor noneternal—how can that which does not exist be said to do so either eternally or noneternally? Buddha-nature escapes description by either of these categories because—just like the essence of mind and the absolute self—it does not exist.

The nonexistence of buddha-nature also makes sense of Hui-neng's claim that although a "barbarian" (himself) and the fifth patriarch are different physically, there is no difference in their buddha-nature (68). If there were some sort of individual essence or nature that defines individual persons, then there clearly would be something that differentiates a renowned Buddhist sage from an uncultured rube. In the absence of any such inherent nature, however, there is nothing that essentially distinguishes them. Their respective buddha-natures—i.e., their fundamental lack of any personal essence—are necessarily identical. The features that appear to distinguish them—station, prestige, background, etc.—are merely provisional and ultimately meaningless, and that which would hypothetically differentiate them in a more profound fashion does not exist. Therefore, there is no essential difference between Hung-jen and Hui-neng: their mutual buddha-nature (fundamental emptiness) is identical.

Hui-neng's claim that his enlightenment experience entailed the realization that "all things in the universe are the essence of mind itself" must be interpreted as meaning nothing other than emptiness. To take the experiential claim in its totality, however, would suggest that all the varied phenomena of the universe are also empty or lacking essence. This, in fact, is exactly what Hui-neng means to say:

> In all things there is nothing real,
> And so we should free ourselves from the concept of the reality
>   of objects.
> He who believes in the reality of objects
> Is bound by this very concept, which is entirely illusive. (146)

Just as there is nothing essential or inherently real in the mind or the self, there is no essential reality to objects. In claiming that all things in the

universe are of the same nature as the essence of mind, Hui-neng claims
that both are ultimately empty.

The failure to realize this essential emptiness or voidness of phenomena
has profound implications for the manner in which one engages the world.
From the Buddhist perspective, there is a fundamental link between one's
experience of the world and the supposed nature of "the world itself." It is
the manner in which one approaches or conceptualizes phenomena that
defines their nature as experienced by the subject. Insofar as an individual
regards phenomena as consisting of some deeper essence or as having
some sort of inherent value or meaning, they exercise a detrimental hold
on that individual. One thereby becomes invested in phenomena and
develops the harmful habit of "grasping" after objects. One becomes
attached to phenomena, and these phenomena exert an injurious influence
over oneself.

This, however, is entirely a result of the way in which phenomena are
construed. In Hui-neng's language, this grasping is to subject oneself to
"discrimination or particularization"—to draw distinctions between different phenomena, to impute to them some sort of meaning or reality that
is taken to define them and thereby suggests that they have some kind of
inherent value that the self then either desires or avoids (106). Both attrac-
tion to phenomena that are construed as desirable and repulsion from
phenomena that are construed as undesirable constitute forms of attachment that militate against the experience of enlightenment. In contrast to
this attitude, Hui-neng counsels that "all things—good or bad, beautiful or
ugly—should be treated as void" (96). The cure to the self-defeating investment in things is to regard them as they actually are: void, or empty of
essence.

Hui-neng's mystical experience therefore consists of the realization
that both his own self or mind and all the various phenomena of the
world are essentially empty. He emphasizes, however, that this realization must obtain in a manner that goes beyond merely acknowledging
the truth of it as stated in Buddhist doctrine. Hui-neng ridicules the man
who, in failing to realize this essential emptiness personally, instead
regards it as a philosophical doctrine to be explored through rational
investigation. Such an individual, the patriarch claims, may "furnish spa-
cious lecture halls for the discussion of realism or nihilism," but he fails to
realize the essential emptiness of things and thereby thwarts his own
enlightenment (144).

Acknowledging the emptiness of things in the correct way is a delicate matter; one must accept and understand this universal emptiness without becoming attached to the notion of emptiness (or, here, the notion of "vacuity") itself: "Let your mind be in a state such as that of the illimitable void, but do not attach it to the idea of vacuity. Let it function freely. Whether you are in activity or at rest, let your mind abide nowhere. Forget the discrimination between a sage and an ordinary man. Ignore the distinction of subject and object. Let the essence of mind and all phenomenal objects be in a state of thusness. Then you will be in *samadhi* all the time" (126). Letting one's "mind abide nowhere" means avoiding allowing one's attention or interest to become rooted in any particular thing. This avoidance, however, cannot consist of becoming fascinated with emptiness itself. That would be merely to substitute the idea of vacuity for phenomena as the object of attachment; in either case, attachment arises, and one fails to remain detached. Rather than suggest emptiness as an appropriate object of attachment, Hui-neng exhorts his audience to give up ideas such as the difference between subject and object. His rejection of the distinction between subject and object is particularly telling. Objects may be said to exist only in a relative state; an object is only an object by virtue of the fact that there is a subject to regard it as such. Similarly, subjects are subjects only insofar as they inhabit that particular relationship to a phenomenon that construes it as an object. Subjects and objects are therefore mutually constitutive. It is in regarding a phenomenon as an object that one constitutes the self as subject, and vice versa. Undercutting either therefore dissolves both.

Hui-neng describes this undercutting as allowing both the essence of mind and all phenomenal objects to "be in a state of thusness." Again, it is important to recall that in denying the essential reality of phenomena (including the self), Hui-neng is not denying that things exist at all; he merely insists that things must be regarded as having only conventional, impermanent existence. Therefore, phenomena do have the attributes they appear to have: apples are red, stars are bright, and ham sandwiches are soft. But that is all they are. Beyond their phenomenal attributes, objects have no deeper essence or reality. Therefore, one is to regard all objects merely as they appear to consciousness through their phenomenal attributes, no more and no less.

This may be regarded as at least part of the key to avoiding attachment to the idea of vacuity (the doctrine of emptiness). Attachment to that doctrine would suggest the belief that it represents a kind of essential truth—perhaps the idea that emptiness constitutes the essence of things in some significant manner. Hui-neng insists, however, that the notion of emptiness is not any such essential truth; nor is it, in fact, an especially esoteric or even profound doctrine. In truth, the idea of vacuity is merely the observation that phenomenal objects are as they appear and only as they appear. Regarding phenomena in this fashion is precisely what Hui-neng means when he directs his listeners to let "objects be in a state of thusness" without becoming attached to the idea of vacuity.

The comportment vis-à-vis phenomena that Hui-neng endorses is a delicate balancing act between denying the total existence of phenomena and taking them to have a kind of reality that is existentially deeper than what appears. Navigating a path between the Charybdis of nihility and the Scylla of essential reality is precisely the perspective that characterizes his enlightenment experience and that he exhorts others to follow: "When [common people] are able to free themselves from attachment to objects when in contact with objects, and to free themselves from the fallacious view of annihilation on the doctrine of void they will be free from delusions within and from illusions without" (112).

This nuanced ontology pervades both *The Diamond Sutra* and Hui-neng's commentary on it. In the latter text, Hui-neng attributes the denial of phenomenal entities to the Buddha himself. Significantly, he also suggests that language referring to phenomenal entities is, like language that refers to the self, heuristic: "The Realized One says that appearances of self, person and so on ultimately can be destroyed and are not substantial realities. 'All beings' is nothing but a provisional term: if you detach from the errant mind, then there are no graspable 'beings'—so it says they 'are not beings'" (118). Just as descriptions of the self must be regarded as provisional, so must descriptions of beings. References to the self and to other entities serve the didactic purpose of allowing the Buddhist teacher to address the presuppositions of his unenlightened audience in order to deconstruct them.

In his commentary on *The Diamond Sutra*, Hui-neng emphasizes the dual nature of the realization of emptiness that characterizes his experience of enlightenment: "Awakening has two meanings. One is outward awakening, seeing the emptiness of all things. The other is inward seeking knowing the emptiness and silence of the mind, not being influenced by objects of the six senses" (89). Realization of the essentially empty nature of phenomena is equally important to realizing the empty nature of the self.

The Diamond Sutra is even clearer in its denial of the ultimate reality of phenomena. It records the Buddha teaching that "all things are devoid of selfhood, devoid of personality, devoid of entity, and devoid of separate individuality."[14] The repetition of this denial in different terms signals two things. First, in denying both "selfhood" and "personality" (which are generally attributed to living beings) and "entity" (which may be applied to inanimate objects), the sutra places living beings such as human persons and objects on the same ontological level, suggesting that they are both equally devoid of essence and in precisely the same way. Like phenomenal objects, human persons are neither more nor less than what they appear to be to phenomenal experience. Second, the repetition of the phrase itself—a formula that reappears throughout the text—serves the rhetorical purpose of underscoring the radical nature of the denial. It leaves little doubt about the extent to which things in the world are fundamentally lacking in essence. The passage goes on to say that it is the realization of this lack of selfhood or essence in all things that distinguishes enlightened bodhisattvas from other men, suggesting the fundamental importance of this ontological truth and the experience of realizing it.

This "negative ontology" underscores apparently paradoxical statements, such as the Buddha's claim that "characteristics are not characteristics" and that "all living beings are not, in fact, living beings."[15] Here, *The Diamond Sutra* employs the same deconstructive language that Hui-neng deploys in *The Sutra of Hui-neng*. In denying that characteristics are characteristics, *The Diamond Sutra* does not mean to suggest that traits that we perceive as defining entities are completely illusory—they obtain insofar as they heuristically describe the traits of entities that are impermanent and have only conventional existence. But insofar as such traits are taken as denoting permanent attributes or necessary qualities, they are illusory. Similarly, living beings are living beings insofar as living beings are regarded only as temporary, nonessential collections of phenomenal attributes; insofar as they are taken as anything else, they are also illusory.

Like Hui-neng, *The Diamond Sutra* also emphasizes that the denial of the essential nature of phenomenal entities must not itself be viewed as a kind of ultimate truth:

> If such men allowed their minds to grasp and hold on to anything they would be cherishing the idea of an ego entity, a personality, a being, or a separated individuality; and if they grasped and held on

to the notion of things as having intrinsic qualities they would be cherishing the idea of an ego entity, a personality, a being, or a separated individuality. Likewise, if they grasped and held on to the notion of things as devoid of intrinsic qualities they would be cherishing the idea of an ego entity, a personality, a being, or a separated individuality. So you should not be attached to things as being possessed of, or devoid of, intrinsic qualities.[16]

Accepting the nonessential nature of things is relatively easy from the Buddhist perspective. What is more difficult is avoiding the tendency to grasp the truth of this nonessentiality of things as a kind of essential ontological insight. Attachment to either the being of things or the lack thereof constitutes a fundamentally mistaken attitude, according to *The Diamond Sutra* and Hui-neng. Therefore, care must be taken to cultivate an attitude of disinterested nonattachment, rather than one of nihilism or commitment to essential voidness.

The Diamond Sutra offers an illustrative verse that captures the metaphysical attitude that accompanies Hui-neng's enlightenment experience:

> Thus shall ye think of all this fleeting world:
> A star at dawn, a bubble in a stream;
> A flash of lightning in a summer cloud,
> A flickering lamp, a phantom, and a dream.[17]

Morning stars, bubbles, and flashes of lightning are all impermanent—they appear and then disappear, just as the various phenomena of the world arise and then dissolve. In this sense, the metaphysical status of the world is what we naturally take dreams to be: passing phenomena, often replete with emotions and experiences that may even be profoundly affecting but that are ultimately transitory and of no deeper significance than what we invest in them. Hui-neng's mystical experience consists largely of this realization and the radically different attitude that it fosters toward existence.

There is, however, one remaining possibility that could serve as the realm of the metaphysically real from the Buddhist perspective: nirvana. Buddhist thought unanimously employs the term nirvana for the soteriological goal toward which it aims; it is thus the relevant form of ultimacy in the Buddhist context. This could easily suggest that nirvana names something—either a metaphysical location or a personal state of being—that is possessed of a deeper or more valuable kind of reality than the mundane world or the self, which are fleeting and transitory. This would, after all, explain its preeminent value for Buddhism. And such an assumption is natural; if the quotidian world is illusory and impermanent, then it seems reasonable that salvation would consist of leaving behind this illusory realm for one (nirvana) that is essentially real. In many ways, this concept echoes the Abrahamic dichotomy between heaven and earth.

The Sutra of Hui-neng is not very forthcoming about nirvana; compared to the space Hui-neng devotes to analyzing the metaphysical nature of the self, worldly phenomena, and the necessary epistemological comportment for realizing the nature of both (to be discussed shortly), the subject of nirvana receives comparatively little attention. But Hui-neng does suggest how nirvana should be understood: "At any one moment, *nirvana* has neither the phenomenon of becoming, nor that of cessation, nor even the ceasing of operation of becoming and cessation. It is the manifestation of perfect rest and cessation of changes, but at the time of manifestation there is not even a concept of manifestation; so it is called the everlasting joy, which has neither enjoyer nor nonenjoyer" (121). Significantly, Hui-neng describes nirvana using the apparently self-contradictory dialectic he employs in discussing the essence of mind and the nature of phenomena. It neither becomes nor ceases, nor is it the absence of either becoming or ceasing. As with the nature of the self and the fundamental being of phenomena, Hui-neng refuses either to attribute traits to nirvana or to deny them. Although the wordplay itself may seem obscurantist, his repetition of the same linguistic trope in discussing nirvana, the self, and worldly phenomena is telling. The use of the same self-deconstructing wordplay in all three cases suggests that the term nirvana should be viewed in the same manner as discourse about both the self and worldly objects: as merely conventional language that serves certain heuristic ends without actually denoting anything of an essential nature. Just like worldly entities and the self, therefore, nirvana should be understood as metaphysically empty—it also has no deeper essence.

Insofar as nirvana is taken as the soteriological goal and form of ultimacy toward which the Buddhist mystic aspires, this understanding of nirvana might appear to be a radical departure from Buddhist thought. In fact, however, it is very much in line not only with Hui-neng's own metaphysics but with trends of Buddhist thought that play a major role in the Zen tradition. First, given that Hui-neng takes such pains to undercut the assumption of the ontological essence of all worldly phenomena, including the self, it would be a surprising departure to suggest that nirvana does have some deeper essence. If the realization of the nonessential nature of things is fundamental to his enlightenment experience, it would be surprising if enlightenment led to the discovery of something else that did have some sort of essence.

Second, denial of the essential nature of nirvana is actually a well-established concept in Zen thought, and especially in those thinkers whose work clearly influenced Hui-neng's own. Some scholars believe that *The Diamond Sutra*—the text at the center of Hui-neng's narrative of his own enlightenment experience—was written by Nagarjuna, the second-century Indian Buddhist thinker and fourteenth patriarch of Zen Buddhism. Even if Nagarjuna's authorship of *The Diamond Sutra* cannot be established with certainty, the continuity of thought between other examples of his work, *The Diamond Sutra*, and Hui-neng's own work suggests that their agreement on the nature of nirvana is likely. Significantly, Nagarjuna is credited with originating the claim that nirvana and *samsara* (the continuing process of death and rebirth that characterizes worldly existence) are identical.[18] And if nirvana is identical with *samsara*, this can only mean that nirvana is also empty and without essence.

The identity of *samsara* with nirvana and nirvana's essential emptiness are consistent themes in Nagarjuna's most influential contribution to Buddhist thought, the *Mūlamadhyamakakārikā* (*The Fundamental Wisdom of the Middle Way*). For instance, Nagarjuna repeatedly refuses to describe nirvana in any specific terms or to attribute to it any particular characteristics. Doing so would suggest that nirvana possessed some sort of defining or essential characteristics, and since there are no such characteristics— even in the case of nirvana—Nagarjuna refuses to apply any predicates to it.[19] Nagarjuna thus demonstrates an awareness of the temptation to view nirvana as essentially real or valuable, and in *The Fundamental Wisdom* he works consistently to thwart this inclination. Rather, Nagarjuna explicitly states that nirvana is merely *samsara* seen "without reification, without attachment, without delusion."[20]

Nirvana is not, as it turns out, some essential state of being or mode of existence to be sought in contrast to the metaphysically empty mundane world. It is the very same world, experienced without attachment and in full acceptance of the ultimately nonessential and empty nature of the self and all phenomena. Therefore, it can only be empty as well. To view nirvana as anything but empty would be to engage in precisely the mistaken kind of ontological thinking that Hui-neng takes such pains to resist: to attribute essential reality to some phenomenon and therefore to "grasp" it as an object of desire. Such a view only fosters further suffering and is therefore antithetical to the revelatory mystical experience to which Hui-neng seeks to lead his listeners.[21]

The form of ultimacy that Hui-neng encounters in his mystical experience is therefore radically different from that encountered by either Ibn al-'Arabi or Meister Eckhart. For both of them, ultimacy is God. While both mystics employ similarly self-deconstructing language in describing ultimacy, they clearly see that ultimacy as something other than emptiness. Even if predicates such as "existence" cannot be applied to God because of his radical transcendence, it is clear that the divine enjoys a mode of metaphysical being that is "something" rather than nothing.

Despite this difference in the *content* of ultimacy, however, there is a distinct similarity in the *structure of the relationship* to ultimacy for all three mystics: *an ontological resonance in which the fundamental nature of the mystic's being is linked to or reflects that of ultimacy.* For Eckhart and Ibn al-'Arabi, this ontological resonance is manifest in the fact that the most essential aspect of the mystic's being (his soul) is essentially identical with God. In both cases, the most basic aspect of the self is seen as a shard or dimension of divinity, essentially constituted of the same metaphysical nature as that of ultimacy. For Hui-neng, the content of that ontological resonance is different (namely, emptiness rather than divinity) but structurally identical: the being of the mystic, again, mirrors that of ultimacy. In the case of Hui-neng, the ontological resonance is manifest in the fact that both the mystic and ultimacy are lacking in essence; they share the fact of being ultimately metaphysically empty. In all three cases, mystical experience reveals an identical structure in the relationship between mystic and ultimacy: the ultimacy the mystic encounters in the midst of his experience is identical to his own nature. This deep structural similarity obtains regardless of the significant differences in metaphysical content among the three mystics and their respective experiences.

Hui-neng's Epistemology of Mystical Experience

In the key passage quoted above, Hui-neng describes himself as having become "thoroughly enlightened" after listening to Hung-jen's exposition of *The Diamond Sutra*. That Hui-neng explicitly links his enlightenment to *The Diamond Sutra* (in two separate passages of *The Sutra of Hui-neng*) would seem to suggest that enlightenment depends on the learning of Buddhist doctrine in general, and perhaps *The Diamond Sutra* in particular. In discussing the epistemological nature of his enlightenment, however, Hui-neng consistently emphasizes that his experience, to the contrary, has very little to do with Buddhist texts or technical instruction. In fact, he repeatedly challenges the supposition that enlightenment is a distinct and special kind of knowledge: "the wisdom of enlightenment [*bodhiprajna*] is inherent in every one of us. It is because of the delusion under which our mind works that we fail to realize it ourselves. . . . You should know that so far as buddha-nature is concerned, there is no difference between an enlightened man and an ignorant one. What makes the difference is that one realizes it, while the other is ignorant of it" (79). The potential for enlightenment is found in each and every human being. Rather than suggest that enlightenment is the end result of sustained training in Buddhist doctrine (perhaps in combination with superior intellectual capabilities), Hui-neng emphasizes that the potential for it is in fact inherent in all persons, regardless of background or formal training. The difference between an enlightened individual and an unenlightened one, according to Hui-neng, is only that the former realizes his own buddha-nature while the latter does not; the difference consists of the recognition of a certain state or potential that is universal, rather than in the possession of a kind of knowledge or ontological quality that is available only to a select few.

This notion is consistent with Hui-neng's own autobiography. Given that the narrative of his life is as much legend as fact, it may be that his background as an uneducated, illiterate commoner from a provincial town was invented in order to underscore precisely the point that enlightenment does not depend on formal education or extensive Buddhist training. In fact, Hui-neng undercuts the notion of enlightenment itself, stating that the attainment of buddhahood consists not in achieving enlightenment but in "holding aloof" from the notions of both enlightenment and ignorance, and "doing away" with the notions of truth and falsity (103).

Hui-neng thereby consistently argues that enlightenment should not be construed as a kind of intellectual achievement available only to a chosen few. Rather, it is a potentiality that anyone may achieve. Throughout *The Sutra of Hui-neng*, Hui-neng repeatedly underscores this theme, going so far as to denigrate the intellectual study of Buddhist scripture. Even if a student were to lock himself in a shed and isolate himself entirely from the world in order to focus single-mindedly on the continual study of Buddhist literature, he would be a "*dhyana* scholar of second-hand knowledge only" (137). In other words, this kind of approach may allow one to become a learned expert on *dhyana* (meditation), but only in the manner of one who has indirect knowledge of what he seeks to know. Those who seek enlightenment in the correct manner realize that it is independent of scriptural authority (83).

One recurrent theme in Buddhist thought is the teaching that one must cultivate a state of nonattachment. On a superficial level, nonattachment describes a lack of concern with material things and a lack of personal investment in the world in general; one realizes the ultimate impermanence of all things and this realization fosters a kind of healthy indifference with regard to the material world. Beyond this, however, Hui-neng and many other thinkers in the Zen tradition acknowledge the temptation of aspiring students to become attached instead to the teachings and concepts of Zen training itself. This kind of attachment is no less detrimental than attachment to worldly, material entities; both kinds of attachment foster delusive investment in *samsara* and thereby militate against the achievement of *moksa* (liberation from *samsara*).

Therefore, Hui-neng consistently contrasts two approaches to the attainment of enlightenment: one, an outer method that depends on scripture, speculation, and recitation of the sutras, and the other, an inner method that recognizes the dispensability of such exterior practices and tools. He likens the student who recites sutras to a yak that is infatuated with his own tail—the endless and ignorant repetition of an action that is ultimately useless (113).

It is not only repetition of sutras that Hui-neng discredits as a technique for achieving enlightenment. In a larger sense, all Buddhist scripture and doctrine is finally of little if any value. The wisdom sought by the Zen student ultimately consists only of realizing the true nature of his own essence of mind, rather than relying on any exterior source (81). The claim may seem surprising, given that Hui-neng is himself a Zen teacher and that his narrative of his own enlightenment experience relies centrally on a Zen text. But the notion that Zen teaching and thought may be dispensed with—and may even function as hindrances to enlightenment, if regarded incorrectly—is found in many other Zen texts.

One of those, the *Blue Cliff Record*, is a collection of famous Zen stories and koans that originated in China roughly four centuries after Hui-neng's death. Current editions often contain both the original material (produced in the twelfth century), and commentaries by the famous Zen masters Hakuin Ekaku (1685–1768), of the Rinzai sect, and Tenkei Denson (1648–1735), of the Soto sect. In the *Blue Cliff Record*, stubborn attachment to Zen doctrine and the mistaken reification of Zen teachings as "truths" is referred to as the "stink of Zen." That notion is captured by the following vignette:

> Obaku said to a crowd, "You are all gobblers of dregs. If you go on like this, where will you have Today? Do you know that there are no Zen teachers in all of China?"
>
> Then a monk came forward and said, "Then what about those who order followers and lead communities all over the place?"
>
> Obaku said, "I don't say there's no Zen, just that there are no teachers."

This recondite exchange is clarified by Tenkei's commentary:

> *Gobblers of dregs*—Everywhere they say that people who consume writings and sayings are gobblers of dregs, but Daie explained that if writings were dregs, then "the oak tree in the yard" and "three pounds of flax" would also be dregs.[22] So it cannot be seen as limited to writings and sayings. From the perspective of the Zen eye, even practice is gobbling dregs, even travel for study is gobbling dregs, even talk about doing meditation or reading scripture is all involvement in writings and sayings. Therefore even to speak of enlightenment and delusion, views of Buddha or views of *Dharma*, is all gobbling dregs.[23]

Obaku makes a subtle distinction between "Zen" and "Zen teachers"— while the latter are lacking in all of China, Obaku does not deny the presence of the former. Clearly, however, he cannot mean to deny the presence of individuals who claim to have authoritative insight into Zen and who have collected groups of students who look to them for leadership and guidance. As the unnamed monk states, such people are "all over the place." The distinction Obaku draws becomes clear in light of Tenkei's comments. "Gobblers of dregs" is a pejorative term for all who claim to practice Zen but do so inappropriately. Although "people who consume writings and sayings" are "gobblers of dregs," Tenkei does not believe that this indicates that all writings and sayings are merely "dregs," for this would include koans such as the famous "three pounds of flax" story, also included in the *Blue Cliff Record*. Therefore, writings and sayings themselves (including koans) are not the target of this criticism.

Tenkei then expands the collection of activities that he dismisses as merely gobbling dregs: travel for study, practice, talk about meditation, reading scripture, and speech about enlightenment, the views of the Buddha or of dharma. "Dregs" are those sediments left in a cup after a drink (presumably, given the context, tea) has been consumed, the unwanted residue left over after a substance has been used. The dregs of which Tenkei writes, then, are the residue or by-products of enlightenment. None of them are enlightenment itself, but they are peripheral accretions that are thought to either precede or follow enlightenment: philosophical disquisitions on enlightenment, classic Zen scriptures, and meditation. All of these activities are merely "dregs" compared to what is of real value.

But these things are also the tools of Zen teachers. Meditation, scriptural study, and explanation of the nature of enlightenment are all techniques by which a teacher of Zen operates. As Obaku's epithet "dregs" makes clear, however, there is nothing of real value in any of these things. Zen cannot, in fact, be taught, especially since these "dregs" are the only tools available. Rather, Zen must be grasped or experienced oneself, individually and without dependence on "teachers" or other respected but ultimately barren activities. Zen does exist in China, Obaku allows, but the Zen teacher is nowhere to be found because what he would teach cannot be taught.

Hui-neng expresses similar sentiments in discussing *prajna*, or wisdom: "*prajñā* . . . means wisdom. . . . People in ignorance or under delusion do not see it; they talk about it with their tongues, but in their minds they remain ignorant. They are always saying that they practice *prajñā*, and they talk incessantly about voidness; but they do not know the absolute void. The heart of wisdom is *prajñā*, which has neither form nor characteristic" (81). While it may be easy to discuss or to speculate about *prajna* or voidness, it is quite another thing to "know" either of these in the authentic sense Hui-neng intends. Like the "teachers" whom Obaku subtly criticizes, Hui-neng holds that most people who speak of either wisdom or emptiness are only gobblers of dregs.

Hui-neng thus relativizes the importance of Zen's central tenets: "He who realizes the essence of mind may dispense with such doctrines as *bodhi*,[24] nirvāna, and knowledge of emancipation. Only those who do not possess a single system of law can formulate all systems of law, and only those who can understand the meaning [of this paradox] may use such terms. It makes no difference to those who have realized the essence of mind whether they formulate all systems of law or dispense with all of them. . . . They are free from obstacles or impediments. They take appropriate actions as circumstances require. . . . They attain liberation" (132). Notions such as *bodhi* and nirvana, Hui-neng implies, are only "skillful means." These are techniques that Zen teachers use to help students along the path to enlightenment. Skillful means, however, are only teaching tools; while they may be presented or received as "truths," eventually they must be forfeited if a student is to successfully free himself from mental constraints. To retain what are only skillful means as doctrines or tenets of belief is the "stink of Zen." This is what Hui-neng means by possessing "a single system of law." The "possession" of or sole adherence to any one system implies that other such systems, insofar as they disagree with one's own, are incorrect. One thereby becomes convinced of the truthfulness of one's own system of law and is thereby trapped by duality. In truth, the system of law then "possesses" the man, and his belief in its tenets ultimately functions as an obstacle or impediment to his own progress.

As in discussing ontological notions such as the essence of mind or the existence of worldly phenomena, even terms denoting apparently central Zen concepts such as nirvana must be kept in a state of dialectical limbo; insofar as phenomena, the self, nirvana, or enlightenment are understood as merely heuristic designations—skillful means—these terms may be used to help students achieve enlightenment. As Hui-neng claims, only those who fully understand the meaning—and the fundamentally conventional nature—of such terms may use them. The moment such terms are regarded as essential in any way, they become obstacles to enlightenment. Ultimately, therefore, all views—including the supposedly fundamental doctrines of Buddhism itself—must be forsaken. Hui-neng makes this point explicitly in *The Sutra of Hui-neng*:

> Right views are called transcendental;
> Erroneous views are called worldly.
> When all views, right or erroneous, are discarded
> Then the essence of *bodhi* appears. (87)

Only by sacrificing attachment to any views and the attendant dichotomy of "right/transcendental" and "erroneous/worldly" may the student achieve enlightenment. A nearly identical notion is found in the final chapter of Nagarjuna's *The Fundamental Wisdom of the Middle Way*:

> I prostrate to Gautama
> Who through compassion
> Taught the true doctrine,
> Which leads to the relinquishing of all views[25]

Jay Garfield suggests that this verse entails *all* views, including Nagarjuna's own ideas as put forth in *The Fundamental Wisdom*.[26] The verse, then, would mean that one must not adhere to any specific philosophical view, including Nagarjuna's. Nagarjuna is known to have stated (paradoxically, according to some) that he did not put forth his own system of thought, and Garfield's interpretation of this verse is supported by that disclaimer. The holding of any views at all, whether in apparent accord with Zen teaching or not, is contradictory to the achievement of enlightenment. Nagarjuna writes earlier in his seminal text:

> Those who develop mental fabrications with regard to the Buddha
> Who has gone beyond all fabrications,
> As a consequence of those cognitive fabrications,
> Fail to see the Tathāgata[27]

In his commentary on *The Diamond Sutra*, Hui-neng is explicit about the merely heuristic nature of Zen teaching. One revealing tactic he deploys in this regard is to liken Buddhist instruction to medicine (102). Medicine is applied not because it is valuable in and of itself but to treat illness; once the illness has been cured, the medicine is no longer necessary and has no further value.

As with other aspects of his thought, Hui-neng sometimes makes dramatic claims to convey his point about the heuristic nature of Zen teaching. He often cites equally extreme statements in *The Diamond Sutra*, suggesting that his striking denials of the meaning and importance of Zen doctrine are perfectly orthodox: "Lest people get fixated on the verbal expressions used by the Realized One, fail to realize the formless truth, and mistakenly create interpretations, Buddha says they are not to be grasped. How could there be any fixity in explanations given by the Realized One according to potential and capacity to edify all sorts of people? . . . That is why the sutra says the doctrines are not to be preached" (102). *The Diamond Sutra* presents the Buddha claiming that "doctrines are not to be preached." It also states unequivocally that "the Tathagata has nothing to teach."[28] According to Hui-neng, this is not to say that the sutra claims that Buddhist teachers ought not to seek students or attempt to liberate other sentient beings; rather, the warning about not preaching the doctrines is a hyperbolic restatement of the nonessential nature of Buddhist teaching.

In fact, Buddhist doctrine and practice exist only because of their utility in guiding unenlightened beings to realization of their empty nature and thereby facilitating their release from *samara*. If not for the illusions concerning the nature of existence within which sentient beings are trapped, there would be no need for the Buddha or his teaching (85). The doctrine that Hui-neng expounds and the truth contained in *The Diamond Sutra* are only means to an end—mere "expedients," as he calls them (136). In the absence of the need to achieve that end (i.e., if there were no sentient beings in need of release from the cycle of death and rebirth), or if the end were eventually achieved universally (i.e., if all sentient beings reached enlightenment), the teaching would become unnecessary. *The Diamond Sutra* corroborates this attitude with regard to Buddhist teaching. Echoing a familiar Buddhist image, the text depicts the Buddha describing his teaching as a raft that must ultimately be relinquished; upon reaching the far shore (enlightenment), the traveler no longer requires the vehicle that transported him there.[29]

In suggesting that Buddhist doctrine is not essential to enlightenment—or therefore to his own mystical experience—Hui-neng gestures toward a broader epistemological theme in Buddhist thought, one that resonates strongly with both Meister Eckhart's and Ibn al-'Arabi's descriptions of mystical experience: the lack of intellectual content. If Buddhist doctrine itself is ultimately devoid of essential teachings, then it follows that intellectual knowledge in general is unnecessary. In fact, Hui-neng argues that the very process of ratiocination is not only unnecessary but often counterproductive in seeking enlightenment. This is why he insists that the advice and guidance of "the pious and learned" are not necessary for liberation (84–85).

Hui-neng is not, of course, alone in advocating such a view. As his predecessor puts it, "deliberation is quite unnecessary and of no use" in pursuing enlightenment (69). Following Hung-jen's lead, Hui-neng also emphasizes that progress in Zen training is not achieved through philosophizing. In response to a student's questions about a sutra, Hui-neng explains, "The reason why *shrāvakas*, *pratyekabuddhas*, and bodhisattvas cannot comprehend the buddha-knowledge is because they speculate on it. They may combine their efforts to speculate, but the more they speculate, the farther they are from the truth" (114). *Shravakas*, *pratyekabuddhas*, and bodhisattvas are all advanced students of Buddhism who, in Hui-neng's view, have reached the edge of enlightenment and yet still lack the ability to cross the final threshold. In his estimation, their ultimate hindrance is precisely the fact that they attempt to speculate or philosophize about "buddha-knowledge." This resistance to speculation goes hand in hand with Hui-neng's devaluation of Buddhist teaching and doctrine; if the latter are only valuable as tools for the end they facilitate, then it follows that fascination with them and focus on them would only be a distraction. These students are like a carpenter who devotes all of his time and energy to building a perfect hammer rather than to constructing the house for which the hammer is intended.

It is therefore unsurprising that Hui-neng claims that liberation is "to attain *samādhi* of *prajñā*, which is *thoughtlessness*" (85). Thoughtlessness, however, is not simply a state of being unconscious. The simple suppression of thought is not sufficient, and actually renders one "dharma-ridden," indicating a kind of residual connectedness to phenomena of the world that is counterproductive for the ascetic path of Zen Buddhism. "Thoughtlessness," in Hui-neng's sense, consists of an awareness of the world that is detached from it. It "pervades everywhere" (it is alert and responsive to the world), but it "sticks nowhere" (it is not invested in or committed to the world, realizing the empty nature of all phenomena). This could be seen as heightened awareness of the world, in that the mind is not centrally absorbed in any one thing but is broadly attentive to all that it encounters. Hui-neng's following verse captures the character of this nonanalytical awareness:

The mirrorlike wisdom is pure by nature.
The equality wisdom frees the mind from all impediments.
The all-discerning wisdom sees things intuitively without going
    through the process of reasoning.

The all-performing wisdom has the same characteristics as the
mirrorlike wisdom. (116–17)

Reasoning actually obscures the pure functioning of the mind. The image
of the mirror—common to Buddhist texts—represents the cleansed
mind's ability to engage with or reflect its environment unimpeded by
cognition. The "mirrorlike wisdom" reflects all that it encounters (awareness) but does not engage in reasoning concerning anything, instead leaving itself open and unhindered to engage "intuitively" with whatever it
encounters.

In order to bring about this unattached awareness, both concepts and
the negation of concepts must be sacrificed:

> To realize that nothing can be seen but to retain the concept of
>   invisibility
> Is like the surface of the sun obscured by passing clouds
> To realize that nothing is knowable but to retain the concept of
>   unknowability
> May be likened to a clear sky disfigured by a lightning flash
> To let these arbitrary concepts rise spontaneously in your mind
> Indicates that you have misidentified the essence of mind, and
>   that you have not yet found the skillful means to realize it.
> If you realize for one moment that these arbitrary concepts are
>   wrong,
> Your own spiritual light will shine forth permanently. (118)

Recognition of the "unknowability" of things is incomplete or artificial as
long as one retains the concept of unknowability. That concept, Hui-neng
emphasizes, is just one more arbitrary phenomenon that is ultimately devoid
of significance. The "thoughtlessness" he espouses is not the intellectual
opinion that phenomena are ultimately unknowable because the concepts
by which we know them are arbitrary constructs. Rather, true "thoughtlessness" is neither knowing things by their concepts nor believing them to be
unknowable; it is the nondiscursive and unfettered engagement with them
as merely transient phenomena. Such an attitude is characterized by inter-
acting with phenomena precisely as they appear to phenomenal consciousness, no more and no less. To let go of arbitrary concepts is not to hold such
concepts *to be* arbitrary, but to *treat them as such* by having no further

concern for them beyond their appearance to phenomenal consciousness. Given the essential ontological emptiness of phenomena, this attitude is apropros.

The Diamond Sutra endorses a nearly identical attitude, characterizing enlightenment as a state devoid of both sensation and thought: "bodhisattvas should leave behind all phenomenal distinctions and awaken the thought of the consummation of incomparable enlightenment by not allowing the mind to depend upon notions evoked by the sensible world—by not allowing the mind to depend upon notions evoked by sounds, odors, flavors, touch contacts, or any qualities. The mind should be kept independent of any thoughts that arise within it."[30] Three different denials of thought may be discerned here. First, the bodhisattva must free his mind of attachment to sensory phenomena. Second, he must keep his mind "independent of any thoughts"; he ought not to be actively speculating on anything. Third, the sutra advises the aspirant to "leave behind all phenomenal distinctions," and this introduces another intriguing dimension of the state of "thoughtlessness" that Hui-neng espouses.

This avoidance of fascination with phenomenal distinctions echoes themes that pervade the ontological dimension of Hui-neng's thought about mystical experience, and specifically his claims concerning the empty nature of phenomena. If all phenomena are ultimately devoid of inherent nature and lack essential being, then they lack the intrinsic qualities that would distinguish them from one another. This denial of essential ontological distinctions is reflected in Hui-neng's admonition to students not to speak "in terms of consciousness of subject and object" (110–11). The denial of phenomenal distinctions may therefore be interpreted as the rejection of the most basic aspects of the intellectual apprehension of the world—including the apparently fundamental difference between subject and object, self and other. Only by undercutting intellectual discrimination in this radical sense does the bodhisattva develop a mind that "alights upon nothing whatsoever."[31]

Unsurprisingly, this radical state of "thoughtlessness" has dramatic implications for the ability of language to capture this state of being. This is an issue that *The Sutra of Hui-neng* addresses both directly, through Hui-neng's own statements about the role of language, and indirectly, through his biography. As we have seen, *The Sutra of Hui-neng* emphasizes that Hui-neng was a provincial, illiterate "barbarian" with no formal education (72, 109, 112). The text gives no indication that he ever learned to read, even after being officially installed as the sixth patriarch. This fact naturally provides Hui-neng's critics with ammunition—ammunition that the master, of course, parries easily. When his authority as a Zen teacher is challenged because of his illiteracy, Hui-neng responds that the "profundity of the teachings of the various buddhas has nothing to do with the written language" (109).

Given Hui-neng's devaluation of intellectual knowledge and Buddhist doctrine, the claim that language itself is irrelevant with regard to enlightenment is not surprising. If the core doctrinal ideas of Buddhism are ultimately only a means to an end, then it follows that the language in which those ideas are expressed is only valuable, if at all, as a heuristic. In fact, the terms and discourses that constitute Buddhist teaching must be regarded in this manner, because what Hui-neng and other Zen teachers attempt to communicate cannot actually be grasped by words:

> Here I am trying to describe to you something that is ineffable
> So that you may get rid of your fallacious views.
> But if you do not interpret my words literally
> You may perhaps learn a wee bit of the meaning of *nirvana*! (122)

The experience of ultimacy to which Zen practice leads cannot be described in words. Yet Hui-neng undertakes the apparently paradoxical task of describing that experience in order to purify his audience of the mistaken ideas and false assumptions that typically bar an individual from enlightenment. Ironically, his listener can derive true understanding from Hui-neng's discourse only insofar as his words are not taken literally. Because the experience of ultimacy is ineffable, the only way in which something of its meaning may be transmitted in words is if they are taken metaphorically—as indicating only indirectly something that the words themselves cannot capture.

Throughout *The Sutra of Hui-neng*, Hui-neng employs this self-deconstructive dialectic that immediately subverts the claims he appears to make. This is a strategy that he deploys self-consciously and that he imparts to his students. When they are asked about nirvana or the nature of enlightenment, Hui-neng advises that they answer with denials and self-reversals: if a question seems to require an affirmative answer, he tells them to answer in the negative; if asked about ordinary men, they are to make reference to a sage, and so on (142, 145). Hui-neng suggests that the consistent use of apparently confusing language will ensure that one's discourse will never be far from the truth (145). The intent of this Buddhist version of apophatic discourse is to undercut the meaning not just of individual terms but of language itself; by juxtaposing the apparent truth of opposites and maintaining a creative tension between questions posed and answers provided, Hui-neng implicitly indicates the inadequacy of language for the truth it seeks to capture. These linguistic feints and ploys disturb the listener's reliance on language as the medium of truth and meaning, and thereby consistently thwart the temptation to erroneously construe enlightenment as a kind of truth that can be spoken or heard. "If you only believe that Buddha speaks no words," Hui-neng writes, "then the lotus will blossom in your mouth" (111).

The ultimate ineffability of enlightenment is a repeated theme not only in *The Sutra of Hui-neng* but in both *The Diamond Sutra* and Hui-neng's commentary on it. Just as the Buddha, according to Hui-neng, speaks no words, *The Diamond Sutra* "is not written in letters" (86).

> All verbal and literary expressions are like labels, like pointing fingers. Labels and pointers mean shadows and echoes. You obtain a commodity by its label, and you see the moon by way of the pointing finger—the moon is not the finger, the label is not the thing itself. Just getting the teaching by way of the sutra—the sutra is not the teaching. The sutra literature is visible to the physical eye, but the teaching is visible to the eye of insight. Without the eye of insight, you just see the literature, not the teaching. (104)

Just as the finger that indicates the moon is not the moon and the names that designate goods are not the goods themselves, so also the sutra is not the truth that it may be taken to indicate. Hui-neng's narrative of his experience of enlightenment conforms to the repeated insistence that such a realization is ineffable—the experience occurs suddenly, without prior training or background learning, and cannot itself be described. In many ways, Hui-neng's own enlightenment experience echoes that of Mahakasyapa, the monk whose enlightenment and consequent inheritance of the dharma from Shakyamuni Buddha was signaled by a silent smile in response to the Buddha's twirling of a single flower.

Throughout *The Diamond Sutra*, various terms are dismissed as "mere names," disposable once they have served their purpose. "Stream-entrant,"

"once-to-be-reborn," "non-returner"—all terms that would describe spiritually advanced individuals such as bodhisattvas—and more mundane
terms such as "cosmos" are all dismissed as ultimately meaningless.[32] The
"religion" taught by the Buddha is not a religion, because such a description implies the setting down of some sort of doctrinal truth that can be
taken as essentially meaningful. In fact, according to *The Diamond Sutra*,
the Buddha insists that "truth is uncontainable and inexpressible."[33]

Conclusion

Hui-neng clearly means to suggest that the experience of enlightenment is
ineffable, and in this he is in accord with *The Diamond Sutra* and other
thinkers in the Zen tradition. He is also, intriguingly, in accord with
Meister Eckhart and Ibn al-'Arabi, both of whom describe the pinnacle of
their own mystical paths as culminating in an experience that cannot
be described in language. Their unanimity on this point, especially given
the vast differences in their cultural contexts and religious backgrounds,
is striking.

As intriguing as this commonality is, it must be noted that the internal
theological reasons for it take two distinctly different forms. According to
Hui-neng, merely having an image or concept of the Buddha militates
against "seeing" him; attachment to doctrines or language functions as a
stumbling block to one's advancement toward enlightenment. These
exhortations echo those of Ibn al-'Arabi and Meister Eckhart, who both
suggest that the deity to which the mystic must direct his attention surpasses the ability of language to capture him. For both Eckhart and the
Sufi, that claim is motivated by the fact that the infinite being of God
simply cannot be captured by the restricting and finite boundaries of a
single image, notion, or term comprehensible by a mortal mind. God is
transcendent; the human mind and the language it uses are temporal and
limited and therefore insufficient to describe ultimacy.

For Hui-neng, concepts and terms fail for a very different reason. It is
not the transcendent and metaphysically unlimited nature of ultimacy
that sabotages "mental fabrications" and language itself. Rather, the fault
is traced to the fact that doctrines and terms imply that nirvana, the Buddha, or the Buddha's teaching *are* somehow eternal, significant realities
that can be meaningfully represented. Here, ineffability arises for precisely

the opposite reason than in the case of the theistic mystics. Language fails with regard to Hui-neng's notion of ultimacy precisely because nirvana is *not* essential or transcendent, and the use of language to describe it can erroneously imply otherwise. Whereas God *exceeds* any and all possible concepts and images, nirvana *subverts* them.

The metaphysical status of the two forms of ultimacy (God and nirvana) are therefore radically different from each other; in many ways, God and nirvana are even polar opposites. Yet each form of ultimacy resists being captured in words or concepts (including the religious doctrines of the traditions to which the mystics respectively belong), and is ultimately known through a kind of immediate experience that is distinctly different from the modality of mundane kinds of knowledge. Despite the differences in the reasons underlying the nature of the mode of knowing represented in all three accounts, they are all described in strikingly similar ways—as unmediated, nonconceptual, and ineffable.

Further, these epistemological themes are supplemented by a common metaphysical structure. In all three cases, the encounter with ultimacy consists of an event that ultimately reveals the fundamental nature of the mystic's own self. For Ibn al-'Arabi and Meister Eckhart, this is the realization that their own fundamental selves are extensions of God's essence. In the case of Hui-neng, this realization takes a substantively different form: his "essence"—like that of the ultimacy he seeks to encounter—is void, a radical and nonessential emptiness. But the structural relation described is identical: an ontological resonance in which the fundamental nature of the being of the mystic reflects and participates in the fundamental nature of ultimacy. In all three cases, the realization of that resonance takes place without mediation, and in the absence of both concepts and language.

CONCLUSION

Theory and Interpretation

In 2000, Robert Forman, Steven Katz's most prolific critic, published an article with Jensine Andresen calling for an end to the "methodological war" Katz's work had initiated.[1] Four years later, Katz published an essay reiterating the theoretical position he first advanced in 1978, with no alteration of its substance or mitigation of its categorical tone.[2] These dual publications suggest that in more than twenty years, little consensus had been reached concerning the appropriate method for the analysis of mystical experience or the possibility of cross-cultural similarities.

In attempting to infuse the study of mysticism and mystical experience with greater philosophical sophistication and methodological rigor, Steven Katz, Robert Forman, Wayne Proudfoot, and other contemporary scholars have deployed various epistemological models and theories of consciousness to explain the nature of mystical experience. In the ensuing debate, scholars have dismissed contrary theories as "self-contradictory," "empty,"[3] "dogmatic,"[4] and "naïve."[5] The sometimes vitriolic nature of this debate is symptomatic of an intellectual climate in which opposing positions have been fervently defended, and in which the interpretation of mystic experiential accounts has been overshadowed by scholars' own theories about mystical experience. Michel de Certeau commented in 1968 that "the attention directed by European analyses toward the mysticism of others is guided more or less explicitly by internal interrogations and disputes, even when these analyses consider foreign traditions."[6] His statement was prescient in noting the limited philosophical horizons within which most scholarship in this area has proceeded. Debate has focused primarily on neither mystical experience as reported by mystics nor interpretation per se, but on the purported truth or philosophical soundness of scholars' own proposed models of experience. Philosophy—specifically, the construction and defense of theories of experience and consciousness—has supplanted and suppressed hermeneutics.

I do not seek to resolve the debate Katz initiated. Rather, I suggest that the debate itself has distracted scholars from the properly hermeneutical question of how to interpret texts based on fundamental assumptions about the nature of experience that drastically contradict those regnant in twentieth- and twenty-first-century academic thought. By distinguishing between the interpretation and the explanation of mystical experience, the hermeneutical difficulties created by the interpolation of a scholar's own philosophical commitments into the interpretation of mystical experience can be avoided. A phenomenological approach, divested of explanatory claims, fulfills this interpretive task. This phenomenological approach consists of two main mechanisms. First, *epoché* brackets or temporarily suspends the analyst's own philosophical commitments, including the explanatory theory he may legitimately employ in the later, separate task of explaining mystical experience. *Epoché* thereby reinforces the descriptive/explanatory bifurcation that Proudfoot advocates. The employment of an explanatory hypothesis, such as Katz's single epistemological assumption, is thereby restricted to the explanatory phase of analysis, preventing explanatory theory from being used as interpretive method.

The objectivity toward which *epoché* gestures may remain a theoretical ideal. Interpretation—as opposed to philosophical critique—depends on foregrounding the foundational assumptions of the text or subject under consideration, independently of the theoretical commitments of the interpreter. Even if the interpreter can approach this ideal only asymptotically, *epoché* represents a necessary heuristic, particularly in the study of texts and experiential accounts whose basic assumptions contradict those of the interpreter.

Second, I recommend semantic holism as the method by which to incorporate context into analysis and to foreground the subject's or text's own concepts and beliefs for interpretation. Katz's work is valuable in underscoring the importance of context for understanding accounts of mystical experience. His particular method of incorporating context, however, is problematic. As Katz himself emphasizes, the analyst has no access to the mystic's actual experience; all the analyst has access to, in fact, is the mystic's *account* of her experience. This suggests that any interpretive theory based on claims about the structure or nature of the mystic's experience itself is, at best, empirically unsecure.

Holism acknowledges this fact.[7] As a semantic rather than an epistemological principle, holism focuses on the mystic's experiential *account*, rather than presuming knowledge of the experience itself. Holism incorporates context into interpretation not as a delimiting function of consciousness but as the source of additional beliefs, concepts, and assumptions whose relations to an experiential account are keys to meaning. Whereas Katz's method assumes that context inscribes boundaries to the possibilities for experience, holism regards the mystic's experiential report and its related contextual sources on an equal plane, and harnesses the latter as guides to interpretation. The principle of charity assumes that there will be a minimal degree of consistency between the mystic's account and other, related concepts and beliefs. It is from this relationship that meaning is derived.

Holism is also better able to acknowledge instances of mystical innovation or divergence from mainstream doctrine and orthodoxy because it does not assume, prior to inquiry, a necessary concordance between experience and context. The hermeneutic circle through which holism operates emphasizes that the meaning an interpreter derives is subject to constant revision upon further engagement with a text or experiential account. This deters an interpreter from overreliance on his own projected meaning of the text (or assumptions based on a given epistemological theory) and promotes hermeneutic focus on the account itself. This method seeks to open up an experiential account for interpretation, rather than to impose semantic horizons based on the interpreter's own philosophical perspective.

As employed in chapters 3, 4, and 5, this method reveals intriguing similarities between different, historically unrelated accounts of mystical experience.

Analysis of the metaphysics of experience in Ibn al-'Arabi, Meister Eckhart, and Hui-neng reveals the common theme of an ontological resonance: in all three cases, the mystics propose the prior existence of a linkage or concordance in basic metaphysical structure between self and ultimacy. The commonality of this notion in Neoplatonic traditions is well known. However, the presence of this commonality beyond the influence of Neoplatonism—specifically, in the tradition of Zen Buddhism— indicates that the theme of ontological resonance is not limited to only those traditions influenced by Neoplatonic thought. In addition to the example of Zen Buddhism, one might also include the Advaita Vedanta school of Hinduism, where the dual nature of Atman/Brahman represents a very similar notion of ontological resonance.

In the cases of Meister Eckhart and Ibn al-'Arabi, this ontological resonance takes a similar form, not only in terms of the structural relationship between mystic and ultimacy but also in terms of content. In both cases, there is the clear suggestion that some sort of prior ontological connection or linkage in basic metaphysical or spiritual structure holds between the self and ultimacy. Both thinkers describe this connection in numerous ways; the prior existence of the human soul in or with the divine is a common form of this notion. In both cases, that prior linkage makes possible the more intimate encounter with ultimacy that the mystic seeks. Therefore, for both thinkers, the realization of that encounter in ontological terms is the realization of a state of affairs that has always already been true.

This ontological resonance takes a different form in the work of Huineng. On the basis of the ontology expounded in Nagarjuna's *Fundamental Wisdom* and Zen thought in general, there is no essence or metaphysical foundation that can be said to link the Buddhist mystic with ultimacy. However, a correspondence is present that is similar in structure, if not content, to that found in both Eckhart and Ibn al-ʿArabi. Specifically, the empty nature of all phenomena, *sunyata*, is recapitulated in the notion of *anatman*, or no-self. Just as all things are empty of essence, so too is the aspiring mystic. The importance of this equation between the nature of the mystic and the world is drastically enhanced in light of the fact that one of the central insights of Mahayana Buddhism, due to Nagarjuna, is the equation of nirvana with *samsara*.[8] Like *samsara* and all its various inhabitants, nirvana is empty. Thus the ontological structure of the Buddhist mystic is identical to that of nirvana in that they are both *sunyata*, empty. Despite the lack of an underlying essence, within trends of mystical Buddhism the same relationship of shared metaphysical structures between mystic and ultimacy obtains, albeit in terms of emptiness.

This ontological resonance indicates something of the nature of mystical experience in these traditions. In each case, mystical experience is described as an encounter in which the mystic achieves a relationship with ultimacy that is far more profound than would be possible within a normal ontology by subverting the subject/object dichotomy. Qualitatively, this ontological resonance indicates an experience that, rather than the detached knowing of an object distinct from the self, takes the form of a more intimate, non-conceptual encounter. The similarity or identity in ontological foundation between mystic and ultimacy suggests that ultimacy is felt or experienced as in some sense familiar, rather than as a radically distinct "other." From a certain perspective, the encounter with ultimacy ultimately turns out to be an encounter with the most basic nature of the mystic's own self (even if that self is empty).

This structural similarity between mystical traditions does not efface the significant differences between them. It would be a mistake to suggest, for instance, that emptiness is a fundamental essence comparable with either Eckhart's or Ibn al-'Arabi's understanding of God. In terms of content, these mystical traditions present different and incommensurable metaphysical doctrines. These differences, however, are particular forms of a concordance in *structure* between mystic and ultimacy that is posited by mystical trends in all three of the traditions I examine. Notably, Bernard McGinn comments that similar notions of the human soul's metaphysical connection to God can be found in all three monotheistic traditions: "It is true that mystics from all three [Abrahamic] religions have stressed the person's virtual preexistence in God as the root for the possibility of what I have called the union of indistinction."[9] Intriguingly, this suggests that an ontological resonance obtains in the works of prominent mystics not only from Christianity, Islam, and Buddhism but also from Judaism (see chapter 1) and, I would add, at least some streams of Hindu thought. This suggests that the ontological resonance represents a structural similarity in the mystical traditions of five of the world's major religions.

Epistemological analysis of the three mystics reveals additional shared themes. In all three cases, the mystics clearly suggest that what is occurring in the midst of mystical experience cannot merely be described as "knowledge" in the usual sense of the term: the form of experiential knowing that takes place there is something distinctly different. Eckhart, building on earlier mystics like Pseudo-Dionysius and echoing near contemporaries like the author of *The Cloud of Unknowing*, argues that God cannot be known by the normal discursive intellect. Even as he resists the idea of a distinct, ecstatic mystical experience, he suggests that the mystic can come to enjoy a more intimate knowledge of God that has little to do with cognitive functions. Concepts, including that of God himself, must ultimately be surpassed in order to achieve an authentic encounter with ultimacy. Concurrently, language becomes drastically attenuated—and then is transcended entirely—in the mystical encounter.

Similarly, Ibn al-'Arabi states that philosophers and academics—because of their immersion in theology and their scholarly intellectual orientations—are permanently barred from the highest forms of mystical experience. Echoing themes found in Eckhart, Ibn al-'Arabi suggests that beliefs about God actually militate against mystical experience. The mystic, Ibn al-'Arabi suggests, eschews logic and doctrine in favor of an "immediate experience" of ultimacy. The name "God," he suggests, is "but a verbal expression."[10] Again like Eckhart, Ibn al-'Arabi also suggests that the encounter with ultimacy is something that resists linguistic articulation and therefore can be known only through direct experience.

Mystical trends of Buddhism similarly suggest that the encounter with ultimacy can occur only once concepts of ultimacy have been transcended. Speculating about enlightenment, reading scripture, and other skillful means of Zen teachers are mere "dregs" compared with the experience of emptiness Hui-neng describes. Significantly, this experience is facilitated by the drastic subversion of the intellect and its discursive function. Although koans and other linguistic tools may be used to this end, language is only another conventional aspect of *pratityasamutpada* (co-dependent origination), and must therefore also eventually be abandoned.

In all three traditions, then, mystical experience is construed as immediate, lacking in conceptual content, and nonlinguistic. These commonalities transcend differences in doctrine, history, and tradition, and their shared presence indicates the erroneousness of the assumption that differences in context necessitate incomparability between mystical experiences. Interpretation, therefore, cannot be guided by that assumption.

These epistemological features of mystical experience as emically represented also have important implications for the interpretation of experiential accounts in general. These mystic epistemologies reflect a common belief that experience can occur largely independently of context and doctrine, and this belief is implicated in the experiential accounts themselves. Rather than contravene orthodox doctrine and teaching, mystics often envision experience as surpassing modes of knowledge and belief that characterize normative religious practice and thought. This shared belief that experience transcends doctrine and theology suggests that mystics commonly understand and represent experience as "underdetermined" by doctrine and context. For the interpreter, I suggest that these aspects of mystical epistemologies function as hermeneutical markers. They indicate that interpretation may be misled if guided by the prior assumption of conformity between experience and context or mainstream doctrine. The preinterpretive assumption of conformity between context and experience overlooks the possibility for divergence, spontaneity, or poetic license on the part of mystics—an aspect of mystical experience emphasized by their own epistemologies.

In citing this shared belief, I do not mean to argue that mystics' appraisals of their own experiences are immune to critique. Recognition of mystical epistemologies as hermeneutical markers does not render reading against the grain either impossible or illegitimate. An analyst may still search for indications of contextual influence, contrary to mystics' claims. Such a procedure, however, requires historical evidence and exegetical substantiation; otherwise, the claim that mystical experience must always be contextually mediated remains speculative and dogmatic.

Mystical claims of unmediated experience or other types of unusual consciousness are tremendously difficult to either confirm or disprove. Given the (probably irredeemably) subjective nature of consciousness and experience, claims to unfiltered, nonlinguistic, and other types of philosophically suspect modes of experience may remain impossible to confirm and therefore controversial.[11] It is difficult to imagine what sort of investigative technique—interpretive, technological, or otherwise—could ever allow subjective experiential claims to become corrigible in a robust, scientific manner. For precisely that reason, claims to unusual types of experience ought not to be dismissed out of hand. That they can be neither proved nor disproved establishes neither their truth nor their falsity. The cross-cultural and transhistorical similarities I identify here, however, represent significant anecdotal evidence that contemporary theories of experience and consciousness may require reconsideration.

Philosophical exploration of consciousness is a relevant enterprise, and one that could benefit by considering the kind of experiential reports examined here; they are, after all, a kind of evidence. Clearly, the contextualist position is problematic as a method for analyzing accounts of mystical experience. While it may accurately describe the typical structure of cognition, these accounts suggest that there are clear limitations to it. This could seem to tip the scales back in favor of the essentialist position: the cross-cultural similarities in these mystical experiences that cannot be explained by shared historical or contextual factors could be seen as evidence for some sort of universal, transcendent "source" that all mystics engage, the experience of which is then colored by subconscious interpretive filters derived from context. This, however, would be too strong a conclusion. First, there clearly are important differences between the "objects" of mystical experience for, on one hand, Hui-neng, and, on the other, Meister Eckhart and Ibn al-'Arabi: while some Abrahamic mystics may resort to negative language in describing God, they clearly do not understand God as *sunyata*. Second, while the interpretive procedure I deploy does identify intriguing cross-cultural similarities, it does not explain *why* those similarities obtain, and a variety of explanations—of both the supernatural and natural varieties—are plausible. It may be, for instance, that certain brain structures universal to the human species may predispose humans to the kinds of experiences described here. In that case, while the essentialist argument would be vindicated, technically speaking, it would not suggest the existence of any sort of shared mystical object common to all or even multiple mystic traditions. Cognitive scientists and neuroscientists are making very interesting headway in uncovering the brain structures and neurological processes that underlie consciousness, and naturalistic explanations for shared types of experience from this quarter cannot be ruled out.[12]

Rather than seek to solve the essentialist versus contextualist debate, I have instead sought to formulate a more effective method for the interpretation of mystic experiential accounts. While this method can produce results that should inform that debate, it provides no easy answers. Neither the assumption of necessary difference nor that of sameness can function as a legitimate guide for the interpretation and comparison of mystic experiential accounts. Such similarities must first be discovered through investigative methods that do not prejudge that question, and this requires an analytical perspective that allows for the possibility of cross-cultural similarities without assuming them as a foregone conclusion. Once found, explanations for such similarities may be offered, which then must be assessed not only on their theoretical merits but also for their ability to attend to and explain the relevant evidence (actual experiential accounts) without interpolation or eisegesis.

As is apparent, I regard mystic experiential accounts as evidence concerning the structure of consciousness and the possible modalities of experience. Doing so raises provocative questions about epistemology and current theories of consciousness. Rather than deriving their authority solely or predominantly from given philosophical traditions or thinkers, theories of consciousness—philosophical, neuroscientific, psychological, etc.—should be informed by empirical evidence. The evidence presented here strongly suggests that current theories need to be revised. Rather than regard mystical experiences as a sui generis type radically divorced from other kinds of experience, I view these experiences as evidence of experiential possibilities that are naturally latent in human consciousness.[13] As such, they indicate that not all experience is necessarily mediated, nor is it always or entirely conceptual or linguistic in nature. Neither do these examples suggest that the mediation thesis is entirely wrong. Rather, what seems to be the case is this: human consciousness is, *for the most part*, mediated, linguistic, and conceptual in nature, but *it may also take forms that are unmediated, nonlinguistic, and nonconceptual.*

It may in fact be that we need to revise the vocabulary with which we approach questions in this domain by distinguishing between thought or cognition, on one hand, and experience, on the other. Thought or cognition, as humans perform it, does seem to be essentially linguistic and conceptual; it is hard to imagine how what we commonly refer to as "thought" could be understood otherwise. And there is strong evidence to suggest that specifically cognitive functions of consciousness are largely mediated.

But this is not to say that all *experience* is always mediated, conceptual, or linguistic. While thought seems to require language and concepts, it also seems to be the case that some forms of experience—like those described by many mystics—do not. This does suggest that such experiences will be more difficult to analyze, if only because the very process of analysis is constituted by those capabilities—language use and conceptualization— that appear to be absent in these cases. But this does not mean that such experiences are meaningless, illusory, or irrelevant. As de Certeau puts it, "The literature placed under the sign of mysticism is very prolific, often even confused and verbose. But it is so in order to speak of what can be neither said nor known."[14] Although the language of mystics is often paradoxical and opaque, this seems to be because mystics are attempting to articulate states of consciousness that resist articulation but are nevertheless meaningful.

By revising our epistemological vocabulary to acknowledge the difference between thought and experience—where the former is understood to be typically mediated, linguistic, and conceptual while the latter may not be—we position ourselves to be better able to comprehend the variegated panoply of states and forms of consciousness attested to by the historical record, whether these come in the form of mystical treatises, religious doctrines, poetry, or the reports of subjects in scientific laboratories. This will require the development of new theories of consciousness, most especially to account for those pesky types of experience that escape our current theoretical categories. Acknowledging mystical experiences as evidence of real modalities of consciousness is the first step in this direction.

Those are philosophical issues. Hermeneutically, the question of the reality of unmediated and other unusual types of experience is secondary to the primary concern in the interpretation of mystic experiential accounts: disclosure of the meanings of the texts themselves. Regardless of the philosophical disagreements modern readers may have with medieval Christian preachers and ancient Chinese monks, accurate interpretations of their writings must identify the underlying notions that are central to them and incorporate these into analysis. The interpretation of mystic experiential accounts demands the recognition that mystical texts frequently operate on the assumption that experience can take forms that radically contradict many of the established theories of modern philosophy. Proper interpretation of these texts incorporates those assumptions into analysis and considers them in relation to both the larger philosophical and theological frameworks and the particular experiential accounts with which they are related. Rather than limiting interpretation to the familiar theoretical territory inscribed by the philosophical presuppositions of our own heritage, hermeneutic theory opens up the semantic horizons of a text into a panoramic perspective whose landscape is shaped by those assumptions that define the text under interpretation. Construed in this manner, theory facilitates interpretation by making itself subservient to it. In this way, interpretation reveals surprising and intriguing similarities in mystical experience that transcend context, doctrine, and tradition, and that raise challenging and provocative questions about our own understanding of the nature of consciousness and experience.

NOTES

INTRODUCTION

1. Andresen and Forman, "Methodological Pluralism," 8.
2. Idel, *Ascensions on High*, 209 (emphasis added).
3. Chittick, "Between the Yes and the No," 96.
4. Idel, *Ascensions on High*, 209.
5. My use of the term "placeholder" echoes its use by Wayne Proudfoot in *Religious Experience*. This does not indicate assent on my part to Proudfoot's argument concerning the obscurantist "placeholder function" of certain emic religious and mystic terms. My term "ultimacy" remains underspecified in order to facilitate comparison.
6. Katz, "Language, Epistemology, and Mysticism," 25, 46.
7. See Katz's essays "'Conservative' Character of Mysticism"; "Mystical Speech and Mystical Meaning"; and "Mysticism and the Interpretation."
8. In *Mysticism and Philosophical Analysis*, see particularly articles by Carl Keller, Robert Gimello, and Peter Moore; in *Mysticism and Religious Traditions*, see articles by John E. Smith, Hans Penner, Robert Gimello, and H. P. Owen.
9. Eckhart, German Sermon 5b, in *Essential Sermons, Commentaries, Treatises*, 183.
10. King, "Two Epistemological Models," 268.

CHAPTER 1

1. Wayne Proudfoot seems to concur with Katz on this point, but Proudfoot also suggests a methodological distinction that is lacking in Katz's work and that alters the impact of this claim. I discuss that distinction in chapter 2.
2. Katz, "Language, Epistemology, and Mysticism," 23, 25.
3. Katz, "'Conservative' Character of Mysticism," 30.
4. Ibid.
5. Katz, "Introduction," in Katz, *Mysticism and Philosophical Analysis*, 1.
6. Ibid., 2.
7. Katz, "Language, Epistemology, and Mysticism," 25.
8. Ibid., 65.
9. Katz, "Introduction," in Katz, *Mysticism and Sacred Scripture*, 3.
10. Katz, "Language, Epistemology, and Mysticism," 25.
11. Forman, *Mysticism, Mind, Consciousness*, 31.
12. Katz, "Language, Epistemology, and Mysticism," 26.
13. De Certeau, "Mysticism," 21.
14. Katz, "Diversity and the Study of Mysticism," 189.
15. Katz, "Language, Epistemology, and Mysticism," 26.
16. Ibid., 40 (emphasis added).

17. J. William Forgie makes the earlier point, while both Robert Forman and John V. Apczynski emphasize the latter. Apczynski attempts to rectify this lacuna by suggesting that Michael Polanyi's epistemological work provides an appropriate mechanism to fill in the gap in Katz's theory. See Forgie, "Hyper-Kantianism in Recent Discussions," 208; Forman, "Construction of Mystical Experience," 257; Apczynski, "Mysticism and Epistemology," 196–97.

18. Forman, "Construction of Mystical Experience," 258–59.

19. Ibid., 259; Stoeber, "Constructivist Epistemologies of Mysticism," 108.

20. Clooney, "Response to Steven Katz," 215; King, "Two Epistemological Models," 260; Price, "Objectivity of Mystical Truth Claims," 92; Forgie, "Hyper-Kantianism in Recent Discussions," 216–18.

21. Evans, "Can Philosophers Limit What Mystics Can Do," 55, 56.

22. Forman, "Paramartha and Modern Constructivists," 409; Shear, "Mystical Experience, Hermeneutics, and Rationality," 394; Price, "Mysticism, Mediation, and Consciousness," 117.

23. King, "Two Epistemological Models," 260; Price, "Objectivity of Mystical Truth Claims," 92; Forgie, "Hyper-Kantianism in Recent Discussions," 216–18.

24. Katz, "Language, Epistemology, and Mysticism," 22–23 (hereafter cited parenthetically in the text).

25. Katz, "'Conservative' Character of Mysticism," 29.

26. See also ibid., 14.

27. Proudfoot, Religious Experience, 122.

28. Scholem, Major Trends in Jewish Mysticism, 5.

29. Idel, Kabbalah: New Perspectives, 60.

30. See Brody, "'Open to Me the Gates'"; and Fishbane, "Mystical Contemplation."

31. Zohar: The Book of Enlightenment, 34.

32. MS Oxford Christ Church 198, fol. 73b, and MS Moscow 131, fol. 186b, quoted in Idel, Kabbalah: New Perspectives, 145.

33. Brody, "'Open to Me the Gates,'" 7.

34. Scholem, Major Trends in Jewish Mysticism, 243.

35. Fishbane, "Book of Zohar," 115n.

36. See also Katz, "Mysticism and the Interpretation," 33.

37. MS Jerusalem 1959 80, fol. 200a, quoted in Idel, Ascensions on High, 43.

38. Zohar: The Book of Enlightenment, 36.

39. Vital, Sha'ar ha-Mitzvot, quoted in Idel, Kabbalah: New Perspectives, 57.

40. The term "Neoplatonism" refers to a religious or mystical extrapolation of certain philosophical themes in Plato originating with the philosopher Plotinus (204–70 C.E.). Neoplatonism envisions God as an abstract principle rather than a personal deity. This deity, or "One," gives rise to creation through progressive emanations, each of which embodies, if imperfectly or incompletely, something of the original divine essence. The highest goal of the human person, according to Neoplatonism, is to return to and reunify with the One by retracing the hierarchy of the original emanation, usually through some sort of spiritual or meditative practice.

41. Quoted in Idel, Ascensions on High, 39–40.

42. Quoted in Schimmel, Mystical Dimensions of Islam, 266–67.

43. Schimmel, "Sufism and the Islamic Tradition," 134.

44. Sells, Mystical Languages of Unsaying, 110.

45. Katz pursues this argument explicitly in "The 'Conservative' Character of Mysticism" (1983) and "Mysticism and the Interpretation of Sacred Scripture" (2000).

46. Katz, "'Conservative' Character of Mysticism," 43.

47. Ibid., 31.

48. Katz, "Mysticism and the Interpretation," 17.
49. Ibid., 28–29.
50. Katz, "'Conservative' Character of Mysticism," 17.
51. Ibid., 32–33; Katz, "Mysticism and the Interpretation," 18.

CHAPTER 2

1. Proudfoot, *Religious Experience*, 73 (hereafter cited parenthetically in the text).

2. While I do not endorse Proudfoot's preference for naturalistic forms of explanation or his understanding of experience, I accept his argument that an interpretive theory that requires the rejection of naturalistic explanations constitutes a protective strategy. The interpretive method I develop, while not specifically favoring naturalistic forms of explanation, does not deny their validity prima facie.

3. Proudfoot's restriction of the authority of the first-person perspective results from his particular understanding of the nature and constitution of experience, which he explains at length in *Religious Experience* and which underwrites his preferred approach to the explanation of mystical experience. In short, Proudfoot does not mean to suggest that a subject has greater insight into his own experience than a third party does. He means to say only that it is the subject's own beliefs, desires, etc. that should be foregrounded in description, or in what I call interpretation. My use of Proudfoot's analytical bifurcation here does not signal my assent to his epistemology.

4. Proudfoot's approving references to both James and Eliade support this claim. While James is sometimes taken as employing a phenomenological approach, Eliade is perhaps its foremost historical representative in religious studies.

5. Eliade, *Quest*, 8–9.
6. Ibid.
7. Katz, "Language, Epistemology, and Mysticism," 28–29.
8. Eliade, *Quest*, 29.
9. Ibid., 35.
10. Ibid., 9.
11. See Davidson's essays "Radical Interpretation" (in his *Inquiries into Truth and Interpretation*) and "Radical Interpretation Interpreted."
12. Frankenberry and Penner, "'There Needs No Ghost Come,'" 71–72.
13. Davidson, "Radical Interpretation Interpreted," 124.
14. Katz, "Mystical Speech and Mystical Meaning," 4.
15. The obvious exception here is that case in which a researcher seeks to interpret or explain her own mystical experience. In such a case, the researcher does have access to the experience itself, or at least to her memory of it. Such a scenario is not unknown (see Forman's *Mysticism, Mind, Consciousness*), and it may raise other methodological issues. However, this case is rare in the context of contemporary academic research on mystical experience.
16. Penner, "Holistic Analysis," 980.
17. Ibid., 981, 983.
18. This is Penner's summary of Bjorn T. Ramberg's thinking. Ibid., 982.
19. Katz, "'Conservative' Character of Mysticism," 26.
20. Gadamer, *Truth and Method*, 267.
21. While allowing understanding to be led entirely and only by "the thing itself" may be an unattainable ideal, that goal may remain the "necessary" guiding intention of the interpreter. See Lammi, "Gadamer's 'Correction' of Heidegger," 496.
22. Gadamer, *Truth and Method*, 267.

23. Gadamer describes the task of interpretation as "centrifugal." Ibid., 291.

24. De Certeau, "Mysticism," 17.

25. Long, *Significations*, 152.

26. Gadamer, *Truth and Method*, 299. David Halliburton reads Gadamer as appealing to the "phenomenological procedure of *epoché*." See his review of Gadamer's *Truth and Method* and *Philosophical Hermeneutics* in "Review: The Hermeneutics of Belief," 7.

27. Gadamer, *Truth and Method*, 299.

28. Ibid.

CHAPTER 3

1. Ibn al-'Arabi, *Bezels of Wisdom*, 2, 3 (hereafter cited parenthetically in the text).

2. This last epithet signals the Neoplatonic influence in Ibn al-'Arabi's writing, which was widespread in all three Abrahamic religions.

3. Schimmel, *Mystical Dimensions of Islam*, 76.

4. Ibn al-'Arabi's own polemics against the more scholastically minded Islamic theologians should be a strong indicator that it is problematic to interpret his writing through a filter defined by mainstream Islamic thought.

5. Quoted in Morris, "Spiritual Ascension," Part II, 72–73.

6. Ibn al-'Arabi, *Meccan Revelations*, 2:6.

7. Morris, "Spiritual Ascension," Part I, 629–30.

8. Ibn al-'Arabi, *Meccan Revelations*, 1:131.

9. Morris, "Spiritual Ascension," Part I, 640.

10. Quoted in ibid.

11. Sells, "Ibn 'Arabi's Garden Among the Flames," 304.

12. Quoted in Morris, "Spiritual Ascension," Part I, 639.

13. Sells, "Ibn 'Arabi's Garden Among the Flames," 297.

14. Sells, "Bewildered Tongue," 110.

15. Sells, "Ibn 'Arabi's Polished Mirror," 131.

16. Quoted in Morris, "Spiritual Ascension," Part II, 76.

17. Ibid.

18. Schimmel, *Mystical Dimensions of Islam*, 41.

19. O'Leary, "Al-Hallaj," 60.

20. Ibn al-'Arabi, *Meccan Revelations*, 1:47.

21. Ibid., 2:226.

22. Ibid., 1:144.

23. Ibid., 1:46.

24. Sells, "Ibn 'Arabi's Garden Among the Flames," 291–92.

25. Hoffman, "Annihilation in the Messenger of God," 352.

26. Quoted in Morris, "Spiritual Ascension," Part I, 636.

27. Hoffman, "Annihilation in the Messenger of God," 352.

28. *Dhikr* is the common Sufi practice of remembering or meditating on God's names, traditionally considered to number ninety-nine.

29. Ibn al-'Arabi, *Meccan Revelations*, quoted in Morris, "Ibn 'Arabī's Rhetoric of Realisation," 72–73.

30. Corbin, *Alone with the Alone*, 230.

31. Sells, "Bewildered Tongue," 105.

32. Quoted in Morris, "Ibn 'Arabī's Rhetoric of Realisation," 73.

33. Schimmel, *Mystical Dimensions of Islam*, 218.

34. Ibn al-'Arabi, *Meccan Revelations*, quoted in Morris, "Ibn 'Arabī's Rhetoric of Realisation," 74.

35. Morris, "Spiritual Ascension," Part II, 64.

36. Ibn al-'Arabi, *Meccan Revelations*, 1:227.

37. Ibid., quoted in Morris, "Spiritual Ascension," Part II, 65.

38. Ibid.

39. Ibn al-'Arabi, *Meccan Revelations*, 2:234.

40. Schimmel, *Mystical Dimensions of Islam*, 140.

41. Ernst, "Mystical Language and the Teaching Context," 192.

42. Quoted in Morris, "Ibn 'Arabī's Rhetoric of Realisation," 77–78.

43. Ibn al-'Arabi, *Meccan Revelations*, 2:11.

44. Schimmel, *Mystical Dimensions of Islam*, 128.

45. Ibid., 100.

46. Ibid., 109–24.

47. Ibn al-'Arabi, *Meccan Revelations*, 2:11.

48. Ibid., quoted in Morris, "Ibn 'Arabī's Rhetoric of Realisation," 74.

49. Morris, "Spiritual Ascension," Part II, 73.

50. James, *Varieties of Religious Experience*, 300.

51. Ibn al-'Arabi, *Meccan Revelations*, 1:48.

52. Ibid.

53. Ibid., 1:49.

54. Sells, "Ibn 'Arabi's Polished Mirror," 128–29.

55. Quoted in Schimmel, *Mystical Dimensions of Islam*, 407.

56. See Wayne Proudfoot's *Religious Experience*.

CHAPTER 4

1. Eckhart, *Essential Sermons, Commentaries, Treatises*, 6 (hereafter cited parenthetically in the text).

2. Dobie, "Meister Eckhart's 'Ontological Philosophy,'" 565.

3. Radler, "Losing the Self," 115.

4. McGinn, *Flowering of Mysticism*, 239.

5. Like other mystics in the Christian tradition, Eckhart believed that scripture was susceptible to various interpretations, and that multiple theologically true meanings could be discerned in one statement or passage.

6. These two dimensions of creation ought not to be understood as actually distinct. Eckhart would have held that there is no passage of time between God's act of conceiving a thing and that thing's creation.

7. Dobie, "Meister Eckhart's 'Ontological Philosophy,'" 574.

8. Ibid., 571.

9. This has implications for the nature of the soul that will be discussed shortly.

10. I discuss the notion of the annihilation of the self below.

11. Pseudo-Dionysius, *Complete Works*, 109.

12. *Epistle of Privy Counsel*, 181.

13. *Cloud of Unknowing*, 67.

14. Radler, "Losing the Self," 114.

15. *Cloud of Unknowing*, 61.

16. Ibid., 67.

17. Dobie, "Meister Eckhart's 'Ontological Philosophy,'" 578.

18. *Cloud of Unknowing*, 111.

19. Pseudo-Dionysius, *Complete Works*, 135.

20. See also Sermon 15, 191.

21. McGinn also notes the radical distinction that Eckhart draws between knowledge operating in its normal mode and knowledge as it functions with regard to God. See his *Harvest of Mysticism*, 86.

22. McGinn, *Foundations of Mysticism*, xix–xx.

23. Dobie, "Meister Eckhart's 'Ontological Philosophy,'" 581, 583.

24. Pseudo-Dionysius, *Complete Works*, 136.

25. *Cloud of Unknowing*, 65.

26. Quoted in McGinn, *Harvest of Mysticism*, 265.

27. Pseudo-Dionysius, *Complete Works*, 55.

28. Ibid., 136.

29. Radler, "Losing the Self," 112.

30. *Cloud of Unknowing*, 108.

CHAPTER 5

1. Faure, "Fair and Unfair Language Games," 161.

2. Surekha V. Limaye, in *Zen [Buddhism] and Mysticism*, explicitly discusses the Zen tradition in articulating the relationship between Buddhism and mysticism. F. Samuel Brainard, in *Reality and Mystical Experience*, and Pyysiäinen, in *Beyond Language and Reason*, both focus on Nagarjuna's *Fundamental Wisdom of the Middle Way* in their discussions of Buddhist mysticism. Faure also addresses Zen in his discussion of language and mysticism.

3. The notion of ultimacy in Buddhism, naturally, must be understood differently from its counterparts in Islam and Christianity. I address this below.

4. Hui-neng, *Platform Sutra of the Sixth Patriarch*, 77.

5. Ibid., 8–9.

6. Ibid., 60.

7. Hui-neng, *Diamond Sutra*, 72.

8. Hui-neng, *Platform Sutra of the Sixth Patriarch*, 114.

9. Ibid., 91.

10. Hui-neng, *Sutra of Hui-neng*, 67 (hereafter cited parenthetically in the text).

11. Red Pine, however, translates this line as "possession of a self gives rise to sin." See his translation of *The Platform Sutra*, 226.

12. Hui-neng, *Diamond Sutra*, 52.

13. Ibid., 19, 32.

14. Ibid., 38.

15. Ibid., 33.

16. Ibid., 22.

17. Ibid., 53.

18. Nagarjuna, *Fundamental Wisdom of the Middle Way*, 250.

19. Ibid., 323.

20. Ibid., 351.

21. Ibid., 229.

22. "The oak tree in the yard" and "three pounds of flax" are references to other famous koans.

23. *Secrets of the Blue Cliff Record*, 38–39.

24. *Bodhi* literally means "awakening" and is commonly used by Buddhist writers to refer to enlightenment.

25. Nagarjuna, *Fundamental Wisdom of the Middle Way*, 352.

26. See Garfield's comment in ibid., 357.

27. Ibid., 282.

28. Hui-neng, *Diamond Sutra*, 31.

29. Ibid., 23.

30. Ibid., 33.

31. Ibid., 28.

32. Ibid., 26, 46, 51.

33. Ibid., 24.

CONCLUSION

1. Andresen and Forman, "Methodological Pluralism," 8.

2. Katz, "Diversity and the Study of Mysticism," 189.

3. Katz, "Language, Epistemology, and Mysticism," 26.

4. Evans, "Can Philosophers Limit What Mystics Can Do," 55, 56.

5. Bagger, "Ecumenicalism and Perennialism Revisited," 400, 409.

6. De Certeau, "Mysticism," 13.

7. Frankenberry and Penner, "'There Needs No Ghost Come,'" 71–72.

8. Nagarjuna, *Fundamental Wisdom of the Middle Way*, 250.

9. McGinn, "Comments," in Idel and McGinn, *Mystical Union in Judaism*, 188.

10. Ibn al-ʿArabi, *Bezels of Wisdom*, 231.

11. It should be noted that *all* types of experience—mundane, mystical, or otherwise— resist objectively verifiable analysis.

12. See, for example, the work of Antonio Damasio, Jaak Panksepp, and Francisco Varela.

13. This neither rules out nor requires the existence of a supernatural "object."

14. De Certeau, "Mysticism," 16.

WORKS CONSULTED

Adam, Martin T. "A Post-Kantian Perspective on Recent Debates About Mystical Experience." *Journal of the American Academy of Religion* 70, no. 4 (2002): 801–17.

Alles, Gregory D. Review of *Religious Experience*, by Wayne Proudfoot. *History of Religions* 27, no. 2 (1987): 226.

Almond, Philip C. "Mysticism and Its Contexts." In *The Problem of Pure Consciousness: Mysticism and Philosophy*, ed. Robert K. C. Forman, 211–19. New York: Oxford University Press, 1990.

Andresen, Jensine, and Robert K. C. Forman. "Methodological Pluralism in the Study of Religion." In *Cognitive Models and Spiritual Maps: Interdisciplinary Explorations of Religious Experience*, ed. Jensine Andresen and Robert K. C. Forman, 7–14. Thorverton, UK: Imprint Academic, 2000.

Apczynski, John V. "Mysticism and Epistemology." *Studies in Religion* 14, no. 2 (1985): 193–205.

Bagger, Matthew. "Ecumenicalism and Perennialism Revisited." *Religious Studies* 27 (1991): 399–411.

———. *Religious Experience, Justification, and History*. New York: Cambridge University Press, 1999.

Barbiero, Daniel. Review of *The Problem of Pure Consciousness*, edited by Robert K. C. Forman. *Philosophy East and West* 43, no. 4 (1993): 766–69.

Barnard, G. William. "Explaining the Unexplainable: Wayne Proudfoot's *Religious Experience*." *Journal of the American Academy of Religion* 60, no. 2 (1992): 231–56.

Barthwal, Pitambar Datt. *Traditions of Indian Mysticism Based upon Nirguna School of Hindi Poetry*. New Delhi: Heritage, 1978.

Bernhardt, Stephen. "Are Pure Consciousness Events Unmediated?" In *The Problem of Pure Consciousness: Mysticism and Philosophy*, ed. Robert K. C. Forman, 220–36. New York: Oxford University Press, 1990.

Bhutia, Thinley Dorjey. *Beyond Eternity Through Mysticism*. New Delhi: Doma Dorji Lhaden, 1994.

Blumenthal, David R. *Understanding Jewish Mysticism: The Merkabah and Zoharic Tradition*. New York: Ktav, 1978.

———. *Understanding Jewish Mysticism: The Philosophic-Mystical Tradition and the Hasidic Tradition*. New York: Ktav, 1982.

Brainard, F. Samuel. *Reality and Mystical Experience*. University Park: Pennsylvania State University Press, 2000.

Brody, Seth. "'Open to Me the Gates of Righteousness': The Pursuit of Holiness and Non-Duality in Early Hasidic Teaching." *Jewish Quarterly Review* 89, nos. 1–2 (1998): 3–44.

Byrne, Peter. "Mysticism, Identity, and Realism: A Debate Reviewed." *International Journal for Philosophy of Religion* 16 (1984): 237–43.

Carman, John B. "Conceiving Hindu 'Bhakti' as Theistic Mysticism." In *Mysticism and Religious Traditions*, ed. Stephen T. Katz, 191–225. New York: Oxford University Press, 1983.

Chittick, William A. "Between the Yes and the No." In *The Innate Capacity: Mysticism, Psychology, and Philosophy*, ed. Robert K. C. Forman, 95–110. Oxford: Oxford University Press, 1998.

Clooney, Francis. "Response to Steve Katz." In *The Future of the Study of Religion: Proceedings of Congress 2000*, ed. Slavica Jakelić and Lori Pearson, 211–16. Boston: Brill, 2004.

The Cloud of Unknowing. Translated by Clifton Wolters. New York: Penguin Books, 1978.

Comans, Michael. "The Question of the Importance of Samadhi in Modern and Classical Advaita Vedanta." *Philosophy East and West* 43, no. 1 (1993): 19–38.

Corbin, Henry. *Alone with the Alone: Creative Imagination in the Sufism of Ibn Arabi.* Princeton: Princeton University Press, 1969.

Corless, Roger J. "Parables of Deconstruction in the Lotus Sutra." In *The Innate Capacity: Mysticism, Psychology, and Philosophy*, ed. Robert K. C. Forman, 82–94. Oxford: Oxford University Press, 1998.

Coward, Harold G. "Levels of Language in Mystical Experience." In *Mystics and Scholars: The Calgary Conference on Mysticism, 1976*, ed. Harold G. Coward and Terence Penelhum, 93–107. Waterloo: Canadian Corporation for Studies in Religion, 1977.

Davidson, Donald. *Inquiries into Truth and Interpretation.* Oxford: Oxford University Press, 2001.

———. "Radical Interpretation Interpreted." *Philosophical Perspectives* 8 (1994): 121–28.

de Certeau, Michel. "Mysticism." *Diacritics* 22, no. 2 (1992): 11–25.

Deutsch, Eliot, and J. A. B. van Buitenen. *A Source Book of Advaita Vedanta.* Honolulu: University of Hawaii Press, 1971.

Dobie, Robert. "Meister Eckhart's 'Ontological Philosophy of Religion.'" *Journal of Religion* 82, no. 4 (2002): 563–85.

Eckhart, Meister. *Meister Eckhart: The Essential Sermons, Commentaries, Treatises, and Defense.* Edited and translated by Edmund Colledge and Bernard McGinn. Mahwah: Paulist Press, 1981.

Eliade, Mircea. *The Quest: History and Meaning in Religion.* Chicago: University of Chicago Press, 1969.

The Epistle of Privy Counsel. Translated by Clifton Wolters. New York: Penguin Books, 1978.

Ernst, Carl W. "Mystical Language and the Teaching Context in the Early Lexicons of Sufism." In *Mysticism and Language,* ed. Steven T. Katz, 181–201. New York: Oxford University Press, 1992.

Evans, Donald. "Can Philosophers Limit What Mystics Can Do?" *Religious Studies* 25 (1989): 53–60.

Faure, Bernard. "Fair and Unfair Language Games in Chan/Zen." In *Mysticism and Language,* ed. Steven T. Katz, 158–80. New York: Oxford University Press, 1992.

Fishbane, Eitan. "Mystical Contemplation and the Limits of the Mind: The Case of the *Sheqel ha-Qodesh.*" *Jewish Quarterly Review* 93, nos. 1–2 (2002): 1–27.

Fishbane, Michael. "The Book of *Zohar* and Exegetical Spirituality." In *Mysticism and Sacred Scripture,* ed. Steven T. Katz, 101–17. New York: Oxford University Press, 2000.

Fitzgerald, Timothy. "Experience." In *Guide to the Study of Religion,* ed. Willi Braun and Russell T. McCutcheon, 125–39. New York: Cassell, 2000.

Forgie, William J. "Hyper-Kantianism in Recent Discussions of Mystical Experience." *Religious Studies* 21 (1985): 205–18.

Forman, Robert K. C. "Bagger and the Ghosts of GAA." *Religious Studies* 27 (1991): 413–20.

———. "The Construction of Mystical Experience." *Faith and Philosophy* 5, no. 3 (1988): 254–67.

————, ed. *The Innate Capacity: Mysticism, Psychology, and Philosophy.* Oxford: Oxford University Press, 1998.

————. "Mystical Knowledge: Knowledge by Identity." *Journal of the American Academy of Religion* 61, no. 4 (1993): 705–38.

————. *Mysticism, Mind, Consciousness.* Albany: State University of New York Press, 1999.

————. "Paramartha and Modern Constructivists on Mysticism: Epistemological Monomorphism Versus Duomorphism." *Philosophy East and West* 39, no. 4 (1989): 393–418.

————, ed. *The Problem of Pure Consciousness: Mysticism and Philosophy.* New York: Oxford University Press, 1990.

Foster, Genevieve, and David Hufford. *The World Was Flooded with Light: A Mystical Experience Remembered.* Pittsburgh: University of Pittsburgh Press, 1985.

Frankenberry, Nancy. "Consequences of William James's Pragmatism in Religion." In *God, Values, and Empiricism: Issues in Philosophical Theology,* ed. Creighton Peden, 64–72. Macon: Mercer University Press, 1990.

————. "The Empirical Dimension of Religious Experience." *Process Studies* 8, no. 4 (1978): 259–76.

————. "Inquiry and the Language of the Divine: A Response to Proudfoot." *American Journal of Theology and Philosophy* 14, no. 3 (1993): 257–62.

————. "Reconstructing Religion Without Revelation, Foundations, or Fideism: A Reply to My Critics." *American Journal of Theology and Philosophy* 13, no. 2 (1992): 117–35.

————. *Religion and Radical Empiricism.* Albany: State University of New York Press, 1987.

Frankenberry, Nancy, and Hans Penner. "'There Needs No Ghost Come from the Grave to Tell Us This': A Response to Ivan Strenski." *Religion* 34 (2004): 65–74.

Franklin, R. L. "Experience and Interpretation in Mysticism." In *The Problem of Pure Consciousness: Mysticism and Philosophy,* ed. Robert K. C. Forman, 288–304. New York: Oxford University Press, 1990.

Franks Davis, Caroline. *The Evidential Force of Religious Experience.* Oxford: Oxford University Press, 1989.

Friedrichs, Robert W. Review of *Religious Experience,* by Wayne Proudfoot. *Sociological Analysis* 48, no. 2 (1987): 179–80.

Gadamer, Hans-Georg. *Truth and Method.* New York: Continuum, 1999.

Gilson, Etienne. "Unitas Spiritus." In *Understanding Mysticism,* ed. Richard Woods, 500–520. Garden City, N.Y.: Image Books, 1980.

Gimello, Robert M. "Mysticism in Its Contexts." In *Mysticism and Religious Traditions,* ed. Stephen T. Katz, 61–88. New York: Oxford University Press, 1983.

Godlove, Terry. "Religious Discourse and First Person Authority." *Method and Theory in the Study of Religion* 6, no. 2 (1994): 147–61.

————. Review of *Religious Experience,* by Wayne Proudfoot. *Journal of Religion* 67, no. 3 (1987): 405–6.

Gold, Daniel. "Experiencing Scriptural Diversity: Words and Stories in Hindu Traditions." In *Mysticism and Sacred Scripture,* ed. Steven T. Katz, 210–31. New York: Oxford University Press, 2000.

Grant, Sara. *Sankara's Concept of Relation.* Delhi: Motilal Banarsidass, 1998.

Green, Arthur. "The Zaddiq as Axis Mundi in Later Judaism." *Journal of the American Academy of Religion* 45, no. 3 (1977): 327–47.

Griffin, David Ray. "Religious Experience, Naturalism, and the Social Scientific Study of Religion." *Journal of the American Academy of Religion* 68, no. 1 (2000): 99–125.

Griffiths, Paul J. "Pure Consciousness in Indian Buddhism." In *The Problem of Pure Consciousness: Mysticism and Philosophy,* ed. Robert K. C. Forman, 71–97. New York: Oxford University Press, 1990.

Grimes, John. "Some Problems in the Epistemology of Advaita." *Philosophy East and West* 41, no. 3 (1991): 291–301.

Halliburton, David. "Review: The Hermeneutics of Belief and the Hermeneutics of Suspicion." *Diacritics* 6, no. 4 (1976): 1–9.

Hamilton, Sue. *Identity and Experience: The Constitution of the Human Being According to Early Buddhism*. Oxford: Luzac Oriental, 1996.

Hardwick, Charley D. "New Openings for Religious Empiricism." *Journal of the American Academy of Religion* 56, no. 3 (1988): 545–51.

Hoffman, Valerie J. "Annihilation in the Messenger of God: The Development of a Sufi Practice." *International Journal of Middle Eastern Studies* 31, no. 3 (1999): 351–69.

Hollenback, Jess Byron. *Mysticism: Experience, Response, and Empowerment*. University Park: Pennsylvania State University Press, 1996.

Hui-neng. *The Diamond Sutra and The Sutra of Hui-neng*. Translated by A. F. Price and Wong Mu-lam. Boston: Shambhala, 1990.

———. *The Platform Sutra: The Zen Teaching of Hui-neng*. Translated by Red Pine. Berkeley: Counterpoint Press, 2008.

———. *The Platform Sutra of the Sixth Patriarch*. Translated by Philip B. Yampolsky. New York: Columbia University Press, 1967.

———. *The Sutra of Hui-neng, Grand Master of Zen: With Hui-neng's Commentary on the Diamond Sutra*. Translated by Thomas Cleary. Boston: Shambhala, 1998.

Ibn al-'Arabi. *Ibn al-Arabi: The Bezels of Wisdom*. Edited and translated by Ralph W. J. Austin. Mahwah: Paulist Press, 1980.

———. *The Meccan Revelations*, vols. 1 and 2. Edited and translated by Michel Chodkiewicz, William C. Chittick, and James W. Morris. New York: Pir Press, 2002, 2004.

Idel, Moshe. *Abraham Abulafia: An Ecstatic Kabbalist*. Lancaster, Calif.: Labyrinthos, 2002.

———. *Ascensions on High in Jewish Mysticism*. Budapest: Central European University Press, 2005.

———. *Kabbalah: New Perspectives*. New Haven: Yale University Press, 1988.

———. "The *Zohar* as Exegesis." In *Mysticism and Sacred Scripture*, ed. Steven T. Katz, 87–100. New York: Oxford University Press, 2000.

Idel, Moshe, and Bernard McGinn, eds. *Mystical Union in Judaism, Christianity, and Islam: An Ecumenical Dialogue*. New York: Continuum, 1999.

Indich, William M. "Can the Advaita Vedantin Provide a Meaningful Definition of Absolute Consciousness?" *Philosophy East and West* 30, no. 4 (1980): 481–93.

Jackman, Henry. "Charity, Self-Interpretation, and Belief." *Journal of Philosophical Research* 28 (2002): 143–65.

James, William. *The Varieties of Religious Experience*. New York: Simon and Schuster, 1997.

———. "A World of Pure Experience." *Journal of Philosophy, Psychology, and Scientific Methods* 1, no. 20 (1904): 533–43.

Janz, Bruce. "Mysticism and Understanding: Steven Katz and His Critics." *Studies in Religion* 24, no. 1 (1995): 77–94.

Katz, Steven T. "The 'Conservative' Character of Mysticism." In *Mysticism and Religious Traditions*, ed. Steven T. Katz, 3–60. New York: Oxford University Press, 1983.

———. "Diversity and the Study of Mysticism." In *The Future of the Study of Religion: Proceedings of Congress 2000*, ed. Slavica Jakelić and Lori Pearson, 189–210. Boston: Brill, 2004.

———. "Language, Epistemology, and Mysticism." In *Mysticism and Philosophical Analysis*, ed. Steven T. Katz, 22–74. New York: Oxford University Press, 1978.

———. "Mystical Speech and Mystical Meaning." In *Mysticism and Language*, ed. Steven T. Katz, 3–41. New York: Oxford University Press, 1992.

————, ed. *Mysticism and Philosophical Analysis*. New York: Oxford University Press, 1978.

————, ed. *Mysticism and Religious Traditions*. New York: Oxford University Press, 1983.

————. "Mysticism and the Interpretation of Sacred Scripture." In *Mysticism and Sacred Scripture*, ed. Steven T. Katz, 7–67. New York: Oxford University Press, 2000.

————. "Recent Work on Mysticism." *History of Religions* 25, no. 1 (1985): 76–86.

Katz, Steven T., Sallie B. King, and Huston Smith. "On Mysticism." *Journal of the American Academy of Religion* 56, no. 4 (1988): 751–61.

Keller, Carl A. "Mystical Literature." In *Mysticism and Philosophical Analysis*, ed. Steven T. Katz, 75–100. Oxford: Oxford University Press, 1978.

King, Sallie B. "Two Epistemological Models for the Interpretation of Mysticism." *Journal of the American Academy of Religion* 71, no. 2 (1988): 257–79.

Klein, Anne C. "Mental Concentration and the Unconditioned: A Buddhist Case for Unmediated Experience." In *Paths to Liberation: The Mārga and Its Transformations in Buddhist Thought*, ed. Robert E. Bushwell Jr. and Robert M. Gimello, 269–308. Honolulu: University of Hawaii Press, 1992.

Lamberth, David C. "Putting 'Experience' to the Test in Theological Reflection." *Harvard Theological Review* 93, no. 1 (2000): 67–77.

Lammi, Walter. "Hans-Georg Gadamer's 'Correction' of Heidegger." *Journal of the History of Ideas* 52, no. 3 (1991): 487–507.

Lao Tzu. *Tao Te Ching*. Translated by Gia-Fu Feng and Jane English. New York: Random House, 1972.

Limaye, Surekha V. *Zen (Buddhism) and Mysticism*. Delhi: Sri Satguru, 1992.

Long, Charles. *Significations: Signs, Symbols, and Images in the Interpretation of Religion*. Aurora: Davies Group, 1995.

Loy, David. "The Path of No-Path: Sankara and Dogen on the Paradox of Practice." *Philosophy East and West* 38, no. 2 (1988): 127–46.

Matilal, Bimal Krishna. "Mysticism and Ineffability." In *Mysticism and Language*, ed. Steven T. Katz, 143–57. New York: Oxford University Press, 1992.

Matt, Daniel C. "*Ayin*: The Concept of Nothingness in Jewish Mysticism." In *The Problem of Pure Consciousness: Mysticism and Philosophy*, ed. Robert K. C. Forman, 121–62. New York: Oxford University Press, 1990.

Mayeda, Sengaku, trans. *A Thousand Teachings: The Upadeśasāhasri of Sankara*. Tokyo: University of Tokyo Press, 1979.

McCutcheon, Russell T. "'It's a Lie. There's No Truth in It! It's a Sin!': On the Limits of the Humanistic Study of Religion and the Costs of Saving Others from Themselves." *Journal of the American Academy of Religion* 74, no. 3 (2006): 720–50.

McGinn, Bernard. *The Flowering of Mysticism*. New York: Crossroad, 1998.

————. *The Foundations of Mysticism*. New York: Crossroad, 1991.

————. *The Growth of Mysticism*. New York: Crossroad, 1994.

————. *The Harvest of Mysticism in Medieval Germany*. New York: Crossroad, 2005.

Morris, James Winston. "Ibn 'Arabī's Rhetoric of Realisation: Keys to Reading and 'Translating' the *Meccan Illuminations*, Part I." *Journal of the Muhyiddīn Ibn 'Arabī Society* 33 (2003): 54–99.

————. "The Spiritual Ascension: Ibn 'Arabi and the Miraj, Part I." *Journal of the American Oriental Society* 107, no. 4 (1987): 629–52.

————. "The Spiritual Ascension: Ibn 'Arabi and the Mi'raj, Part II." *Journal of the American Oriental Society* 108, no. 1 (1988): 63–77.

Nagarjuna. *The Fundamental Wisdom of the Middle Way*. Translation and commentary by Jay L. Garfield. New York: Oxford University Press, 1995.

Nishitani, Keiji. *Religion and Nothingness*. Berkeley: University of California Press, 1982.

Okasha, Samir. "Holism About Meaning and About Evidence: In Defense of W. V. Quine." *Erkenntnis* 52, no. 1 (2000): 39–61.

O'Leary, De Lacy. "Al-Hallaj." *Philosophy East and West* 1, no. 1 (1951): 56–62.

Ong, Walter J. *Interfaces of the Word: Studies in the Evolution of Consciousness and Culture.* Ithaca: Cornell University Press, 1977.

Otto, Rudolf. *The Idea of the Holy.* Translated by John W. Harvey. New York: Oxford University Press, 1958.

———. *Mysticism East and West: A Comparative Analysis of the Nature of Mysticism.* Wheaton: Theosophical Publishing House, 1987.

Pedersen, Kusumita P. Review of *Religious Experience*, by Wayne Proudfoot. *Philosophy East and West* 38, no. 2 (1988): 209–12.

Penner, Hans H. "Holistic Analysis: Conjectures and Refutations." *Journal of the American Academy of Religion* 62, no. 4 (1994): 977–96.

———. "The Mystical Illusion." In *Mysticism and Religious Traditions*, ed. Steven T. Katz, 89–116. New York: Oxford University Press, 1983.

Perovich, Anthony N., Jr. "Does the Philosophy of Mysticism Rest on a Mistake?" In *The Problem of Pure Consciousness: Mysticism and Philosophy*, ed. Robert K. C. Forman, 237–53. New York: Oxford University Press, 1990.

Pflueger, Lloyd. "Discriminating the Innate Capacity: Salvation Mysticism of Classical Samkhya-Yoga." In *The Innate Capacity: Mysticism, Psychology, and Philosophy*, ed. Robert K. C. Forman, 46–82. Oxford: Oxford University Press, 1998.

Phillips, Stephen H. "Could There Be Mystical Evidence for a Nondual Brahman? A Causal Objection." *Philosophy East and West* 51, no. 4 (2001): 492–506.

Price, James Robertson. "Mysticism, Mediation, and Consciousness: The Innate Capacity in John Ruusbroec." In *The Innate Capacity: Mysticism, Psychology, and Philosophy*, ed. Robert K. C. Forman, 111–222. Oxford: Oxford University Press, 1998.

———. "The Objectivity of Mystical Truth Claims." *Thomist: A Speculative Quarterly Review* 49, no. 1 (1985): 81–98.

Prigge, Norman, and Gary E. Kessler. "Is Mystical Experience Everywhere the Same?" In *The Problem of Pure Consciousness: Mysticism and Philosophy*, ed. Robert K. C. Forman, 269–87. New York: Oxford University Press, 1990.

Proudfoot, Wayne. "Inquiry and the Language of the Divine." *American Journal of Theology and Philosophy* 14, no. 3 (1993): 247–56.

———. "Religious Belief and Naturalism." In *Radical Interpretation and Religion*, ed. Nancy K. Frankenberry, 78–92. Cambridge: Cambridge University Press, 2002.

———. *Religious Experience.* Berkeley: University of California Press, 1985.

———. "Responses and Rejoinders: Explaining the Unexplainable." *Journal of the American Academy of Religion* 61, no. 4 (1993): 793–812.

———. "William James on an Unseen Order." *Harvard Theological Review* 93, no. 1 (2000): 51–66.

Proudfoot, Wayne, and Phillip Shaver. "Attribution Theory and the Psychology of Religion." *Journal for the Scientific Study of Religion* 14, no. 4 (1975): 317–30.

Pseudo-Dionysius. *Pseudo-Dionysius: The Complete Works.* Edited and translated by Colm Luibheid. Mahwah: Paulist Press, 1987.

Puligandla, Ramakrishna. Review of *The Problem of Pure Consciousness*, edited by Robert K. C. Forman. *Philosophy East and West* 50, no. 2 (2000): 304–8.

Pyysiäinen, Ilkka. *Beyond Language and Reason: Mysticism in Indian Buddhism.* Helsinki: Suomalainen Tiedeakatemia, 1993.

Radler, Charlotte. "Losing the Self: Detachment in Meister Eckhart and Its Significance for Buddhist-Christian Dialogue," *Buddhist-Christian Studies* 26 (2006): 111–17.

Ram-Prasad, Chakravarthi. "Saving the Self? Classical Hindu Theories of Consciousness and Contemporary Physicalism." *Philosophy East and West* 51, no. 3 (2001): 378–92.

Rashke, Carl. Review of *Religious Experience*, by Wayne Proudfoot. *Journal of the American Academy of Religion* 55, no. 3 (1987): 620–22.

Rorty, Richard. "Method, Social Science, and Social Hope." In Rorty, *Consequences of Pragmatism*, 191–210. Minneapolis: University of Minnesota Press, 1982.

———. *Objectivity, Relativism, and Truth*. New York: Cambridge University Press, 1991.

Rothberg, Donald. "Contemporary Epistemology and the Study of Mysticism." In *The Problem of Pure Consciousness: Mysticism and Philosophy*, ed. Robert K. C. Forman, 163–210. New York: Oxford University Press, 1990.

Schimmel, Annemarie. *Mystical Dimensions of Islam*. Chapel Hill: University of North Carolina Press, 1975.

———. "Sufism and the Islamic Tradition." In *Mysticism and Religious Traditions*, ed. Steven T. Katz, 130–47. New York: Oxford University Press, 1983.

Schleiermacher, Friedrich. *On Religion: Speeches to Its Cultured Despisers*. Translated by John Oman. Louisville: Westminster John Knox Press, 1994.

Schmidt, Leigh Eric. "The Making of Modern 'Mysticism.'" *Journal of the American Academy of Religion* 71, no. 2 (2003): 273–302.

Scholem, Gershom. *Major Trends in Jewish Mysticism*. New York: Schocken Books, 1954.

Secrets of the Blue Cliff Record: Zen Comments by Hakuin and Tenkei. Translated by Thomas Cleary. Boston: Shambhala, 2000.

Sells, Michael. "Bewildered Tongue: The Semantics of Mystical Union in Islam." In *Mystical Union in Judaism, Christianity, and Islam: An Ecumenical Dialogue*, ed. Moshe Idel and Bernard McGinn, 87–124. New York: Continuum, 1999.

———. "Ibn 'Arabi's Garden Among the Flames: A Reevaluation." *History of Religions* 23, no. 4 (1984): 287–315.

———. "Ibn 'Arabi's Polished Mirror: Perspective Shift and Meaning Event." *Studia Islamic* 67 (1988): 121–49.

———. *Mystical Languages of Unsaying*. Chicago: University of Chicago Press, 1994.

Sharf, Robert H. "Experience." In *Critical Terms for Religious Studies*, ed. Mark C. Taylor, 94–116. Chicago: University of Chicago Press, 1998.

Shear, Jonathan. "Mystical Experience, Hermeneutics, and Rationality." *International Philosophical Quarterly* 30, no. 4 (1990): 391–403.

Shodo Harada Roshi. "Zazen Meditation in Japanese Rinzai Zen." Translated by Thomas Kirchner. In *The Experience of Meditation: Experts Introduce the Traditions*, ed. Jonathan Shear, 1–21. St. Paul: Paragon House, 2006.

Skoog, Kim. "Śamkara on the Role [of] Sruti and Anubhava in Attaining Brahmajnana." *Philosophy East and West* 39, no. 1 (1989): 76–74.

Smart, Ninian. Review of *Religious Experience*, by Wayne Proudfoot. *Journal of Philosophy* 85, no. 3 (1988): 151–54.

———. "Understanding Religious Experience." In *Mysticism and Philosophical Analysis*, ed. Steven T. Katz, 10–21. New York: Oxford University Press, 1978.

Smith, Huston. "Is There a Perennial Philosophy?" *Journal of the American Academy of Religion* 55, no. 5 (1987): 553–66.

Smith, Jonathan Z. *Relating Religion*. Chicago: Chicago University Press, 2004.

Staal, Frits. *Exploring Mysticism*. Berkeley: University of California Press, 1975.

Stoeber, Michael. "Constructivist Epistemologies of Mysticism: A Critique and a Revision." *Religious Studies* 28 (1992): 107–16.

Stout, Jeffrey. "Radical Interpretation and Pragmatism: Davidson, Rorty, and Brandom on Truth." In *Radical Interpretation in Religion*, ed. Nancy Frankenberry, 25–52. Cambridge: Cambridge University Press, 2002.

Suzuki, Daisetz Teitaro. *Mysticism Christian and Buddhist: The Eastern and Western Way.* New York: Collier Books, 1962.

Taylor, Eugene. "Metaphysics and Consciousness in James's *Varieties*: A Centenary Lecture." In *Williams James and the Varieties of Religious Experience: A Centenary Celebration*, ed. Jeremy Carrette, 11–26. New York: Taylor and Francis, 2005.

———. "Radical Empiricism and the New Science of Consciousness." *History of the Human Sciences* 8, no. 1 (1995): 47–60.

Thurman, Robert A. F., and David B. Gray. "Tsongkhapa on the Integration of Quiescence and Insight Meditation." In *The Experience of Meditation: Experts Introduce the Traditions*, ed. Jonathan Shear, 145–69. St. Paul: Paragon House, 2006.

Underhill, Evelyn. *Mysticism: A Study in the Nature and Development of Man's Spiritual Consciousness.* New York: Penguin Books, 1955.

Vajda, G. "Jewish Mysticism." In *Understanding Jewish Mysticism: The Merkabah Tradition and Zoharic Tradition*, ed. David R. Blumenthal, 6–8. New York: Ktav, 1978.

Vedanta-Sutras: With the Commentary of Sankaracarya. Translated by George Thibaut. Delhi: Motilal Banarsidass, 1977.

Wainwright, William J. *Mysticism: A Study of Its Nature, Cognitive Value, and Moral Implications.* Madison: University of Wisconsin Press, 1981.

———. Review of *Religious Experience*, by Wayne Proudfoot. *Faith and Philosophy* 5, no. 2 (1988): 208–13.

Woodhouse, Mark B. "On the Possibility of Pure Consciousness." In *The Problem of Pure Consciousness: Mysticism and Philosophy*, ed. Robert K. C. Forman, 254–68. New York: Oxford University Press, 1990.

Woods, Richard, ed. *Understanding Mysticism.* Garden City, N.Y.: Image Books, 1980.

Zaehner, R. C. *Mysticism Sacred and Profane.* New York: Oxford University Press, 1969.

Zohar: The Book of Enlightenment. Translated and edited by Daniel C. Matt. New York: Paulist Press, 1983.

INDEX

Page numbers in italics refer to figures; those followed by n refer to notes, with chapter and note number.

on essential difference in existences of Creator and creation, 94

on existence as secondary to and derivative from God, 96–98

on external religious practice, inadequacy of, 107–8

on God's retention of Creation within Himself, 95–96

on heresy *vs.* error, 90–91

and hermeneutic method, 119

on human soul: birth of the Son in, 93, 103–5, 114, 118; existence of within ongoing creation, 98–99, 104–5; as identical with God, 99–100, 101–7, 118, 153, 156–57; shared ground with God, 93–94, 101, 105–6, 112, 113–14, 116, 117; unity of with unified ground of Trinity, 105–6, 114, 118

on images of God as barrier to knowing God, 109–10

on impossibility of understanding God, 110–11

on increased intimacy with God through annihilation of self, 99–101

on ineffability of encounter with God, 115, 116–17

influence of, 89, 91

influences on, 106, 113, 119, 158

on knowledge of God as purely experiential, 114–15

on language: as barrier to knowing God, 116–17; insufficiency of to describe mystical experience, 93–94, 152–53; similarity of views in Ibn al-'Arabi and Hui-neng, 124, 152–53

life of, 89–91

and living in the moment, necessity of, 108

on names of God, 115

on names of God as barrier to knowing God, 116–17

Neoplatonism of, 96–97, 98, 99, 119, 156

ontology of, 94–107; shared features with Ibn al-'Arabi, 101; similarity to other Christian mystics, 106–7

personal experience of God as theme in, 90, 92

and pre-existing connection between God and humankind, 101

in quantum ("insofar as") principle in, 93–94, 97

and self-awareness as obstacle to knowing God, 110–13, 119

sermons, provocative nature of, 89–90

on shared ground of God and human soul, 93–94, 101, 105–6, 112, 113–14, 116, 117

theology of: consistency across sermons and treatises, 91–92; departures from Church doctrine, 100, 102, 107–8, 110, 115–16, 117, 118, 119; guiding themes in, 92

on unity of God, Jesus, and human soul, 104–5, 114, 118

on unity with God within active life, 92, 115, 118

on unmediated knowledge of God, 114

on worldly attachments as barrier to knowing God, 108–9

Eliade, Mircea, 39–41

Elias (prophet), Ibn al-'Arabi on, 66, 74

encounter, definition of, 5

Enoch, 24

epistemology. *See also under* Eckhart, Meister; Hui-neng; Ibn al-'Arabi, Abu Bakr Muhammad

as interrogative category in this book, 50, 56

similarities in Eckhart, Ibn al-'Arabi, and Hui-neng, 118–19, 124, 127, 139, 146, 152–53, 156–60

Ernst, Carl, 79

essentialism, 2

contextualist critique of, 2, 15–18

Eliade and, 39–40

on irrelevance of context to mystical experience per se, 16–17

on pure consciousness events, 2, 17

revision of in response to contextualist critique, 2, 17

similarities in accounts of mystical experience and, 160–61

Evans, Donald, 19

experience, unmediated

Eckhart on, 114

Katz on impossibility of, 17–18

need for further research on, 161–62

experiential account of mystical experience, interpretation as means of achieving, 35–36

explanation of mystical experiences

vs. descriptive accounts: and hermeneutic approach, 35, 52, 155; phenomenological epoché and, 51, 155; Proudfoot on, 34–35, 37–39, 40, 49, 167nn2:2–3

in hermeneutic approach, 53

vs. interpretation: benefits of distinguishing between, 33, 35–36, 154–55, 163; and interpretation as necessarily prior, 51–52

in one's own experience, 167n2:15